I0236617

A
HISTORY
of
LIVERMORE
MAINE

Reginald H. Sturtevant

With drawings by S. W. Hilton

Order this book online at www.trafford.com
or email orders@trafford.com

Most Trafford titles are also available at major online book retailers.

REVISED 2nd EDITION

© Copyright 1970, 2010 Reginald H. Sturtevant.
All rights reserved. No part of this publication may be reproduced, stored in a retrieval system, or transmitted, in any form or by any means, electronic, mechanical, photocopying, recording, or otherwise, without the written prior permission of the author.

Printed in the United States of America.

ISBN: 978-1-4269-3567-1 (sc)
ISBN: 978-1-4269-3568-8 (dj)
ISBN: 978-1-4269-3569-5 (e-b)

Library of Congress Control Number: 2010908702

Our mission is to efficiently provide the world's finest, most comprehensive book publishing service, enabling every author to experience success. To find out how to publish your book, your way, and have it available worldwide, visit us online at www.trafford.com

Trafford rev. 07/21/2010

Trafford PUBLISHING   www.trafford.com

North America & international
toll-free: 1 888 232 4444 (USA & Canada)
phone: 250 383 6864 ♦ fax: 812 355 4082

Table of Contents

Reginald H. Sturtevant

Foreword

The historical value of this book will be immediately obvious to the reader. What is not immediately obvious (other than to those who knew him) is that this work is a monumental witness to the fortitude and courage of the man who wrote it.

For years, the author looked forward to having time in his retirement to fulfill a long-standing ambition to write a comprehensive history of Livermore. As a writer, he had an admirable knack of incorporating a large measure of entertainment into a great deal of well-documented historical content; and, by reason of this talent, he was for decades looked upon as a sort of unofficial area "Historian" - often called upon to author newspaper and magazine articles and historical booklets.

Where he could perhaps have, at one time, completed this work in a matter of months, two severely disabling strokes resulted in the laborious, nearly insurmountable task of preparing it over a period of years. With boundless determination and a will to do his best with the God-given talents remaining at his disposal, he overcame the formidable obstacles of paralysis (of his right side - including his writing hand) and aphasia (loss of ability to communicate by speech and writing): he learned to write with his left hand; and, through painstakingly slow therapy, he relearned language and the ability to communicate ideas by both speech and writing.

Unfortunately, a third stroke once again deprived him of the ability to speak and write. His history was published in its incomplete state, as he desired that it be released in conjunction with the State's sesquicentennial year, 1970 - (which was also the 175th anniversary of Livermore).

Rewarded with the pleasure of seeing this book at last published, he died in 1974, having lived a life of distinguished achievement and public service.

PREFACE

Of the many criticisms aimed at the society and culture of these United States by people of other lands, one of the most frequent is that "it has no roots." Europeans are generally amazed by the mobility of our population, when they learn that it is not at all unusual for a family in one generation to move to three or four different locations, often in different States; that it is unusual to find more than one or two generations of a family in the same location.

They are equally impressed by the impermanence of our buildings. Jean Paul Sartre, for example, says of our structures, "Their house is a shell; it is abandoned on the slightest pretext. Changes are continually being made. An apartment house is bought to be demolished and a larger apartment house is built on the same plot. After five years the new house is sold to a contractor who tears it down to build a third one. The result is that, in the States, a city is a moving landscape. You feel from your first glance that your contact with these places is a temporary one; either you will leave them, or they will change around you."

Not to be forgotten is that this willingness to change, this constant search for something better; is one of the basic reasons for our rapid economic progress. On the other hand, this does not imply, necessarily, a concurrent forgetfulness or ignorance of the past. The attitude so often expressed by, "Let the dead past bury the dead; we are not interested in where we have been, but only in where we are going," can be very costly. By it, we can lose much of our national pride and unity which comes from a common knowledge of the hardships, sufferings, and triumphs of past generations; by it, we can lose valuable lessons from the past, for, as has been said, "those who fail to learn from history are doomed to repeat it"; most important of all, by it we can lose the sense of continuity, the realization that we are neither beginning nor end, and so have both an obligation to the past, and a responsibility to the future.

This book, then, is designed not so much as a work of scholarly, historical research, as a presentation of the salient facts and personages in the history of the Towns of Livermore, in what I hope to be a readable form for the general public. Thus, perhaps, it may contribute to the realization that these towns, like so many others in New England, do have roots that are strong and deep; and, hopefully, may contribute to the nourishing of those roots.

ROCKOMEKA
The Indian Period

MAINE WAS NOT AN UNINHABITED LAND when the white men first came here. According to Williamson and other early historians, there were in 1615 about 40,000 Indians living in what is now Maine. These consisted of two families - the Etechemins, occupying the area from the Penobscot River to the East; and the Abnakis, holding the territory West of the Penobscot into New Hampshire.

The Etechemins comprised three tribes - the Tarratines (or Penobscot), the Marechites (or St. John), and the Openangos (or Passamaquoddy). The total Etechemin population was somewhat over 20,000, including 6,000 warriors; and their largest tribe was the Tarratine, which numbered over 8,000, of which 2400 were warriors.

The Abnakis, in Maine, were made up of four tribes the Sokokis (or Saco), the Anasagunticook (or Androscoggin), the Canibas (or Kennebec) and the Wawenocks (or Sheepscot). These four tribes numbered slightly less than 20,000 persons, of which 5,000 were warriors; and their largest tribes were the Anasagunticooks (or Androscoggin) and the Canibas (or Kennebecs), each of whom totaled about 6,000.

The Sokokis lived on both sides of the Saco River, and into New Hampshire. The Anasagunticooks claimed dominion of the waters and territories of the River Androscoggin from its sources to Merrymeeting Bay, and on the west side of the Sagadahoc to the sea. The Canibas held the valley of the Kennebec from its sources to Merrymeeting Bay, and on the east side of the Sagadahoc to the sea. The Wawenocks occupied the territory adjacent to the Sheepscot River, and particularly along the seacoast to the land of the Penobscots. The story of the Abnakis has never been told as fully and as sympathetically as it deserves. Certainly the maltreatment and eventual annihilation of these Indian tribes by the English is, to say the least, a discreditable page in history.

When we speak of the Indian Wars, we usually think of "Kentucky's Dark and Bloody Ground," or the "Winning of the West"; yet Maine, and particularly the coast of Maine from Kittery to the Penobscot River, was the scene of warfare as cruel and as bloody as any the country has ever seen, and it was almost continuous for nearly a hundred years.

Here were thirteen major towns, numerous small hamlets and uncounted individual homesteads, which were completely wiped out, save only four - the Towns of York, Wells, Kittery and Appledore, or Isle of Shoals. This happened not just once, but several times, between the outbreak of King Philip's War in 1675 and the conquest of Canada in 1760.

Many colonists were killed, some with horrible torture; others were carried off into captivity from which they never returned; while still other captives were eventually ransomed or recovered.

The saddest part of it all was the fact that it was wholly unnecessary, as the French demonstrated in their colonizing of Quebec and Acadia. They treated the natives as brothers; the Jesuits converted them to Christianity and taught them to read and write. French colonists intermarried with the Indians, and absorbed them into their civilization.

The Abnakis, most intelligent and most highly civilized of all New England Indians, met the first English with warm welcome and generous treatment, expecting friendship in return; but the English - from the first landing of Capt. Weymouth in 1605, when, in return for his welcome, he kidnapped five of their Sachems and carried them off to Europe - used the natives shamefully. The English, on numerous occasions, kidnapped Indians and sold them into slavery in Spain; they cheated the natives unmercifully in fur trade; disturbed their fishing and hunting grounds; and steadily encroached on the

Indians' territory. Perhaps most unbearable of all to the proud Abnakis was the arrogant and contemptuous manner in which they were treated by the English – more like animals than human beings. At the last, the English were even paying bounties for Indian scalps

– 100 pounds for an adult and 15 pounds for an Indian child, even as we pay bounties for bears and bobcats.

In Popham's ill-fated colony of Sagadahoc, the English amused themselves by loading a cannon nearly to the muzzle with powder, then getting some Indians to help move it. As the Indians were dragging it along by ropes, an Englishman touched off the charge. Several natives were killed outright, and others horribly burned and mangled. Naturally the Indians retaliated and made life miserable for these Popham colonists, until they fled back to England at the first opportunity.

Captain John Smith, with a second ship under Captain Thomas Hunt, came to the mouth of the Kennebec in 1614. After loading his ship with fur and fish, Captain Smith sailed for home, leaving Captain Hunt to finish his loading. In Captain Smith's own words:

> "Thomas Hunt ... betrayed four and twenty of those poor Savages aboard his ship, and most dishonestly and inhumanely, for their kind treatment of me and all our men, carried them with him to Malaga (Spain) and sold them."

On one occasion, some English sailors, seeing an Indian woman with an infant in her canoe, and having heard that Indian children, like animals, could swim naturally, decided to test the theory, and upset the canoe throwing mother and child into the water. The infant, of course, sank; and the mother, after frantic efforts, was able to recover the child, but too late to save its life. She was the wife of Squando, Sagamore of the Sokokis; and the incident not only incurred for the English the bitter hatred of Squando, but did much to start King Philip's war.

These incidents are quite typical of the English relations with the natives. "The native Indians," said Popham's colonists, "are the outcasts of creation. They have no religion, but are merely diabolical. They are the very ruins of mankind, the most sordid and contemptible part of the human species."

12

On the other hand, the French, who, at about the same time, established a settlement among the Abnakis of the upper Kennebec and lived with them not only on terms of peace, but strong and personal friendship, wrote of them -

"The Indians are docile and friendly, accessible to the precepts of religion, strong in their attachment to their friends, and submissive to the rites and ceremonies of the Catholic faith."

In the subsequent warfare between English and French, it is not hard to understand why the Abnakis were always found on the side of the French territory.

Of the four Abnaki tribes, it is the Anasagunticook, or Androscoggin Indians, who particularly concern us, for they were the earliest known residents of Livermore.

They had a campground or gathering place at Pejepscot, or Brunswick Falls, which was often a meeting place for the several tribes; they had a fort at Laurel Hill, near the Great Falls at Lewiston; two branches of the tribe lived in Leeds (Caghnaugas) and in Sabattus (Pejepscots); but Rockomeka was their tribal headquarters and, reputedly, the largest Indian village in New England. This was a six mile section of the Androscoggin valley, extending from Rockomeka Falls (now Livermore Falls) to Canton Point, and being parts of what the white man was to know as Livermore and Jay. This included some of the best fishing - both brook trout and river salmon and a very large area of rich, alluvial flat land where they planted six or seven hundred acres to corn and other vegetables. The Indian name "Rockomeka" is said to have meant "Place for Corn."

The village itself comprised several hundred acres on which were constructed wigwams made of poles covered with bark or skins; larger council houses, usually about 20' x 40' to 60'; and storehouses or cellars for their food supplies.

The interiors of their dwellings had floors covered with hemlock boughs, and benches, or raised sections, next to the walls, covered with furs for cushioning and warmth. In the center was the fire on a bed of stones, for both cooking and heat; while, directly above, a hole in the roof was arranged for the smoke to escape. They had no windows or doors, entrance being through an opening over which were hung furs and skins.

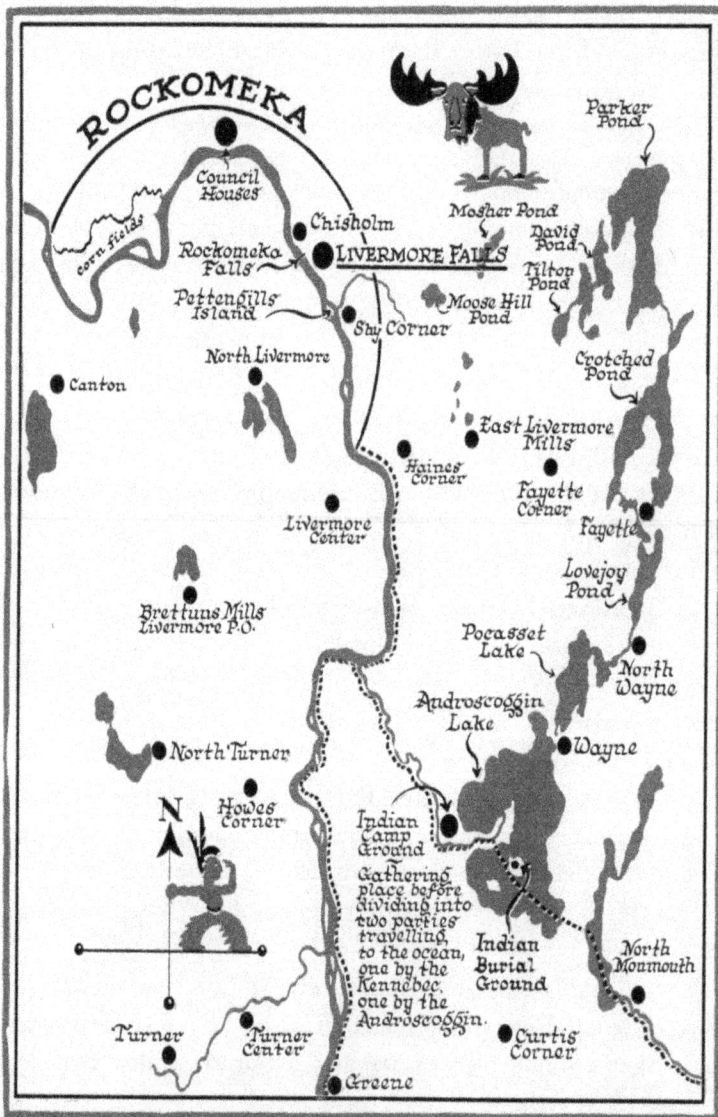

Approximate location of the Indian settlement, the burial ground, gathering place and routes to the ocean.

Their village was located in the shelter of the hills, which, rising sharply from the river valley and blanketed with a heavy growth of both soft and hard woods, afforded some protection for their dwellings from wintry blasts, and provided an abundant supply of game.

Pettingill's Island, just below Livermore Falls, and off the mouth of Red Water Brook, was one of their favorite campsites. This part of town, bordering on Red Water Brook, is called "Shuy" or "Shy"; and got its name from the fact that other Indians from the East, presumably Canibas, occasionally wandered in here to fish, but immediately fled at the sight of either Anasagunticooks or white men. Hence it was referred to as "The Place of the Shy Indians," and later on, simply as "Shy."

The Anasagunticooks roamed over the entire Androscoggin valley, from Umbagog Lake to the ocean, taking quantities of salmon and sturgeon in season at Rockomeka Falls, Great Falls, and Pejepscot Falls; and all the trout they wished, in the many lakes and tributary streams. They feasted on shell fish at the seashore, and caught plentiful supplies of salt water fish, which their women dried and smoked to carry back to Rockomeka. August was the time for duck hunting, when the flocks had shed their quills and feathers, and the young were insufficiently fledged to fly. The Indians drove them into the coves and creeks, and killed great numbers.

In the late summer and early autumn, they had green corn, maize, and other vegetables from their extensive plantings at Canton Point, which were planted, hoed, and harvested by the women.

In the late fall and winter months, they depended mostly on game for their food - principally venison, either fresh killed and broiled, or from their cache of dried and smoked meat together with the dried corn which the women ground into meal.

These people were still in the "Stone Age." They had no metal tools or weapons until the English and French

Spear Throwing stick

Bow Arrow

Harpoon points

Celt or tomahawk

Adz

Stone axe

Bone scrapers

Bone awl

Snowshoes

Clay pot

Shell hoe

Bark pot

Weapons and Tools

settlers came; but were extremely skillful in devising implements of all sorts from stone, wood, horn and shell.

Their bows were of tough elastic wood, requiring great strength to bend; but with them the Indians were deadly accurate, even with moving targets, at forty or fifty yards distance. Their arrows were tipped with heads of selected stone - usually flint, hornstone, jaspar, or quartz - most of which came from Mt. Kineo. They were remarkably well made, perfectly balanced and sharp as razors, as many have noted in the specimens still found around this locality. Their spear heads, too, were of such stone, six to eight inches in length, slender, and equally sharp.

For skinning and scraping hides, they had stone knives and chisel-like scrapers, and sharp sea shells; for hoes, they used stone or shells fastened to wooden handles.

For grinding their corn, they hollowed out a stone for a mortar; and a long, narrow stone, rounded at one end, and with a hole in the other end, served as a pestle. The pestle was usually suspended from a bent sapling which, as a sort of counter weight, made it easy for the squaw to move up and down in grinding. Numerous examples of these mortars and pestles have been found in this locality, and two such may be seen at Berry Hill Orchards and at the Norlands.

About these earliest natives of Livermore, the first question of an interested inquirer is usually, "What did they look like?" Fortunately, from descriptions of many early explorers and colonists, we know quite exactly. In stature, they were above average height, their bodies strong and straight; and their features regular and prominent, much more cleancut than the plains Indians. They had black, sparkling eyes, ivory-white teeth, and jet black hair that was long and coarse. The warriors shaved their heads, leaving only a scalp-lock, which was bound up on top, and brought forward like a crest, held in place by bear's grease, and which made them appear at least seven feet tall.

Their skin was a bright, copperish color, from which came their name, "Red Men"; and which readily distinguished them from any other races. A deformed, cross-eyed person, or dwarf was never found among them: nor were any blind or dumb. None of the men were ever corpulent, and they had no beards - whether from plucking out the hairs, from an ointment they used against insects, or by nature, authorities differ; but Capt. John Smith records that they were fascinated by the beards of his men, which they thought were false - which would indicate that perhaps they were beardless by nature.

In walking, both sexes "toed in," for greater ease in traveling through woods. Their senses were unusually acute, and their perceptions quick and clear. There were few sickly or feeble among them, and many lived to a great age, possessing their energy and faculties to the last.

The women were somewhat shorter, and tended to be more fleshy than the men. It is said that, if only they had our ideas of neatness and cleanliness, many of them would qualify as real beauties.

They had a fondness for bright colors, and used colored beads, shells, feathers, and colored threads in the adornment of their clothing or their person.

Their clothing was made from skins of animals: with fur side next to the body in cold weather; without fur in the warm months. It was the custom of many of the men to wear only a breech clout and moccasins in summer. With red or blue pigment they painted their faces and the exposed parts of the body in a variety of ways, which made their appearance, according to design, truly terrific.

Like all Abnakis, they were grave and taciturn in demeanor, seldom laughing or showing any emotion. Trained to privations,their patience, composure and stoicism were proverbial; and they affected never to dread suffering, and never to have sympathy for the meekest, tortured enemy.

It was characteristic of them always to remember a favor, and never to forget an injury. To retaliate evil for evil, to torture a fallen captive, to keep no faith. with an enemy, and never to forgive, seemed to be maxims according to their ethics. On the other hand, they were invariably faithful in friendship, and hospitable to the fullest extent of their means.

Smoking Fish

Cooking in buried pot

Fair and honest in trade, they were astonished at the crimes white men commited to accumulate property. Among themselves, every right and possession was safe without locks or bars, and they never practiced falsehoods to each other. Except for clothing, weapons and utensils, all property was held by the tribe in common; so greed and avarice for material property were not motives of the individual. Thievery, adultery and crimes of violence were practically unknown among them. An injury to one of the tribe was made a common cause of all.

All domestic work was done by the Women, including all planting, tending, and harvesting of crops; smoking, drying and curing of meat and fish; grinding of corn; collecting and carrying wood and tending fire; and all household chores - as such were considered beneath the dignity of the men, who did the hunting, fishing and fighting.

The Anasagunticooks, like the other Abnaki tribes, were governed by a chief, who was called the Sagamore, and a council of wise men, called Sachems.

Thus it was, in 1600, that the portions of Livermore Falls and Jay that were known as Rockomeka, were the tribal home of these Androscoggin Indians, who were living an almost idyllic existence - at least in 3 of the 4 seasons. If the Maine winters seemed hard, they were accustomed to them by many generations of experience; and with plentiful furs, tight wigwams, and constant fire on the stone hearths, they kept relatively comfortable. In the other seasons, this part of the valley was truly beautiful. In the spring, the river was a raging torrent, roaring over the falls, between banks and hills of lush and variegated green, ranging from the soft, pale green of willows, poplars, and birches to the dark, black-green of spruces and pines, while the silvery salmon brought a welcome change from venison. In the warm, lazy days of summer, the river flowed more quietly and the falls were only a dull rumble, as the tribe drifted down in their birch-bark canoes to Merrymeeting Bay and the open ocean, to hunt ducks, to catch and dry fish, and to feast on clams, mussels. and lobsters. The fall was best of all when, after the squaws had gathered in their crops of corn, squash and pumpkin, Indian summer brought "October's bright blue weather." The hunting was at its best, and the dying year was ending in a bright burst of gorgeous color, which made the picturesque little islands in the river seem like ladies' hats extravagantly decorated.

With the friendly and related Sokokis and Pennacooks on the west; the equally friendly and related Canibas and Wawenocks to the east; the ocean in front, and the wilds of Canada to the north, the Anasagunticooks seemed secure and at peace. Little did they realize what was in store for them with the coming of the white men.

In 1605, Captain George Weymouth on the ship "Archangel" came to Maine, landing first at Monhegan, May 17, 1605; then proceeded to the Boothbay area where he was welcomed by some of the Abenakis (Wawenocks), whose kindness he repaid by seizing and kidnapping five of them. He next proceeded to the mouth of the Androscoggin, where he raised a cross; but the natives were warned of his treachery, and not a single Anasagunticook appeared.

In 1607, George Popham and Raleigh Gilbert came in the ships "Gift of God" and "Mary and John," to establish the "Sagadahoc Colony," sometimes called Fort St. George. Captain Gilbert, in a shallop with nineteen men, went exploring the coast; and on Sept. 24, 1607, reached Merrymeeting Bay. Turning left, he entered the Androscoggin. Early next morning, he reached the falls at Brunswick; and, by ropes, dragged the shallop up through those rapids. About three miles above, they landed and camped for the night.

The next morning a canoe crossed the river carrying an Indian chief, "Sebeona," and four natives. The chief was friendly and courteous, but would not land until they placed one of their men in his canoe as a hostage. As soon as the hostage was received into the canoe, and Sebeona had taken a seat in the shallop, the Indians commenced paddling up river toward their village. The birchbark canoe, light as a bubble, was driven with great rapidity, and it was with difficulty that the shallop kept up.

21

Building a Canoe.

Having ascended the river about three miles more, the canoe landed; and the four Indians, with their one white companion, entered a trail which led back to their village. Leaving
nine men to guard the shallop, Captain Gilbert hurriedly followed, a little apprehensive, since they could only com-

municate by signs, and he was unsure of the intentions of the Indians. The well-trodden path led picturesquely around the forest-crowned hills of the Androscoggin for a distance of about a league. Here they came upon the little hamlet of the chief. The whole village of about 250 persons was, of course, thrown into great commotion by so strange an event.

Captain Gilbert's historian writes - "Here we found near 50 able men, very strong and tall, such as their like before we had not seen. All were newly painted, and armed with bows and arrows."

Their reception was hospitable in all respects and they reported, "Peaceful overtures prevailed, and proposals for trade were made."

This, apparently, is the first recorded confrontation of the English with the Anasagunticooks.

The first white settler inland, in the territory of the Anasagunticooks, was one Thomas Purchase, who took up residence within the Town of Brunswick in about 1628. In 1639, he sold certain of his lands on the Bay, and moved further up the Androscoggin. He developed a very lucrative trade with the Indians, and amassed a large fortune; but no trader along the coast was more harsh in his maltreatment of the natives than was Thomas Purchase. He not only got them drunk and cheated them out of their furs and lands, but he began cheating them of their liquor as well. There is recorded the complaint of one Anasagunticook that he sold Purchase 100 pounds of furs for water taken from Purchase's well.

For more than 50 years, the Abenakis put up with the cheating and maltreatment by the English, and the constant encroachment on their lands, with no signs of open hostilities; but they frequently made complaints to no avail, and their resentment and hatred were building up. As the white men steadily moved into their hunting and fishing grounds, one of their Sagamores warned, "The English will leave you but two alternatives - be driven into exile, or be annihilated."

When at last the pent-up feelings burst out, in 1675, in King Philip's War, the Anasagunticooks struck first at the hated Thomas Purchase, plundering his goods and killing his cattle. Purchase was away at the time; but the Indians did not harm his wife, only warning her, "Others will soon come, and you will fare worse."

Two weeks later, the lonely cabin of Thomas Wakely, in Falmouth, on the east bank of the Presumpscot River was attacked. Mr. Wakely, his wife, his son John, and John's wife and three children were tomahawked. Two children were carried away as captives.

From then on, the next 100 years were almost constant warfare, interrupted by brief periods of truce - King Philip's War 1675-1678, King William's War 1688-1699, Queen Anne's War 1703-1713, Lovewell's War 1722-1725, Spanish or 5-years War 1745-1749, and the French & Indian War 1755-1760.

It is not within the province of this book to go into the details of that long and terrible struggle; but a few incidents will give an idea of its character, in which the Androscoggins were always in the forefront as the most powerful and most hostile of the Abenakis.

Within the short space of 5 weeks, in 1671, 60 miles of the coast eastward of Casco Bay was ravaged and depopulated. Cape Neddick, Scarborough, Casco, Arrowsic, and Pemaquid were in ashes. In the attack on Cape Neddick, among the dead was a nursing mother who had her brains dashed out. Her infant was fastened to her bosom, and was thus found still living, striving to draw nourishment from the cold breast.

Major Waldron was one who had particularly incurred the hatred of the Indians in his dealings with them in trade. When they paid him what was due, he would neglect to cross out their accounts; and in buying beaver skins by weight, he insisted his fist weighed just one pound. In the attack on Dover in 1689, he was captured. The Indians stripped him, tied him in an arm chair, and proceeded to torture him in a most dreadful manner. Some gashed his breast with knives, saying, "I cross out my account." Others cut off joints of his fingers, saying "Now will your fist weigh a pound?" After continuing this torture for some time, they finally let him fall upon his own sword.

In May, 1690, a force of four to five hundred French and Indians, under command of M. Burneffe, attacked Fort Loyal at Falmouth. For four days and nights the Fort was under continuous attack, until most of the garrison were slain. The survivors surrendered on the promise of the French commander that their lives would be spared; but when the gates were opened, M. Burneffe lost all control over his ferocious allies; and the 70 survivors nearly all were slaughtered, many with inhuman tortures.

The General Court of Massachusetts, observing that the Androscoggins were the most hostile of the Maine Indians, determined to attack that tribe. On September 9, 1690, they sent Major Benjamin Church with a force of 300 men, with orders reading:

> "To sail eastward by the first opportunity to Casco or Places adjacent that may be most commodious for landing with safety, and to visit the Enemy, French and Indians at their headquarters at Amerascogen, Pejepscot or any other Plat according as you may have hope or intelligence of the Resident of the Enemy; killing, destroying and utterly rooting out the Enemy wheresoever they may be found."

Major Church landed at Maquoit and marched at night to the Indian Fort at Pejepscot. They found only an abandoned village and empty wigwams at that spot.

Major Church pushed on hurriedly, up the west bank of the Androscoggin River, reaching the junction of the Androscoggin and Little Androscoggin Rivers at about two o'clock in the afternoon of September 14, 1690. His approach was discovered by young Doney, son of Worumbee, who ran for the Indian fort at Laurel Hill, leaving his wife and two English captives behind. The Indian woman was shot, and the two captives released; but young Doney reached the fort and warned the other Indians, who followed him out the north gate, running up the great falls, and disappearing under them. A few Indians, unable to reach the falls in time, were killed.

Several women and children had been unable to escape, among them the wives of two distinguished Sagamores, Kankamagus and Worumbee, with their children. As the Sagamores' wives promised Major Church that 80 English, then held captive upriver at Rockomeka (Canton Point), would be exchanged for their ransom, their lives - (and those of their children) - were spared. But the rest of the Indians (both females and unoffending children) were put to the tomahawk or sword, excepting only 2 old squaws.

The letter from Major Church to Governor Hinckley of Plymouth, reporting this, reads:

> "We left two old squaws that were not able to march; gave them victuals enough for one week, of their own corn, boiled, and a little of our provisions; and buried their dead, and left clothes enough to keep them warm, and left wigwams for them to lie in; gave them orders to tell their friends how kind we were to them, bidding them to do the like to ours. Also, if they were for peace, to come to Goodman Small's at Berwick, within 14 days, who would attend to discourse them."

Major Church learned that the main body of Androscoggins had gone to Winter Harbor (near Saco) to attack the English there.

Hundreds of horrible tragedies of burning, scalping and toturing have never been recorded. Hundreds of colonists were killed or carried into captivity; and some of the worst sufferings were endured by these poor captives, wounded men, feeble women leaving the gory bodies of their husbands behind them, and little children now fatherless.

One woman, carrying her child, began to fall behind; a savage grabbed the child, crushed its skull with his tomahawk, saying, "Now you will travel faster."

One young woman, becoming exhausted, complained that she could go no farther without rest. An Indian took her aside, cut her head off, scalped it, and showing it to the rest of the prisoners, said, "So will I do to any who complain."

A fat man among the prisoners was having trouble in keeping up; but was able to escape and hide in a hollow tree. The Indians easily tracked him to his hiding place; dragged him out, stripped him and tied him to a tree. Then they proceeded to torture him. They cut dollops of flesh from his ample body and threw the bloody pieces in his face; they stuck burning faggots in his body; and finally left him to finish dying by roasting at a slow fire.

One captive they skinned alive, and used his hide for belts.

They had the custom, when they had lost men in a fight, to put to death as many captives as they had men killed. For example, in the summer of 1705 a band of 18 Abnakis rushing from the forest near York, seized 4 children belonging to the family of Mr. Stover. One being too young to travel, they knocked in the head. As one of their own warriors had been shot in their retreat with the children, they took vengeance by putting a little boy to death with awful tortures.

On another occasion, a party sprang from ambush, at Kittery, and seized Mr. Shapley and his son. They gnawed off the first joint of each finger and thumb of the unhappy young man, and stopped the bleeding by inserting the mangled stumps into the bowl of tobacco pipes, heated red hot. This seems to have been one of their favorite modes of torture.

The captives whom Major Church released at Rockomeka, in exchange for the wives and children of Worumbee and Kankamagus, in 1690, are the first record we have of white men being in what is now Livermore; but there were doubtless others still earlier, who were also unwilling guests of the Androscoggins.

Ordinarily, prisoners were held at Rockomeka only temporarily, pending their sale to the French in Canada. However, some were kept permanently as laborers, to help the squaws with hoeing, gathering wood, etc. Also, some children, usually boys, were adopted by the tribe, and became so attached to their red-skinned brothers and the Indian way of life, that they never went back to their white relatives.

Older residents of Livermore Falls may recall George

Chandler, who operated the grist mill here, and his sister Mary Emma Chandler (Mrs. Joseph G. Ham) . Their family of Chandlers lived in North Yarmouth, Maine. One of their family, Joseph Chandler (12 years) together with two Mitchell boys, Soloman (11 years) and Daniel (7), had been watching the men at work at a neighbor's farm. Before the men left, the boys were sent home that they might drive up the cows which were pastured on the protected land below the meeting-house. Beside the road home, 12 or more Anasagunticooks had hidden themselves, planning, it is thought, to attack the men as they returned from their work at night. Here they were discovered by the boys, and not daring to let them go after their discovery, or to remain long in the immediate neighborhood with them in captivity, they immediately made off with them, and started the long trail toward Canada. The older boys had to trudge along as best they could, but when little 7-year old Daniel gave out the Indians took him on their backs, and carried him until he was rested.

The boys were first carried to St. Francois, but here they were separated and years passed before they were all together again.

Joseph Chandler was sold to a Frenchman, who in turn sold him to Cornelius Cuyler of Albany for 25 pounds. He was ransomed from Cuyler by his father, and about six months later, returned home by the roundabout route of France.

The younger Mitchell boy, Daniel, was adopted by the Anasagunticooks at St. Francois, and ten of the most impressionable years of his life were passed among them. He was an Indian in all his habits and speech, and the wild life of the tribe became dearer to him than the home and friends of his childhood. When his father finally located and ransomed him, after 10 years, he was very unwilling to leave the Indians, and even after he was on his way home, he attempted to escape and return to them. For a long time he was closely watched and great care taken lest he return to his red-skinned brothers.

June 20,1703, Governor Dudley requested the Abenaki sagamores to meet with him upon Casco peninsula in Falmouth.

Attended by a considerable retinue of gentlemen belonging to the legislatures of Massachusetts and New Hampshire, he had the pleasure of a conference with a large delegation from the Pennacooks, of New Hampshire; and the Sokokis, the Anasagunticooks, the Canibas and the Tarratines from Maine.

All the Indians appeared to great advantage. They were well armed, handsomely clad, some of them fancifully decorated, and the most of their faces so painted as to give them looks truly terrific. Probably no one tribe (says Williamson) was so fully represented as the Anasagunticooks, for about 250 of them arrived in a flotilla of 65 canoes, with their sagamores

Mesambomett and Wexar.

The headquarters and main village of the Anasgun-ticooks, at Rockomeka on the Androscoggin, was not far from the Canibas village of Norridgewock at the junction of the Kennebec and Sandy Rivers. Because this latter was the mission station of the Jesuits, served at this time by Father Rasle whom the English particularly hated, an expedition of 270 men, under Colonel Hilton, was sent up the Kennebec to attack Norridgewock in the winter of 1705. The Indians, however, had ample warning of his approach and disappeared into the forests. Colonel Hilton, finding the village deserted, burned a large chapel and vestry, together with a cluster of comfortable Indian wigwams; but returned without having seen a solitary Indian.

During these early years of the 18th century, Indians, though invisible, seemed to be everywhere. No man could pass a few rods from the door of a garrison without danger of being shot down. Mr. Pickenel, at Spruce Creek, for example, was leaving his door with his family, when a bullet from a concealed savage struck him dead. His wife also was wounded and his little child scalped. The poor child, left for dead, recovered from the dreadful wound.

By 1707 only six English settlements survived in Maine - Kittery, Berwick, York, Wells, Casco and Winter Harbor.

In the ten years, 1703 - 1713, more than a quarter of the inhabitants of Maine had been killed or captured; but, in the same period, it is estimated that more than a third of the Abenakis perished. Furthermore, the English were being reinforced by a constant stream of new immigrants, while the Abenakis were suffering constant diminution from the warfare and epidemics such as smallpox.

That the English perpetrated cruelties in this warfare, as well as the Indians, is shown by such incidents as that of Colonel Walton who, in 1710, with some soldiers and Massachusetts Indians had captured a sagamore of the Canibas. Because the Indian would not talk freely, Colonel Walton passed him over to the Massachusetts Indians to hack to pieces with their tomahawks.

Two parties of Indians, one from the Androscoggins and one from the Kennebecs, met at Merrymeeting Bay, June 13, 1722, in 20 canoes containing 60 men. By way of reprisal they seized nine families of settlers. All were treated humanely, and they soon liberated the women and children and all but four men, whom they held as indemnities for the safety of four Indian hostages.

It is remarkable that, exasperated as were the natives at this period, they generally treated their prisoners very humanely. The children, even of good families, often became so much attached to their captors that they were unwilling to return to civilized life.

In the winter of 1722, another expedition was undertaken to destroy the village of Norridgewock and kill Father Rasle. This time it was proposed to go up the Androscoggin to Rockomeka, and at the big bend of the river, they would cross country northerly a few miles to the Sandy River. By following down the valley of Sandy River they could reach Norridgewock by a totally unexpected route, and hoped to strike the Indians by surprise. In February 1722, the troops reached the falls at Brunswick. The storms of winter were upon them, and drifting snow encumbered their path.

Painfully they toiled up the river by the banks of the Androscoggin to the vicinity of Rockomeka. Just then occurred a "January thaw"; a warm rain melted the snow; and all the fields were covered more than knee-deep with slush. The icy moisture penetrated leather as though it were brown paper. The discomfort was so extreme that further journeying became impracticable. The soldiers gave up, and returned, not having caught sight of a single Indian.

The attempt was made again in August 1724. The expedition went up the Kennebec; and on August 22nd they advanced cautiously through the woods, and surrounded the settlement. This time the Indians were taken completely by surprise. Their men tried hastily to grab arms and hold off the invaders, while their women, children and old men plunged into the river, trying to escape to the other shore.

Most of those in the water, however, were shot as they swam. Meanwhile, in the village, 80 were slain and scalped - including of course, Father Rasle, whose body was horribly mutilated.

Charlevoix, who was a resident of Canada about that time, in his "Histoire de la France Nouvelle" (Paris, 1744) describes the scene thus:

> "The noise and tumult gave Father Rasle notice of the danger his converts were in. Not intimidated, he shewed himself to the enemy in hopes to draw all their attention to himself, and secure his flock at the peril of his own life. He was not disappointed. As soon as he appeared, the English set up a great shout, which was followed by a shower of shot; when he fell down dead near to a cross which he had erected in the midst of the village. Seven Indians, who sheltered his body with their own, falling around him. Thus died this kind shepherd, giving his life for the sheep, after a painful mission of 37 years."

The Governor Dummer treaty which marked the cessation of hostilities in December 1725, amounted to unconditional surrender of the Indians, and left the English in undisputed possession of all the land they claimed. Governor Dummer, however, recognized the injustices done the Indians, and endeavored to see that they were fairly treated.

In July, 1726, a conference was appointed at Falmouth for ratifying the treaty. About forty chiefs appeared, with Wenemovet, a Tarratine Sagamore, at their head, who declared that he had full power to act for the Anasagunticooks and other Abenaki tribes. It is said that "all were much impressed by the intelligence and high moral qualities manifested by many of these chiefs."

Loron, a sachem, wrote to Mr. Dummer:

> "Never let the trading houses deal in much rum. It wastes the health of our young men. It unfits them to attend prayers. It makes them

carry ill both to your people and their own brethren. This is the mind of all our chief men. I salute you, great Governor, and am your good friend. - Loron"

Wivurna, another Sachem, who had been a brave and bloody warrior, being softened and charmed by the spirit of firmness and justice which he witnessed in Mr. Dummer, wrote:

"Brother - I am fully satisfied; for all the blood, that before lay boiling in my breast, is flowed away. Now I much labor for peace in our land. Should any windy clouds arise, I would make haste to inform you, - that they might do us no harm. In three things you make my heart glad. My grandson, that was dead, is alive and returned to me safe. Canavas, that was taken, comes home well; he is encouraged to do good service. Your kindness to me and my people, I am thankful for. I am now old and gray-headed; I have seen many good gentlemen, English, French, and Indian, - and many of them are dead. But of all, I have not found like Governor Dummer, for steadfastness and justice. If I were a Sagamore and young, the first thing I did, should be to see you. But as I am old and not able to travel, I Heartily salute you, my good friend. Farewell. - Wivurna"

Some of the English settlements were fearful lest the Anasagunticooks, or other Abenakis who had not personally signed the treaty, should make a new attack; and so, to quiet all fears and bind all tribes to the treaty, another conference was called in July 1727, at which all tribes, including the Anasagunticooks, would be present.

The Indians met Governor Dummer's party at Falmouth, July 17, 1727; and this time, all the Maine Indian tribes were represented. Before beginning the negotiations with the English, the Indians selected Auyaummowett, from Rockomeka, as

33

spokesman for all the tribes.

Upon completion of the reading of the treaty, Auyaum-mowett, the Androscoggin, rose and said -

> "What we have heard from your Honour at present we shall take into consideration 'till tomorrow, and then you shall hear from us; as for the Articles which have been read over to us, we have heard of them, but never heard them read so fully to us, and are very glad we have now heard of them for we came for that purpose. As we are now sitting before your Honour and see the faces of one another, we say, This is the place which God has appointed for us to see one another at, and as God is the Master of Prayer, we pray he would direct us all in the ways that may tend to Peace, and desire your Honour would let us know and be so free as to hide nothing from us, and if we say anything that is amiss or look like an affront, that you would let us know it that we may avoid it, and we shall be so on our part as to keep nothing back nor hide anything from you in the Treaty, we ought to join heartily and be strong in the Affair, it is of great Weight and Moment, it weighs heavy, We have said."

The various tribes considered the treaty in tribal councils; but actually they had no choice but to submit. They were in serious condition, both from shortage of firearms and ammunition, and from lack of food, since hostilities had prevented planting of crops, laying in a supply of game, and securing furs for trade.

Final arrangements were made for the return of captives, and the conference concluded with a banquet on Munjoy Hill.

Gov. Dummer knew how to sympathize with the Indians in their wrongs. Had the spirit which animated him prevailed from the beginning, there need have been no war whatever with the Indians. But as a rule, the English settlers hated the Indians, and were anxious to get entirely rid of them.

When questioned as to why they took sides with the French, these are the words of the Indians, as reported by Williamson
(Vol. II, Page 113):

"The French are our friends; they advocate our rights, and become, as it were, one with us. They sell us whatever we want, and never take away our lands. They send the kind missionaries to teach us how worship the Great Spirit; and, like brothers, they give us good advice when we are in trouble. When we trade with them, we have good articles, full weight, and free measure. They leave us our goodly rivers, where we catch fine salmon, and leave us unmolested to hunt the bear, the moose, and the beaver, where our fathers have hunted them. We love our own country, where our fathers were buried, and where we and our children were born. We have our rights as well as the English; we also know as well as they, what is just and what is unjust.

"When you English came, we received you with open arms. We thought you children of the sun; we fed you with our best meat. Never did a white man go hungry from our cabins. But you returned evil for good. You put the burning cup to our lips. It filled our veins with poison. When you had intoxicated us, you took the advantage, and cheated us in trade. You now tell us that our country is yours, that it has passed from us forever.

"You say that you have bought our lands from our Sagamores. It is not true. Our chiefs love their tribes too well, and have too great souls, to turn their children from the homes of their fathers. Where can we go? We own no other land. There is no other land so dear to us. The forts which you have built on our territory are contrary to treaty; and they ought to be laid low."

By 1735, the population of Maine was restored to about 9000. There were nine towns and several settlements called plantations. But again the Indians became alarmed. The increasing settlements were fast encroaching upon their territories, and their thoughtful men saw clearly that the time was fast approaching when they would be driven from all their possessions.

In 1743, there were eleven towns and a population of 12,000. The English, in their hatred of Indians, made little distinction between friends and enemies. If a Canadian Indian engaged in any act of aggression, the English were prompt to take vengeance upon any Indian they might chance to meet. Captain James Cargill, of Newcastle, was commissioned to raise a scouting company. He chanced to meet a band of Indian hunters, peaceful men who no longer thought of any hostile act. He shot down twelve and took their scalps, which were worth to him and his party 2400 pounds. Soon after, they met a friendly Indian woman, Margaret; she was well known, and was returning from a visit to the garrison with her baby in her arms. They shot her down and as the dying woman pleaded with them to protect her child, they killed the baby before its mother's eyes.

Brunswick, on the Androscoggin, was one of the first places repeopled after Lovell's War. In 1730 a chaplain was allowed at this garrison; and it was in this place that Sabiste, the Anasagunticook Sagamore, requested the government to keep some supplies; "For," said he, "in cold winters and deep snows my Indians, unable to go to Fort Richmond, sometimes suffer."

The government always, in such instances, cheerfully administered relief; and the tribe of Androscoggins remained quiet, though constantly viewed with distrust.

The French, in Canada, observing the straits to which their

allies, the Abenakis, were reduced from the continual warfare and the encroachment of the English, offered them asylum and territory of their own around the Chaudiere, at St. Francois and Becancourt; and many of the Indians began moving North, to take advantage of the offer. The Sokokis and the Wawenocks no longer existed as tribes - their remnants joining the Anasagunticooks, or St. Francois colony. The Canibas, too, since the destruction of Norridgewock, were greatly reduced, and were gradually moving up towards the headwaters of the Kennebec, and into Canada.

The Anasagunticooks, while stoutly maintaining their ownership of the Androscoggin valley, and, to a certain extent, continuing occupancy from Rockomeka to the Canadian border, nevertheless shifted their headquarters to St. Francois, where they quickly became the major factor in that settlement. Their language was the language of all the refugees, and their Sagamores were given the lead of the colony.

When, in 1741, the English authorities were made aware that the tribes upon the Androscoggin and Kennebec Rivers were gradually withdrawing from their former places of abode to Canada, this was regarded as an unfavorable symptom and probable preparation to resume hostilities.

Governor Shirley told the Canibas' chiefs that he had decided to build a new fort at Teconnet, on the point of land between the rivers Kennebec and Sebasticook. In 1754 Fort Halifax was here constructed, 100'x40' with flankers and blockhouses, and garrisoned by one hundred men. This and Fort Western were strongly resented by the Indians.

On November 6, 1754, a scouting party of Indians fell upon a party of the Fort Halifax garrison, killed and scalped one soldier, and carried away four other prisoners. Meanwhile five hundred French and Indians were collecting at Quebec, preparatory to assault on Fort Halifax.

The public was greatly aroused against the St. Francois Indians, and many believed that the time had arrived when that tribe, if none other, ought to be utterly exterminated. The Governor and General Court declared war, June 11, 1755, against the Anasagunticooks, and all other tribes east of the

Piscataqua, excepting those upon the Penobscot River; and furthermore offered bounties of one hundred pounds for every Indian scalp, and one hundred and ten pounds for a captive.

Once more typical Indian warfare was resumed, mostly by small parties waylaying or ambushing settlers. For example, on May 18, 1757, a party of Anasagunticooks waylaid Captain Lithgow and eight men near Topsham, and wounded two at the first onset. A severe skirmish ensued in which the Indians on seeing two of their number fall dead, seized their bodies and fled. Two Englishmen were killed further up the river.

In response to the aroused public fear and resentment, and the clamor for annihilation of the Anasagunticooks at St. Francois, General Amherst, having reduced Ticonderoga, dispatched thence, September 13, 1759, Major Robert Rogers, with about two hundred rangers, to destroy the Indian villages at St. Francois and Becancourt. Those familiar with the works of Kenneth Roberts will recall his vivid description of this expedition of "Rogers' Rangers."

After a fatiguing march of twenty-one days, Rogers came within sight of the places which he discovered from the top of a tree. Halting his men, at the distance of three miles, he rested till twilight. In the evening he entered the former village in disguise with two of his officers. The Indians being, unfortunately for them, engaged in a great dance, he passed through them undiscovered. Having formed his men into parties and posted them to advantage, he made a general assault, October 4, just before day, while the Indians, fatigued by exercise, were in a sound sleep. So completely were they surprised, that little resistance could be made. Some were killed in their cottages, and others attempting to flee, were shot or thrust through with bayonets by those placed at the avenues. About twenty were taken prisoners, and five English captives were rescued from suffering. Daylight disclosed to the assailants a horrid spectacle. It was the sight of several hundred scalps torn from the heads of their countrymen, elevated on poles and waving in the air.

St. Francois was a village which had, through a period of many years, been enriched with the plunder of English frontiers and the sale of captives. The church was adorned with plate and the houses were decently furnished. The apprehension of alarm and pursuit did not allow much time for pillage. The rangers took only such things as they could conveniently carry; among which were two hundred guineas in money, a silver image weighing ten pounds, a large quantity of wampum, and some articles of clothing. Having set fire to the village, Rogers made his retreat up the river St. Francois; intending that his men should meet in rendezvous at the upper Coos on the Connecticut River. Rogers, having one man killed and six or seven wounded, found it necessary to dismiss his prisoners on their parole; after this he was pursued and lost seven of his company. The whole party kept in a body about ten days, and then scattered. Some died in the woods, and all the rest suffered the extremes of hunger and fatigue, before they arrived at any habitation of the settlers.

With the fall of Quebec to General Wolfe, also in September 1759, and the annihilation of St. Francois, there were indications that the wars between the New England provincials and the eastern tribes, which at periods for eighty-five years had overspread the land with blood and desolation, were about to terminate - probably forever.

Wasted by war, famine, hardships and disease (particularly the smallpox) and no longer supported by their French allies, the Anasagunticooks were facing inevitable extinction. Since the massacre at St. Francois, not a chief remained to whom they could swear allegiance and under whom they might hope to start a new colony.

Many Anasagunticooks remained in Maine, however. At the time Lieutenant Livermore first came here, in 1770, there were about five hundred of them left in the Androscoggin valley mostly in Leeds, Rockomeka, and the upper reaches of the river. Soon after the opening of Leeds, Livermore and Jay to white settlement, these survivors, save for a few solitary Indians, moved further up the river or into Canada.

Even after they had withdrawn from this area, they continued to make two annual pilgrimages down the river to the sea, to sell their furs, to hunt sea fowl and to fish - but more important, to visit the graves of their dead. Down the river they came, as far as the mouth of Dead River, up which they paddled to their usual campground which is said to have been just East of the present railroad bridge over Dead River in Leeds. There they waited until all their members, scattered on their holy missions to the dead, had joined them.

It was their custom to bury the dead in a sitting position; then once a year, or periodically, to dig up the remains, scrape any remaining flesh from the bones, which they then deposited in the family tomb. One such burying place, we know, was on Norris' Island, in Androscoggin Lake.

One colonist was traveling with them as a prisoner, when one of their number was killed in a skirmish; and he relates how they up-ended the roots of a tree, placed the body beneath it, then let the tree spring back in place, leaving no sign of a burial. Prior to such burial, however, they cut off an arm to take back to the family tomb.

When the scattered members had all gathered, they divided into two parties, one returning to the Androscoggin and following down to the sea, the other crossing from Wayne Pond to Wilson, Annabessacook, Cobbosseecontee into the Kennebec, down which they paddled to the sea.

The last such tribal pilgrimage was in 1796. Even the pathetically few hundreds, of a once mighty tribe of many thousands, must have been an impressive sight, as they came down river in their flotilla of canoes, in full ceremonial tribal dress and freshly painted in bright red and blue colors. For them, it must have been a heart-rending trip, for they knew it was the last, and they were abandoning the graves of their dead forever.

With the dignity and stoicism so characteristic of their race, they accepted the inevitable. Stopping along the way to bid farewell to their few white friends - among whom, we are proud to say, was Deacon Livermore - in their birch bark canoes they glided silently up the river, to disappear in the pages of history.

They deserved a better fate.

It is true that once their enmity was aroused, they fought

with a ferocity and cruelty foreign to our ideas of "civilized" warfare; their ethics taught that, with an enemy, they should never show mercy, never keep faith, and never forgive.

It is true also that their ideas of personal cleanliness did not accord with ours; though their wigwams were always neat and clean, they apparently did not wash even face and hands, to say nothing of clothing and utensils - at least during the cold months.

On the other hand, they were superb physical specimens - tall, lean and muscular, with surprising strength and endurance. But most important, it will be many centuries, if ever, before Livermore again harbors a civilization where there is no crime, where greed and avarice are non-existent, where the social consciousness is such that the good of all comes before the individual, and where friendship is unmeasured, even by death; as was so well demonstrated by those seven unarmed braves who tried to make rampart of their bodies to protect their good friend, the kindly Jesuit, Father Rasle - and who died at his side.

The Androscoggins, like the other Abenakis, had no written language, and so left us no record; their structures were exceedingly frail and quickly vanished. About the only reminder of them we have today are their place names, such as Umbagog, Cupsuptic, Anasagunticook, Pocasset and especially Androscoggin which denominated the river on which their life centered, and by whose name the tribe itself was generally known.

Early in the last century, Amasa Alden, a descendent of John Alden of Plymouth, lived at the junction of the River Road and the North Livermore Road, beside the falls at Livermore. He was a mason by trade, but better known for his avocations of musician and rhymester. At different times, three volumes of his verse appeared. He lived, with the sound of the falls continually in his ears, and its spray almost at his feet. It is not surprising that the river was the inspiration of some of his writing.

One of Alden's verses is a fitting requiem for the vanished race:

"ANDROSCOGGIN, well they named thee
In that mellow Indian tongue;
Thou art named in many legends,
And right worthy to be sung.
Thine is beauty, mighty river,
Throwing up thy sparkling spray,
Rushing on with deafening fury,
As thou passest on thy way.
Gone forever from thy borders, but
IMMORTAL IN THY NAME,
Are the red men of the forest;
Be thou keeper of their fame."

PORT ROYAL
The Pioneer Settlement

THE OWNERSHIP OF MAINE LANDS was so confused by the different grants and annulments of Patents, the different rulings of succeeding Sovereigns, and the conflicting claims on boundaries, that it may be useful to summarize the major facts, as they pertain to this portion of New England before proceeding with the founding and growth of the town of Livermore.

Letters Patent were issued to John Cabot and his sons, Sebastian, Lewis, and Sancius, in 1497, by Henry VII; and several voyages were undertaken by them, from 1497-1499, to the North American coast from Maine to the Carolinas. It is upon these discoveries by the Cabots that the English based their claim to the territory.

In 1605, Captain George Weymouth visited Monhegan and explored the coast of Maine.

1606 - James I designated the whole territory between 34 and 45 degrees of latitude as "North and South Virginia"; and gave Charters to the London Company, or First Colony of Virginia, for the southern part; and to the Plymouth Company, or Second Colony of Virginia, for the northern part (41⁰-45⁰ parallel), with condition that all sales of land be confirmed by the Crown.

1607 - The Popham Colony (Fort St. George) was established on the Sagadahoc peninsula, at the mouth of the Kennebec. This was the beginning of English colonization of New England, and was under the Plymouth Company grant.

1614 - Captain John Smith arrived at Monhegan; and explored the coast from the Penobscot to Cape Cod, of which he made a map designated "New England."

1620 - A new Charter was granted the Plymouth Company under the new name "The Council at Plymouth" or "Council for New England," covering all land between the 40 and 48 N. Latitude, to be called "New England." The three principal men on this council were Lord John Popham, Sir Ferdinando Gorges, and Captain John Mason. Gorges and Mason, with several merchants, organized "The Company of Laconia"; and secured a patent from the Council for all land' between the Merrimack and the Sagadahoc (or Kennebec). This was given the name of "The Province of Maine."

1629 - Mason and Gorges divided their Province between them, with the Piscataqua River as middle boundary - Mason's part being called "New Hampshire," and Gorges', "New Somersetshire."

1635 - Gorges was made Governor General of all New England; and the Plymouth Council surrendered its Patent. New Patents were issued, reserving grants made by them.

1639 - Gorges was granted a Charter from Charles I, giving him the territory between the Piscataqua and Kennebec rivers, extending 120 miles North and South - the tract to be called "The Province and Countie of Maine."

Thomas Purchase and George Way had previously been granted (1632) certain territory on the Androscoggin River and east side of Casco Bay, including Harpswell, Brunswick, and a part of Topsham, and known as Pejepscot, Purchase conveyed to Massachusetts (through Governor Winthrop) his land at Pejepscot, except the portion occupied and improved by himself.

In 1647, after the death of Gorges, the "Province and Countie of Maine" was without proper government and supervision of its affairs; so, the inhabitants of the southern section voluntarily sought the protection and government of Massachusetts, becoming freemen of that Commonwealth. In 1658 that section became the separate and autonomous County of Yorkshire; and Massachusetts continued to extend its authority in Maine.

1660 - Upon the restoration of Charles II, Ferdinando Gorges (grandson of Sir Ferdinando) claimed Maine as his property; and four years later a royal order bade Massachusetts to restore it to him.

1676 - King Charles II decreed that Massachusetts does not. have "Right of Soil" in Maine and New Hampshire.

1677 - Massachusetts finally cleared its title by buying the Gorges' rights for 1250 pounds.

1685 - James II replaced Charles II, and the new King annulled the Massachusetts Charter; land titles were assailed and old deeds declared invalid.

1689 - James II having been. dethroned and replaced by William of Orange, Massachusetts resumed its charter rights.

1692 - A new Provincial Charter for Massachusetts, the "Charter of William and Mary," was brought by the first Royal Governor, Sir William Phips. This included land from Piscataqua to Kennebec as the District of Maine, and from Kennebec to St. Croix as Sagadahoc - all under the Massachusetts Charter, thus confirming to Massachusetts the rights purchased from Gorges.

Meanwhile, Thomas Purchase had died (1678) and Richard Wharton, of Boston, bought from the heirs of Purchase and Way the land covered by their patent of 1632. He also sought and obtained, from Worumbee and five other Sagamores of the Androscoggin tribe, a large tract of land on both sides of the Androscoggin river and "extending to the uppermost falls in said And. river."

Wharton sailed for England for the purpose of securing

from the Crown recognition of his claim; but died before proper confirmation could be obtained. The administrator of his estate sold the whole of his claim to Thomas Hutchins et als, constituting the original PEJEPSCOT COMPANY. This title was confirmed by the General Court of Massachusetts, June 10, 1715.

However, violent disputes arose because of differing interpretations of "Uppermost Great Falls in Androscoggin River"; the Plymouth Company held that this had always been used to describe the falls at Lewiston, while the Pejepscot Company claimed that the falls at Rumford were meant. Consequently, Port Royal was in the disputed area.

The Massachusetts Legislature, March 8, 1787, passed a Resolution which declared "That the Twenty Miles Falls, so called, in ANDROSCOGGIN river, being about twenty miles from BRUNSWICK Great Falls, should be called the Uppermost Great Falls in ANDROSCOGGIN river, referred to in the deed from Warumbee and five other Indian Sagamores, confirming the right of Richard Wharton and Thomas Purchase, executed July 7th, in the year of our Lord 1684, in the thirtyfifth year of the reign of King Charles the second.

"And it is further resolved, as the boundaries of the Pejepscot Company, so-called, have not been ascertained, that the committee on the subject of unappropriated lands in the counties of Lincoln and Cumberland be, and they are hereby directed not to locate or dispose of any lands lying upon And. river, and between said river and lands claimed by the Plymouth Company to the southward of the south line of Bakerstown (Poland) bounded at the said Great Fall in ANDROSCOGGIN river aforesaid, on the west and south line of Port Royal on the east of said ANDROSCOGGIN river."

Thus, the rights of the Plymouth Company and the title of the Commonwealth of Massachusetts, to the land that is now Livermore, were secured; and the validity of the settlers' deeds confirmed beyond question (except by the real owners, the Androscoggin Indians, who were powerless to enforce their rights).

To summarize, then, the chain of title as it pertains to Port

Royal (or Livermore):

    a) Title was claimed by the Crown of England by reason of the discoveries of the Cabots, 1497-99;

    b) King James I gave Charter to the Plymouth Company, granting to them New England;

    c) Sir Ferdinando Gorges obtained from the Plymouth Company the land between Piscataqua and Kennebec rivers;

    d) A new Charter from King Charles I confirmed this grant, and specified its northward extent as 120 miles;

    e) Massachusetts obtained title by purchase of the Gorges rights, and confirmation under the Charter of William and Mary, 1692;

    f) The settlers of Port Royal obtained their titles under land grant from Massachusetts, June 11, 1771.

The events directly connected with the founding of the town of. Livermore really began in the year 1710. The Province of Maine was in sad shape - all but six settlements were destroyed, and the Indians were elusive enemies, striking when least expected, then fading out of sight in the forests. They were aided and abetted by the French, who furnished them arms and ammunition; and, at times, joined them in battle. Governor Dudley, of Massachusetts, felt that the only way to combat them was to strike at their source of supply, French Acadia.

In 1707, two expeditions against the French stronghold of Port Royal ended in failure; but Governor Dudley would not give up. "We shall never," the governor said, "be long at rest, until Canada and Nova Scotia constitute a part of the British empire."

A new attempt was organized in 1710, in which the British Government took an active part. Twelve hundred men, with a formidable armament, were embarked in 36 ships; and landed on

September 24, 1710, from the bay before Port Royal. The batteries were set up, and a heavy cannonading commenced, which forced the French governor, Subercase, to surrender, as his garrison of only 260 men was no match for an attacking force of such size.

Thus Acadia passed into the hands of the English; and in honor of Queen Anne the name of Port Royal was changed to Annapolis Royal, and the province to "Nova Scotia."

The Great & General Court of Massachusetts established a number of land-grants, under certain conditions, as pay for service and compensation for losses in the Port Royal expedition. Sixty participants in that campaign, from Waltham and vicinity, did not get around to filing their petitions for compensation until 1735, in response to which the Great & General Court, on November 24, 1736, granted "Township No.2 on the east side and next adjoining Connecticut River" as a gratuity for services in reducing Port Royal; and authorized Nathaniel Harris to call the proprietors together. He notified them to meet at the house of Isaac Baldwin, innholder, January 28, 1737.

A regular record of the proceedings of the proprietors was kept until November 1, 1743. They laid out the Township, and had the plan approved by the Court. Lots were assigned, roads cleared, and a sawmill built - the whole at a cost of more than 1,000 Pounds. A number of the proprietors began to build their homes there; but their records show that on November 1, 1743, a meeting of the proprietors, held in Weston, was adjourned to the following May on account of the "rumor of war with France, and the winter season approaching." It was not an idle rumor, for in the French & Indian War which followed many of the settlers were killed, and others taken captive.

Then, to cap the climax of misfortune, a new survey settling the dispute over bounds between Massachusetts and New Hampshire, threw this township into the Province of New Hampshire, so that the proprietors lost not only the land, but all their expense, time and labor, as well as the lives of those inhabitants killed or missing.

Nothing further was done to secure adjustment of the

Deacon Livermore house, the first permanent residence (1779) in Livermore and the site of Livermore's first town meeting (1795).

The gravestone of Deacon Elijah Livermore

proprietors'claim, until May 23, 1770, when a meeting was held at Mr. Samuel Harrington's, in Waltham, "to know the minds of the proprietors if they would pursue their claim on the equity of Port Royal." The vote was in the affirmative, and a committee consisting of Major Samuel Livermore, Dr. Leonard Williams, and George Babcock was chosen to petition the General Court to obtain another grant.

The General Court, which assembled October 29, 1770, was petitioned accordingly and, on June 11, 1771, passed a Resolve granting the prayer of the petitioners; and to the original grantees, their heirs and assigns, "a township of the contents of 6 1/2 square miles, in some of the unappropriated lands in the Province of Massachusetts Bay, to the eastward of Saco River, and adjoining some former grant, on the condition that the proprietors:

> "settle sixty families in said town in seven
> years; build a house for the public worship of
> God; settle a learned Protestant minister, and
> lay out 1/64 part for the first settled minister,
> and 1/64 part for the ministry;
> 1/64 part for the use of schools;
> 1/64 part for the use of Harvard College."

On August 9, 1771, Samuel Livermore and Leonard Williams, by virtue of the powers of the grant, sent Elijah Livermore and Elisha Harrington to explore the country and select the land; instructing them:

> "... to take a boat and pilot at Brunswick
> Falls and proceed up the river as' far as Rocky-
> Mico.
>
> "If the land is good, and you can adjoin it to
> any former grant, layout a township 9 mile and
> 40 rods long and five mile wide."

The two men proceeded as directed, and between August 9, 1771, and April 27th, 1772, they explored the Androscoggin valley, and selected 30,220 acres of land lying on both sides of the river, adjoining Sylvester township (now Turner) on the

grinding corn

Indian mortar on the Berry Farm in North Livermore; used by the Andro-scoggin Indians for grinding corn.

south, and extending about a mile above Rockomeka falls on the north. The southeasterly portion was afterwards set off to the Towns of Leeds and Wayne.

At a meeting at the house of Samuel Livermore, in Waltham, June 17, 1772, Lieutenant Elijah Livermore, Captain Ebenezer Learned and Mr. Richard Woodward were appointed to run the lines around the township, and layout 61 one hundred acre lots, i.e. - one for each proprietor and one for the first settled minister. The following is from the "Journal of our Journey To Lot out our Township on Androscoggin River."

"Set out from Waltham for Boston Tuesday August 18, 1772, waited for fair wind till Fryday 8 of clock in the morning. Then set sail in a fine Large Sloop Called the Fenix and had a very good voige Landed near Collon Lithgros - miles up Kennebeck River on the next Day about four 0 clock Afternoon.

23 Set sail 3 0 clock Afternoon went to merry meeting Bay.

24 Set sail 6 0 clock morning and that tide went to Pownalboro, next tide went to Garden town.

25 Set sail 7 0 clock Ran up to Bombay Hook (Hallowell) where we Ran a ground at the turn of Tide then took our stores in Boat up to Snows a mile Below Fort Western. About 5 0 clock Fish and I went forward about 4 mile in order to procure a battoe for our use ether to buy or make or Borrow.

26 a rainey morning spent the whole day without success.

27 our store arrived at Winthrop about noon wee Bought boards to make a BATTOO then went to Mr. Frosts about 2 miles from Wilson pond.

28 wee Hired Icabud How to help us wee paid our Teamster Mr. How and Fish began the

battoo and the rest carried the stores forward toward the pond.

29 battoo finished about noon then lanched into said pond and got safe over about Sunset."

In the following two months, September and October 1772, Ebenezer Waters as surveyor, with Elijah Livermore and Richard Woodward as chairmen, laid out lots on the east side of the river. The following accounts of the survey party of 1772 were allowed and ordered paid:

Ebenezer Waters	19
Capt. Ebenezer Learned	18 6s
Richard Woodward	22
Lieut. Elijah Livermore	46 3s 8d
Thomas Fish	7 18s

At the meeting of proprietors, also held at the house of Samuel Livermore in Waltham, Nov. 11, 1772, at which the above accounts were allowed, it was further voted to open a horse-way to Sylvestertown (Turner) and a cart-way to Pond-town (Winthrop). Elijah Livermore, Ebenezer Learned, and Thomas Fish were appointed to perform this service, and were instructed to have the above roads cleared by the last of October in that year.

As Samuel Livermore, the moderator, had died early in 1773, and Nathaniel Livermore had resigned, Leonard Williams, Esq., Deacon Elijah Livermore (heretofore called Lieutenant Livermore), and Mr. Elisha Harrington were elected on November 3, 1773, as the committee to "manage the prudentials of said proprietary." At this same meeting, the accounts of Deacon Livermore (40 pounds 10 shillings 11 pence) and Thomas Fish (31 pounds 7 pence) for clearing roads to the town, were presented and allowed.

That this was hard-earned money is evidenced by Thomas Fish's Journal, April 26, 1773, to June 26, 1773; and his "Journal of a second visit to Port Royal in 1773," which are here reproduced - but translated into modern language and spelling for ease in reading (original version in the Appendix):

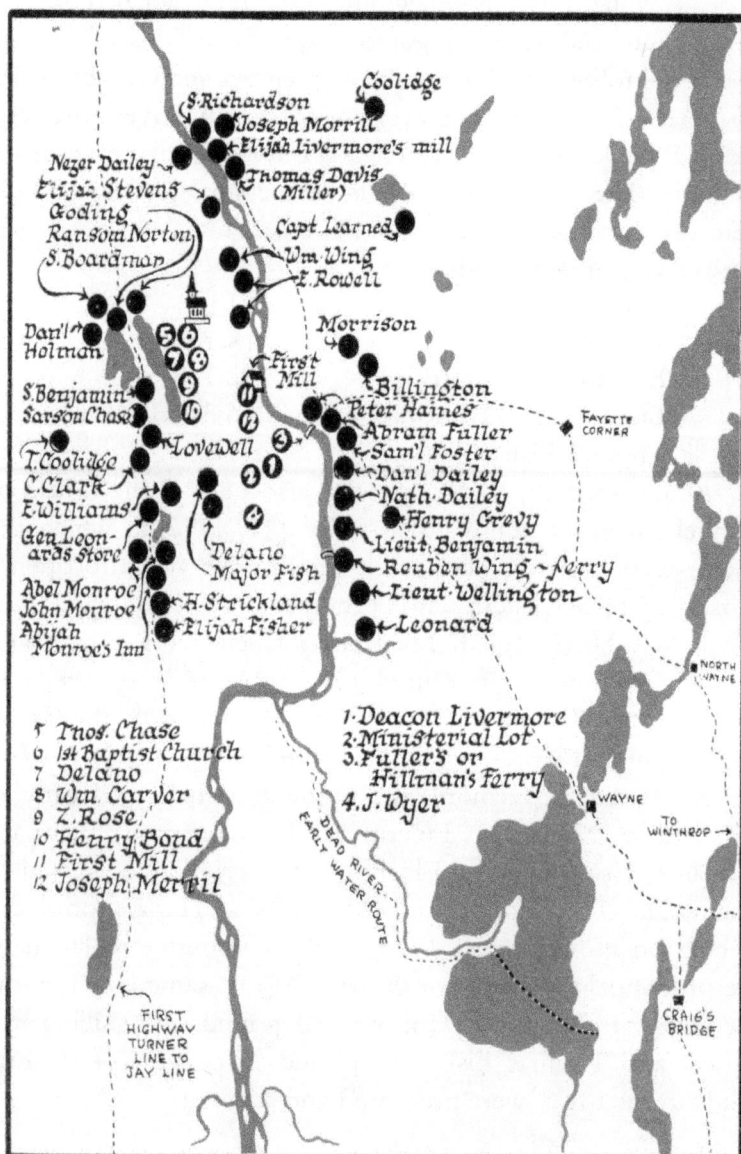

Approximate locations of first settlers'
homes and early roads and ferries.

Elijah Livermore's mill was at the area now
Livermore Falls.

Map labels:

S. Richardson
Joseph Morrill
Elijah Livermore's mill
Thomas Davis (Miller)
Coolidge
Nezer Dailey
Elijah Stevens
Gooding
Ransom Norton
S. Boardman
Capt. Learned
Wm. Wing
F. Rowell
Morrison
Dan'l Holtman
Billington
Peter Haines
Abram Fuller
Sam'l Foster
Dan'l Dailey
Nath. Dailey
Henry Grevy
Lieut. Benjamin
Reuben Wing - Ferry
Lieut. Wellington
Leonard
S. Benjamin
Sarson Chase
Lovewell
T. Coolidge
C. Clark
E. Williams
Gen Leonards Store
Abel Monroe
John Monroe
Abijah Monroe's Inn
H. Strickland
Elijah Fisher
Delano
Major Fish
First Mill

Fayette Corner
North Wayne
Wayne
To Winthrop
Craig's Bridge
Dead River
Early Water Route

5 Thos. Chase
6 1st Baptist Church
7 Delano
8 Wm. Carver
9 Z. Rose
10 Henry Bond
11 First Mill
12 Joseph Merril

1. Deacon Livermore
2. Ministerial Lot
3. Fuller's or Hillman's Ferry
4. J. Wyer

First Highway Turner Line to Jay Line

54

JOURNAL FROM OXFORD TO ANDROSCOGGIN RIVER

April 26, 1773 - Left Oxford. Dinner at _____ Lodged at
    Framingham.

April 27 - To Boston. Spoke for passage aboard Capt. John
    Martin's sloop, named the Sally, belonging to Fal-
    mouth as its home port.

April 28 - Got our stores aboard. Waiting for a fair wind.

April 30 - Sailed at 7 o'clock in the morning. Came up opposite Deer Island with a head wind.

May 1 - Sailed at half past eight; and at sunset was opposite
    Ipswich Bay. Ninety-six sailing vessels all in sight at
    once. Pleasant weather with wind fair but light.

May 2 - Sunday. Put in to Falmouth at one o'clock .in the
    afternoon; and at three o'clock came to anchor at the
    Town.

May 3 - Got our stores out of the vessel, and stored them in
    Mr. Shattuck's store. Left Falmouth at 2 o'clock in
    the afternoon. Traveled eleven miles, carrying our
    packs which were very heavy. Lodged at Mr. Joseph
    Latens in North Casco.

May 4 - Traveled 4 1/2 miles through the woods before break-
    fast. Killed one pigeon and ate it 'for breakfast. At
    night we were at Mr. Stinchfield's in New Gloucester.
    The weather today was very hot. We met Mr. Liver-
    more's team going after the rest of the stores left
    behind.

May 5 - Set out for our township, with Mr. James Stinchfield
    as our guide. Our party consisted of D. Mixer,
    Thomas Fish, William Foster and Ebenezer Gleason.
    Lieut. Livermore stayed behind to bring up our stores.
    We traveled to the Little Androscoggin, 9 miles from
    New Gloucester, and waded the river. William Foster
    fell into the river all over, with 3 axes and a great-coat
    on his shoulders. We killed 4 pigeons and one
    partridge. Camped by Great Wilson pond. It is 30
    miles from Falmouth to the Little Androscoggin,

measured by the chain, and 9 miles more to Wilson pond. In wading the river I wet the works of my watch, but did not stop to take the water out.

May 6 - Began clearing our road. We set the woods afire, and burned our gun stock. We slept very cold, for our blankets are behind with our stores.

May 7 - Lieut. Livermore and his men reached us at ten o'clock, bringing our stores; but they had had bad luck in crossing the Little Androscoggin, as one horse fell in, and the stores he carried were thoroughly soaked. They left us at 2 o'clock, and returned for more stores. We cleared the road to a large brook, which 'will be difficult crossing until a bridge is built. Lieut. Livermore had left Falmouth on May 1st, with his team and hired men.

May 8 - Still at work on our road. We killed 2 partridges and caught some fish. We camped by a pleasant pond; and about sunset our guide returned to us, having marked out the road ahead.

May 9 - Sunday morning. Our guide left us, having been in our employ 3 days, beside Sunday for travel home. I delivered to Mr. James Stinchfield my deed, to keep or leave at the Registers office in Falmouth if he has the opportunity to get my deed of my land in Port Royal Township recorded. - This night there is very sharp lightning and hard thunder until about mid-night.

May 10 - We are clearing our road today, and tormented by the flies. It is a hot day with thunder and lightning very hard and sharp till midnight, A great deal of rain fell, making uncomfortable sleeping this night. We have cleared the road to within 1 mile of Twenty Mile River, but there are bad logs by the mile together to cut out of the road. We have not eaten but two meals of salt provisions since we have been in the woods, - so plentiful are the fish and the partridges. Saw where the lightning struck a tree not far from our camp last night.

The first known photo of Livermore Falls village (c.1852, on completion of the Androscoggin Railroad); from the left are buildings currently owned by Burchard Hall, Robert Dickerman (formerly owned by C. Ham), Blaine Hardy, John Coolidge (formerly owned by George Treat - then Chester Sturtevant) and Richard Brophy..

Norlands Street,Livermore c.1910: schoolhouse, Washburn Library, Washburn house (Norlands) and "Oxford House."

May 11 - Clearing Road. Tonight the Committees for Phips' Canada camped with us, - headed for their township for lotting out (running the lot lines for division of the town among owners).

May 12 - Lieut. Livermore and his men reached us about ten o'clock in the forenoon. Another rainy night.

May 13 - Lieut. Livermore crossed the Twenty Mile River with 4 oxen and 1 horse. Today we carried our baggage over that river, and camped near the river. Crossed the river with the road construction at three o'clock. A rainy night.

May 14 - It was still raining this morning, and continued so all day. We camped on the east side of 20-mile river. Fish here were very plentiful, - trout very large and in great numbers. We lay here with our blankets stretched for shelter all day.

May 15 - Lieut. Livermore and I set out together, to look over the land for laying out a road into our township. The way we went, it was about 15 miles. It was raining some when we started, and turned out to be about as rainy a day as I ever saw. Lieut. Livermore, in trying to circle around a swamp, to locate better land for the road, got lost; and I fired three gun shots, and continued shouting intermittently for two and half hours before he found me; and then we set out for, and arrived at our temporary camp at dusk. We would have lain in the woods all night without a fire; but, to our great joy, Mr. Howe, of Pond Town, was there asleep in the old bunk I had there last year, and had a good fire going. I pulled off my shirt and wrung it out as dry as I could; warmed it, and put it on again. I did the same with my blanket; and lay down in my wet clothes and rested as comfortably as I could. Our plan of the Town had got soaked, and separated into nine pieces, which caused us some trouble, having no other with us.

May 16 - Sunday. We returned to our people on 20-mile river, because of the misfortune we had on Saturday which obliged us to return for lack of provisions. I snapped my gun, well loaded with a ball, at a large bull moose; but the powder, being damp from Saturday's wetting, to my great sorrow did not go off. On our return to our people, we found them all well, and eating some hot partridge broth, which was welcome to us, also, for we had not eaten any hot victual since we left them.

May 17 - Monday. I went with Lieut. Livermore to help him drive his cattle into Town, and got along very well, except that his horse fell down and cut his knee, thus laming himself. We got within one mile of camp at dusk, and wanted very much to reach the camp; so we un-yoked our oxen, and I set my compass. It was so dark that I could not see the needle clearly, and took East to be West, causing us to shear off about a mile and strike the great meadow. We were obliged to lie on an island in the meadow all night; and after long trial, we got a fire going, but had no ax nor provisions with us. It was somewhat rainy, but we camped down as well as we could, and starved it out, having eaten no hot victuals since morning. We wished for daylight long before it came, and finally arrived at our grand camp at eight o'clock in the morning.

May 18 - Tuesday. We were looking the Town over to find the best location for the road. Partridges or pigeons were to be had almost every day. The dog met up with a porcupine, and filled his nose with quills.

May 19 - Wednesday. We returned to Sylvester (Turner) where our people were, and arrived there about 5 o'clock. Just before I got there, the dog stole some cheese and converted it to his own use; and, as he broke the law, he received his punishment just as I arrived. About one hour afterward he treed a very large porcupine. I shot it and skinned it; and he stowed away the whole body, so that he will have no need of stealing more provisions.

May 20 - Thursday. We are once more at the old task of clear-

"This day we had partridge for dinner".

ing the road, past a large brook. About 12 o'clock it began to rain, and drove us from our work, before night. It is very rainy and uncomfortable weather for our business. On the 14th and 15th all our hands laid off by reason of rain, besides several other times for part of a day. This day we had partridge for dinner; and after we had dined, I took the gun and went about 100 rods from the camp, and killed two more for the next day. I Our family is small, - nobody here but Foster, Gleason and I. Father Mixer (Fish was married to Mixer's, daughter), Lieut. Livermore, and his men left us the 17th to go on to our new Oxford Royal (Port Royal) to plant corn and potatoes. We made a drawing of the Plan of our Town from the pieces of the one that had come apart from soaking, and did well enough so that it will answer our need at this time.

May 21 - Set out for Mr. Lane's, on Little Androscoggin River, to get our stores (of provisions). We arrived there just before dark; and packed our provisions for marching the next morning.

May 22 - Saturday. We set out, with heavy packs upon our backs; but we had one keg that we called "The Bull" which helped us carry the rest. At every spring, we "Blooded the Bull". We covered twelve miles before night came on.

May 23 - Sunday. We arrived at our camp this morning, and found all things well.

May 24 - Monday. Moved our road forward about a mile and a half. About 2 o'clock a thunder shower came up, and with the rain very hard and sharp thunder and lightning. It continued raining until night.

May 25 - Tuesday. It is fair and cold, and the Hies did not bite as bad as usual.

May 26 - Wednesday - Election Day. Very rainy, and we had neither bread nor meal. We went on into our Town. It was rainy all the way, and we arrived at the Grand

Camp about two o'clock. Lieut. Livermore had just killed a fat calf, and the sight of the calf, with other good necessaries, restored us to as good condition as ever. Here we found the Phips' Canada men, who had come to see us also, to spend a few sociable hours with us. They told us that they killed a fat calf the day before, to celebrate Election Day; but their cow ran away wild into the woods, and they had not milked her since they killed the calf. It is not to be much wondered at, for she was a native of the land there. We had some further discourse about flies. They asked me if I had seen any; and I told them I had seen a few, but they would not have believed me had not my cheeks, face and hands been almost raw, - which proved I spoke the truth. I should not have been called one of veracity by them. After a little social time, eating some fresh veal and drinking some West Indies rum toddy, we parted from our neighbors; and went to grinding our axes for the next day's work.

May 27 - Thursday. The men are at work on the road next to the River. We could not get any meal to carry with us, but expect some to be brought tomorrow from Pond Town by Mr. Howe. I went up to the Meeting House Lot, and laid out and marked the road down -to the intervale.

May 28 - We are at the old task. A cloud of gnats came down upon us. today, the first we have seen, but we expect thousands directly. The black flies seem to have diminished, but the mosquitos are very numerous among us, and a great many of them will weigh half a pound - not apiece though. There is a high wind today, so that we imagine Mr. Howe could not cross Androscoggin Pond, which is why our meal failed to arrive.

May 29 - Saturday. We worked on the road until noon. Left Foster to fetch out some meal, while Gleason and I went out to our camp in Sylvester, for we were afraid the wild beasts would destroy our provisions and clothes if we left them there any longer. We marked the road across five Lots; and got to our camp just at sunset. A mile and a half from our town line into Sylvester. Found all things well, but no meal nor bread.

May 30 - Sunday. This morning made a breakfast of chocolate, butter, and cheese, but no bread. Dinner, no bread; but about 2 o'clock we heard a cracking in the brush; and I took the gun in hand, thinking the noise was made by a moose; but who should come into sight but our neighbor Foster with a half bushel of meal on his back, - which rejoiced us as much as the sight of a moose. It seems that, though it was Sunday, he thought mercy came before sacrifice; he knew we had no bread, and so came out to us.

May 31 - Monday. An unfortunate but remarkable occurence, - Foster cut his knee, or just above the knee, through 3 thicknesses of garter, 1 thickness of trousers, and 2 thicknesses of stocking. It was not a bad cut, and happened at half past nine. At ten minutes after eleven, he came very near being killed, but was remarkably preserved. I was felling a tree about 20 inches in diameter and very tall. When I saw the tree start to fall, I gave the word, · "Take care." Foster was about 4 rods from me, upon a log about 3 feet from the ground. He stood and looked at the tree as it was falling. The tree fell on the log he was on, and gave it a cant that turned him right under the tree. He fell right under the log he was on and buckled him into a heap. The tree settled on him; knocked the breath out of him; and left him stunned, while the ax flew out of his hands and landed about eight feet from him. His position was such that he could not help himself; but Gleason and I lifted the log about an inch; and I turned his head, which was buckled under his body, so that as he came to he managed to help himself get out. His shoulder was hurt some, and his leg black and blue; and his whole body had received a bad shock.

June 1 - Tuesday. It was rainy this morning until after nine o'clock. We went to work about 3 o'clock, but were driven off by rain again. There was a good deal of thunder, but not near. Came home to our camp and set the girls to washing, and kept them washing until their fingers were sore; and the boys tended the water kettles. This was the first wash time since we left home. Our linens and woolens look very white; but we thought best not to wash our muslins and cambrics because the weather looks doubtful for drying, and we are going to move tomorrow. Thus we thought it would make them yellow, and unfit to be seen in the meeting house. (This, of course, is an example of Major Fish's humor.)

June 2 - Wednesday. Cloudy, loose weather this morning. It was lowery all day; but we worked all day on the road, and fighting mosquitoes, till dusk. About 10 o'clock a bear came within a few rods of our camp, - everyone asleep but myself. I let him come quite near, then waked the dog, thinking he might tree him. The dog stood and sniffed a while; then I took the gun in my hands and the dog jumped into the brush about three rods, but came back scared almost to death, and yelled with his bristles stuck up, and alarmed the whole camp. I let him out and he followed the bear a spell, and came back again, glad he was alive. We had no little laugh at our surprise and the fear that the dog experienced for few minutes. We cleared the road into our township this day.

June 3 - Thursday. Rainy most all day, but we moved about 2 1/2 miles into our town.

June 4 - Friday. We are at the same old work. Broke one axe today.

June 5 - Saturday. I went into town to grind the axe which Foster broke yesterday, and the flies bit me the worst

I have been bitten since I have been in the woods. A wolf came and howled around our camp, and caused much commotion among us.

June 6 - Sunday.

June 7 - Monday. About 10 o'clock the Phips' Canada men arrived. They cooked their dinner with us; and after we had drunk a little brandy toddy and eaten dinner together we parted company. This afternoon, with a little help, I moved all our housing stuff and provisions two miles.

June 8 - Tuesday. This afternoon the dog killed a porcupine, filled his mouth full of quills, and caused a good deal of trouble to get them out. We tied his legs and gagged him, and worked about an hour upon him. He was very glad when it was over.

June 9 - Wednesday. Today was cloudy all afternoon, and rained at night. The wind blew so that we were afraid to go to sleep, - but kept awake all night for fear of being killed by falling trees.

June 10 - Thursday. We travelled in to Lieut. Livermore's, for we were afraid to stay longer in the woods, the trees were falling so. It cleared off about noon, and we returned again to camp.

June 11 - Friday. At work on the road. At night, we went into our camp, from where Mr. Howe had marked out our road into Winthrop.

June 12 - Saturday. It was rainy in the forenoon; but in the afternoon we were at work on the road again.

June 13 - Sunday. Set out for Winthrop at 10 -o'clock and struck our Town Line in the Loar of Tyall(?) near where it crosses a beaver dam, and followed it about 2 miles steering E.S.E. and struck a pond that we thought was Great Androscoggin Pond. We continued E.S.E. and struck Dead River about half past one; still keeping the same course, and struck Winthrop in the northerly part of town, at one Mr. Sears' Improvement. (The term "improvement" was used to designate

"... found two cubs up a tree."

cleared land and buildings.) It was very rainy when we reached this improvement about four o'clock; and we were so hindered by the rain that we did not reach Mr. Howe's until night.

June 14 - Monday. Set out at one o'clock to mark our road to Port Royal, and at night camped by Great Androscoggin Pond. As we were pitching camp, we heard something growling like a bear; and on investigation, found two cubs up a tree. I shot one of them, and Mr. Howe shot the other. We had some for breakfast, - a very good breakfast. Road finished today.

June 15 - Tuesday. Set out this morning, and struck the river by Fish's Island about 11 o'clock. One o'clock, all hands washing up for going home.

June 16 - Wednesday. We went after Lieut. Livermore's cattle that had run away. Started off about noon, and struck their tracks, which we followed until sunset; but could not overtake them. Our hired hands were busy cutting a road to the falls. We camped without blankets or food. I got in the next day.

June 17 - Thursday. We were without food, except one pancake. This afternoon we packed up our things for marching home; and were about four miles on our way when sunset came. Some rain and thunder.

June 18 - Friday. We reached Mr. Lane's about the middle of the afternoon; and rested and refreshed ourselves at Little Androscoggin River.

June 19 - Saturday. We crossed the river, and reached Mr. Stinchfield's about 11 o'clock. After refreshing ourselves, we started for Falmouth, travelling as far as Mr. Winslow's in North Casco, and lodged there for the night.

June 20 - Sunday. At Falmouth. In the afternoon, went to church. Lodged at Mr. Shattuck's.

June 21 - Monday. We were looking for a passage, and found two vessels likely to sail in 2 or 3 days; but it happened that a vessel from the Kennebec, having run into fog, put in here at Falmouth to fill with fresh water; and we met the Captain by chance, who agreed to furnish us passage. We put our stores aboard in about 15 minutes, and sailed down the harbor; but for want of wind we were obliged to anchor again. We had sailed at sunset, and dropped anchor about 9 o'clock.

June 22 - Tuesday. We were lying wind bound, and went ashore again. About 5 o'clock, the wind came around to the North, and we set sail, going out of the harbor on a fair but light wind.

June 23 - Wednesday. We are still in passage, with light but fair wind. When the sun was about an hour high, a small squall came up, with some thunder and rain. It cleared off, and was a pleasant night.

June 24 - Thursday. This morning we rounded Cape Ann, beating all day against a small breeze. A part of the time, we were lashed to another becalmed vessel. About 10 o'clock we got within the Light, and ran up to Gorges Island; but the wind died away and we drifted onto the is land. However, as the tide was rising, we got off soon without any damage. For want of wind, we hove to above Long Island, and lay there until the next tide.

June 25 - Friday. About 2 o'clock we resorted to towing, in lieu of sailing, for we had no wind; and at 4 o'clock we landed our baggage. Foster and I set out for home, and went to Lieut. Livermore's at Waltham about 10 o'clock in the evening.

June 26 - Saturday. A very hot day in which we travelled the rest of the way home, - and a very hard day's work it was for me.

[Major Fish returned to Port Royal in August, 1773, as shown by the following notes copied from his Journal.]

Aug. 23 - Attended the Town Meeting in Winthrop to see if they would lay out a road to meet ours. The 29th and Sunday the 30th at Town Meeting; 31st, Monday, home again.

Sept. 3 - Viewing the Road as marked out by Mr. Howe, to see if it were possible to avoid the swampy land, but found no way; neither did I find a way to cross Fish's Brook with a bridge.

Sept. 4 - This day I went to the Southward of the marks; but found no way for the road to go, within reasonable distance of the marks.

Sept. 6 - This day, I travelled up Fish's Brook, and found it could be passed by a bridge about 1 1/2 miles from the river. Struck out for Beaver Brook, and found where it could be forded about 2 miles from the river.

Sept. 7 - This day I marked from Fish's Brook to Beaver Brook; and viewed the land from Fish's Brook to the river to see if the road could come that way. Found it to be very good land for a road.

Sept. 8 - Today, went to Beaver Brook and, marking E.S.E. course, struck our Town Line about 3 miles from Great Androscoggin Pond. I wept to 30 Mile River to see if the road could not go further to the K and North, to bring it in a straight line with my marks, but found it very swampy.

Sept. 9 - Tried a beech hill near our Town Line, and found it went up with a moderate ascent, arid down with a moderate descent. I then marked North about 2 miles to Beaver Brook, and struck my previous marks about half a mile to the West of our Town Line.

Oct. 5, 1773 - Went to Winthrop to see about a bridge, and to let the contract for it.

Oct. 6 - Today I went up to Mr. Craig's to let out the Bridge contract. Mr. Craig struck off West by South, and struck Braggs' lot.

Oct. 7 - Home today, and surveyed the road with Mr. Howe.

Up until now (1773) the survey and the drawing of lots was concerned only with the land on the west of the river known as the "First Division"; but in November, 1773, it was decided to proceed with division of the land on the east side, called the "Second Division." A meeting of the proprietors was held November 3, 1773, at the Inn of Isaac Gleason, of Waltham, at which the following action was taken according to their records:

> "Voted that they will lay out the remainder of said Township and that they will lay out exclusive of what is drawn 3 Lotts of one hundred acres to each Right, and the remainder in equal parts to each Right. Voted and chose Dea. Elijah Livermore, Capt. Ebenezer Learned and Mr. Thomas Fish a committee for that purpose.
>
> Voted that the committee now chosen sort the lotts in an equal proportion to quality as possible so that each Proprietor draw his lots at one draught.

Brettuns Village, Livermore - c.1900; an early inn, known as "Livermore House" is situated in the center background.

Androscoggin River was always an effective barrier between the East and West settlements of Livermore - leading to the permanent political division of the town, with the incorporation of Livermore Falls.

Voted and granted a tax of forty-eight
shillings on each Right to defray the expenses
of settling and laying our said Township."

Early in 1774, the chosen committee, Deacon Livermore,
Captain Learned, and Major Fish, set out to complete the
survey and lotting of the township as directed by the proprietors; and the following is taken from Major Fish's journal
of that trip:

A MEMORANDUM FROM OXFORD TO PORT ROYAL

April 18, 1774 - Set out for Boston. Dined at Grafton; and, at
night, were at Deacon Livermore's in Waltham.

April 19 - We arrived in Boston to look for passage. Lodged at
the Sign of the Lamb. Very hard thunder and lightning.

April 20 - We found passage available on board Capt. John
Campbell's sloop, "Polly." We travelled back to Waltham and lodged at Deacon Livermore's.

April 21 - Thursday, back in Boston, buying provisions. Again
we lodged at the Sign of the Lamb.

April 22 - Finished buying stores; and now waiting to sail.

April 23 - Saturday. We loaded our stores on board; and a
quarter after 8 in the evening we set sail.

April 24 - Sunday. Made Wood Island; and, at 6 o'clock in the
evening, stood in for Seguin. At 12 o'clock, came to
anchor in the mouth of the Kennebec River for the
night.

April 25 - We set sail at 9 o'clock in the morning, with a head
wind. Beat up the river about five miles, but the tide
then failing us, we hove to.

April 26 - Beat up the river to Long Reach, where we left the
sloop and continued up the river with Mr. Sewall in
his boat. We arrived at Mr. Hargraves' at ten o'clock at
night, in Pownalborough, with hands very sore from
rowing.

April 27 - Rowed up the river, against a very swift current, to

Deacon Clark's. Travelled to Winthrop to hire a team to bring up our stores. Hired Mr. Bragg.

April 28 - We went back to the Kennebec River; and up to Winthrop again. Lodged at Mr. Whiting's.

April 29 - We went to Mr. Howe's, and then set out for Mr. Fuller's, on the way to our town. We missed the right road; went out of our way about one mile, then struck through the woods about 4 miles in order to reach a bridge called "Craig's Bridge," and we came out within 10 rods of that bridge. Killed one partridge along the way. We camped by Fuller's meadow. It was a very rainy day, and a rainy night. Mr. Wellington taken ill.

April 30 - Saturday. Went to show Mr. Ballard our town line. We left Mr. John Babcock with Mr. Wellington. It was very rainy, so we returned to our 'camp, and found Mr. Wellington seized with violent pains in his head, and much distressed at his stomach. Got him in to Mr. Bragg's.

May 1 - Sunday. Still raining, so we went to Mr. Howe's to lodge. While I am now writing, I heard credibly that 4 men were drowned at Vassalboro, - Lieut. Warring from Pepperell, Deacon Brown's son, from Concord, and two others unknown to me.

May 2 - Went to Mr. Hopkins' after my instruments left behind in our chest. Bought a very large pack. On arrival at Mr. Chandler's, I found that Mr. Wellington had been moved here from Mr. Bragg's, and was very sick. I stayed with him this night.

May 3 - Measured the road from Mr. Chandler's, marking every mile on the South side of the nearest tree. We found the road to be 18 1/2 miles, lacking 13 rods. We found our people camped where 30 Mile River empties into great Androscoggin Pond.

May 4 - Set out with part of our stores, and crossed Androscoggin Pond. We went down Dead River to the great Androscoggin River; landed our stores; and fired two guns for a signal that we had arrived. With much joy, they heard the signal; and hastened to make their way to us, for they had not eaten any food cooked with water.

May 5 - Set out to run a line to west part of our town.

May 6 - We spent this day surveying. Saw some ice in a back cove of our river, laid up there by a freshet, on the bank and out of the sun.

May 7 - Went up the river today; and found all things well at my chest, and Deacon Livermore well at his camp."

Once the "Second Division" survey was completed, and Lots drawn, the proprietors moved rapidly to the settlement of the town, offering 4 pounds to each of the first ten who would settle families and build a house in Port Royal, provided they do so before 1776, and agree to dwell there five years. To accommodate such settlers, Leonard Williams, Elijah Livermore, and Elisha Harrington were designated a committee to engage some person or persons to build a saw mill and grist mill in the town.

Once again, however, as in 1735, War disrupted their project, and we find this entry in their records under date of May, 1775:

"The distressing war with Great Britain breaking out April 19, 1775, and all being obliged to resist the enemy, the place to which the meeting was adjourned being so near the theatre of action prevented any meeting whatever."

That a great number of the proprietors and prospective settlers of Port Royal did turn their efforts to "resisting the enemy" is evident from the many we know to have been engaged in that struggle. No complete record exists, but among them we do know the following were numbered:

BENSON, Ichabod

BENJAMIN, Lieut. Samuel

BOND, Henry - son of Col. William Bond, of 25th Cont. Regt.

CHASE, Thomas, - served with John Paul Jones.

CHILD, Abijah, - Capt. 25th Regt. Continental Army

First bridge under construction; this "Haupt Truss" bridge - (invented by Herman Haupt in 1839) - was completed in 1858; it was carried away by the "pumpkin freshet" of 1871.

The first bridge after completion; its location was substantially the same as that of all succeeding bridges.

COOLIDGE, Joseph - 14th Regt. Continental Army

DELANO, Jabez

FISH, Thomas, - Major in Cont. Army

FISHER, Elijah, - member of Cen'l Washington's
    Body Guard

FOSTER, Samuel, - Lieutenant

FULLER, Isaac

GIBBS, Peletiah

GODING, Jonathan C.

GREVY, Henry - a Hessian soldier

HAYWARD, Simeon

HOLMAN, Daniel - one of the "Minute Men" at Concord

LIVERMORE, Elijah - Lieutenant

LEARNED, Ebenezer - General

LEAVITT, Dea. Joseph

MARTIN, William Godfrey - a Hessian soldier

MERRILL, Joseph

MILLS, Joseph - Major (a half-brother of Lieut.
    Samuel Benjamin)

MUNROE, John - served aboard a privateer

STEVENS, Elijah - served aboard a privateer

SAWIN, Samuel

TURNER, Abial

WALKER, John - was with Arnold's expedition to Quebec

WELLINGTON, Elijah - Lieutenant

WILLIAMS, Elisha - Adjutant in Cont. Army, and
    Aide-de-Camp of Washington.

WYER, Josiah - was at the battle of Bunker Hill

Evidently the proprietors felt that by 1779 the war was near enough to a conclusion, and such action as remained was far enough removed, to allow a resumption of the Port Royal project, for on January 19, 1779, they once more called a meeting.

It will be recalled that the grant of the township was given on condition that 60 families be settled in the town WITHIN SEVEN YEARS. This time limit, of course, expired in 1777; so on March 3, 1779, we find this entry:

"Voted and chose Leonard Williams, Esq., Dea. Elijah Livermore, and Mr. Elisha Harrington a Committee to petition the Great and General Court for a further time to fulfil the conditions of the Grant of said township, the times having been such that it has been impossible to fulfil the same in the time allowed."

The request for additional time was granted; and Elijah Livermore moved his family and belongings, via Kennebec River and Winthrop, a month later, in April of 1779, to establish his permanent home in Port Royal, thus becoming the first permanent settler in the town.

As previously noted, Lieutenant Livermore came here in 1771 on a tour of exploration; and again in 1772 as one of the surveying party running the lines and making the "First Division" of lots. In May of 1773, with his hired hands, two pairs of oxen, a horse and other cattle, he arrived at his chosen Lot, and commenced the planting of corn and potatoes. He remained all summer, and possibly through the winter of 1773-74, for when Thomas Fish arrived early in the spring of 1773 he reported finding "Dea, Livermore well at his camp."

However, in 1775, as a Lieutenant of Massachusetts Militia, he abandoned Port Royal, and joined his associates in "resisting the enemy," apparently until January 1779; and so he could hardly be considered a permanent settler before the latter date.

His family stopped in Winthrop while he built a small house, and raised crops of corn and potatoes; then joined him in the fall to commence the "battle with the wilderness."

In the same year came Mrs. Carver, Josiah Wyer, and Elisha Smith, joined soon afterwards by Josiah Norcross. This first year was disturbed by the unfriendly attitude of the Indians at Rockomeka, who could hardly be expected to appear overjoyed at the arrival of white men to take away their homeland. However, by this time only about 500 Androscoggins remained in the valley; and they were more or less resigned to the inevitable. Friendly relations were soon

76

established with Deacon Livermore, and thereafter Indians were frequent callers at his home. It was not unusual for the Livermore family, on arising in the morning, to find one or more "braves" wrapped in their blankets, asleep on the kitchen hearth.

Of the other settlers in 1779, the second was the widow Carver, who came from Duxbury, and brought her seven children, ranging in age from 4 to 21 years. They made their "pitch" on what was later known as the Hunton farm, on the east side of the river. After a short time, the oldest son, William, selected a location on the west side (Lot No. 33 - Later the J. M. Hinds place) which he thought was better; and here the family lived until 1785.

The third settler was Josiah Wyer, who had been serving in the Revolution and was in the battle of Bunker Hill. He built, in 1779, a log house to the east from the road leading past the house of E. H. Beckler. Later, presumably after this road was built, he built the old house and barn that were replaced with more commodious structures by Amos O. Beckler. His daughter, Nancy, was the first female child born in the town.

Elisha Smith, the fourth of the first group of settlers, came from Martha's Vineyard, and cleared the farm later owned by Thomas M. Wyman.

Of those who moved to town between 1780 and 1790, the exact time and order of arrival is not known; but among the first was Major Thomas Fish, who had been closely associated

The second bridge, completed in 1872.

The flood of 1896 destroyed the second bridge (just visible in the background).

with Deacon Livermore from the outset. He was assistant in the survey and lotting of the "First Division," and one of the appointed surveyors who completed the Last Division. Through his efforts the road from Winthrop into Livermore (or Port Royal) was cleared, and the bridge between Dexter and Wilson Ponds, then in Winthrop (or Pondtown) was built and called Craig's Bridge. Like the others, Thomas Fish went to war in 1775, and was a Major in the Continental Army. He left the service in 1780, and returned to his Port Royal lots, No. 28 and part of No. 27, which he had purchased in 1773. Here, at the junction of the "Fish Meadow," as it is still called, and the old discontinued road to Isaac Livermore's, he built his log cabin, the cellar and foundation of which can even now be plainly seen. Major Fish was from Oxford, Worcester County, Massachusetts, and had married Naomi Mixer, of Sutton, June 25, 1767. She had died shortly before his final move to Port Royal, so he came alone to settle here, leaving a daughter, Ruth, back in Massachusetts with relatives.

Another of Major Fish's skills was the making and repairing of shoes. He frequently visited Winthrop, where he was well known, to obtain necessary materials for this trade; and became acquainted with Miss Betsey Marrow, to whom he eventually became engaged to be married.

On December 20, 1781, he called at the house of Nathaniel Fairbanks in Winthrop, to obtain a half side each of sole and upper leather. It was then 3:00 p.m., and a fierce north-east snow storm had begun. The Fairbanks family urged him to stay over night, and wait for the storm to abate; but the Major insisted that he must get back to Port Royal; so he started out in snow already knee-deep, with the 25 pound bundle of leather strapped to his back, to walk the sixteen miles of trail which he himself had laid out. He got as far as the Androscoggin, which he crossed just below the rips, from where there was a direct road to Deacon Livermore's house. When he was within a half mile of safety, blinded by the driving .snow, he swerved off the road toward the Intervale and stumbled along for some time, completely lost, until he fell exhausted on the plain nearly east from Deacon Livermore's house, about six rods from the bottom of the hill, and about 20 rods south of the road from Hillman's ferry to the Livermore house.

At midnight, that night, Deacon Livermore heard a sound in the storm like something in distress. He got up and listened but nothing more being heard, he went back to bed. Two days later, when the Major's departure from Winthrop was learned, search was made, and his body discovered.

Mrs. Anna Livermore Hamlin, daughter of Deacon Livermore and mother of Hannibal Hamlin, was a little child when this happened, and she wrote the following:

> "I was a very little girl when Maj. Fish froze to death, and slept in the trundle bed. It was in the evening when they got Mai, Fish to our house; he was crooked, as he died, and they laid him upon the hearth before the fire to thaw him. Several times I looked out over the headboard of my trundle bed and saw them thawing Maj. Fish so that they could lay him out."

He was buried with military honors at Winthrop; but no headstone was erected. Years later, when his daughter wished to remove his remains to Massachusetts, no one could tell where his grave was. So today the only memorial to the gallant Major, who helped to lay out the town, and survived five years of warfare, is "Fish's Meadow" and an overgrown cellar-hole.

His tragic death, naturally, cast a heavy gloom over the early settlement, for next to Deacon Livermore, he was probably the most active in the Town's organization.

These early settlers, in most cases, did not own the land upon which they settled. It was customary for them to select what seemed to be a favorable site; clear the land, or "make an improvement"; build a log cabin; and plant some crops. If, after a year or two, they decided it was fertile land and a desirable location, they arranged with the owner for its purchase. If, on the other hand, it was disappointing, or some other place was more appealing, they simply moved on, and tried again.

It will be noticed that, for the first ten years, the sites

chosen were within close proximity to the river, whether on the east or west. In spite of the designated "horseway" and "cartway" to Pondtown and Sylvester, the most convenient route still was the water route, via the river and ponds to the Kennebec.

The second group of settlers, those coming between 1780 and 1785, included:

LIEUTENANT SAMUEL BENJAMIN, who had been serving in the Revolution, bought of Deacon Livermore 120 acres in October, 1782, bounded on the East by Long Pond, and on the North by Round Pond. He executed, on Oct. 11, 1782, a mortgage to Deacon Livermore to secure payment of the purchase price, viz., - 25 bushels of corn and 25 bushels of rye within 26 months, and the same amount of corn and rye in 3 years and 2 months. Expressed in the deed, the consideration was given as 30 Pounds.

CUTTING CLARK, a brother of Hannah Clark, Deacon Livermore's first wife, lived on the Northerly part of Fullers Hill, coming from Waltham about 1780-81. He was particularly noted as a famous hunter.

DANIEL DAILEY, with his two sons, NATHANIEL and NEZER, settled on the East side of the river, on the farm later owned by Lewis Hunton. NATHANIEL cleared the farm on the East side of the river, afterward owned by Lieutenant Benjamin. NEZER settled on the West side, below the falls.

JABEZ DELANO, with his three brothers, ZEBEDEE, JAMES and EBENEZER, moved here from Winthrop (Pond town). Jabez was the one who found Major Fish's body while he was living on the Hunton place; he took up the Fish improvement at Fish's Meadow, then later tended for Deacon Livermore the grist mill at the falls. ZEBEDEE settled on the farm later owned by Thomas Chase. JAMES owned the farm later known as the Orin Rich place; while EBENEZER chose the westerly part of town, beyond Isaac Hamlin's.

LIEUTENANT SAMUEL FOSTER, a Revolutionary veteran, lived on the East side of the river.

HENRY GREVY, who came here directly following the close of the Revolutionary war, 1781-82, is a most interesting case, for he fought on the other side. He was a Hessian soldier, i.e., a British mercenary from the province of Hesse. Whether he had been a prisoner of war, or left the British Army voluntarily, is not known; but he evidently liked the country and decided to adopt it as his own. He settled on the farm east of Lieutenant Benjamin's, on the East side of the river.

NATHANIEL LIVERMORE, a distant cousin of the Deacon, built the house on the place where Deacon Sanders afterward lived, later owned by Cyril W. Jackson. His residence here was brief, for he died in 1783.

JONATHAN MORSE was evidently one of the very first - for his wife, Anna Lovering, was killed by a falling barn frame in 1779.

ZEBEDEE ROSE came from Dighton, Mass., through the influence of Deacon Livermore. He settled first on the James Chase place, but later bought the P. E. Dearborn place at Gibbs' Mills.

ABJAL TURNER, who was born in Scituate, Massachusetts, had been a Revolutionary soldier, and came to Livermore to reside with his son, John.

LIEUTENANT ELIJAH WELLINGTON, from Lincoln, Massachusetts, was one of the first settlers on the East side of the river.

COOLIDGE, was the first settler in the Moose Hill area, for he made a clearing and built a log house on the westerly slope of Moose Hill, about 1779. A few years later he sold the place to Philip Smith whose house is still standing, and still occupied by one of his descendants.

SAMUEL RICHARDSON was the first settler north of the falls, on the East side of the river, in what was to become the village of Livermore Falls. He settled on Lot No.1, on the north line of the town; and the Richardson Cemetery, on Main Street, was a part of his farm.

LEONARD, settled near the Norris place at Strickland.

MORRISON and BILLINGTON settled in the East Livermore neighborhood.

PETER HAINES came from Gilmanton, New Hampshire, in 1784, and settled on the East side, near what is now Haines Corner.

On August 29, 1781, a committee was appointed to confer with a committee of Phips' Canada (now Jay) regarding the building of a mill to accommodate both townships, which shows how far back go the interlocking interests of the two towns. For almost 200 years now they have been tied together by combined efforts in highways, water district, sewerage disposal, fire departments, and some attempts have been made to combine the schools, though so far without success.

Sixty pounds, the mill lot (so called) and the island in the river against the same, were granted June 19, 1782, to build a mill on the brook leading from Round and Long Ponds, and Elijah Livermore agreed to erect the mill. A grist mill and a saw mill were constructed near the outlet of Long Pond, which in later years came to be known as Gibbs' Mills.

The first mills at Rockomeka Falls (now Livermore Falls) were not built until 1791. The river here had a natural fall of 14 feet, while a ledge ran out from the east bank several rods; but the variation between high and low water levels, and the tremendous force of the river, particularly in spring freshets, posed a major engineering problem which no one was willing to tackle until Deacon Livermore made the attempt successfully in that year. Much labor and expense went into the effort, and perhaps the hardest part was securing the "crank." One of English manufacture was purchased, and brought by ship to Hallowell.

The so-called "horseway" from Pond town to Port Royal was little more than a trail, with brush and trees cut from its path, and it could not accommodate wheeled vehicles, though a horseman could travel it. To get the heavy iron "crank" over the land, the men fashioned a dray, with one end of the poles attached by straps to either side of the saddle, and the other end dragged along the ground. On this dray they built a sort of platform, on

The third bridge, completed in 1897. With a single span of over 800 feet, it was for many years the longest one-span bridge in New England. A temporary ferry still operates in the foreground; Hugh Chisholm's Umbagog Mill is the large building in the center background

The fourth bridge (completed 1958) shortly before the third bridge was dismantled

which the "crank" was lashed. In this manner it was safely carried to Wayne Pond, where it was transferred to a dug-out canoe. Elijah Stevens took charge of this craft and its cargo, with two men to help at the paddles. To protect against loss in case of an upset, a buoy was attached to the "crank." Elijah and his crew crossed Wayne Pond, traveled down Dead River to the Androscoggin, and up the latter to a point 60 or 70 rods below the falls, where the rapids prevented further navigation. From here to the rising land, where the mill would be located, was a low, sunken swamp land, impossible to negotiate either by boat or by horse. They were faced with the puzzling question of how to get the "crank" to the mill site.

Elijah Stevens was a rugged, athletic man of great determination. He proposed to the others that he would carry it through if they would raise it to his shoulder and steady it. It weighed 211 pounds, English weight, so was no small burden even on good footing. They lifted it to his shoulder, and he bore it across the swamp, up the brow of the hill, and cast it down where it was wanted.

When the mills were completed and ready to run, the inhabitants assembled and held a jubilee on the occasion.

Elijah Stevens, mentioned here, came from Dedham, Massachusetts before 1790, and worked for Deacon Livermore for a year to pay for his lot, the Oldham farm. He had served on board a privateer in the Revolution.

Between 1785 and 1790, the town grew quite rapidly, and among the arrivals, in addition to Elijah Stevens, were:

SYLVANUS BOARDMAN, of Martha's Vineyard, who came to Port Royal in 1788 or 1789, with Samuel Hillman, Ransom Norton and James Norton. These men were known as "The Four Partners"; because they had agreed among themselves to take up lots, and for 1 year share equally the profits and losses. He chose the lot next west of Ransom Norton's, and built his camp on the knoll near Tan House Brook. This burned, and he later built the place known to this day as the Boardman house.

ELIJAH FISHER, of Norton, Massachusetts, was in Livermore in 1789, and settled on a farm on the old highway adjoining and South of the Strickland farm. He was a Revolutionary soldier of excellent reputation, and was a member of "Washington's Life Guard" under Captain Caleb Gibbs. He was in the battle of Bunker Hill, and remained in service six years.

PELETIAH GIBBS, from Milford, Worcester County, Massachusetts, was living here before 1789, and served often in Town office in these early years.

SAMUEL HILLMAN, one of the "four partners" previously mentioned, was 19 years old when he came here in 1788.

DEACON JOSEPH LEAVITT, a Revolutionary soldier, settled on the farm which Clifford R. Thompson later maintained as an orchard.

ISAAC LOVEWELL, of Weston, Mass., was living here prior to 1790, and purchased from Samuel Whiting the farm on the north side of the hill known as Lovewell's (or Water's) Hill on the old highway.

JOSEPH MERRILL first appeared one fall, driving cattle past Deacon Livermore's up to the "Great Meadows" or Phips' Canada to winter. The Deacon tried to get him to buy the lot next north of his; but Joseph, after looking over the land, turned it down, saying "there isn't enough stone on it to fence the land." But later, when he returned in the spring, he made a trade and settled on the lot which, in years afterward, was bought back by the Deacon's youngest son, Samuel.

ABEL MONROE, who came with his brothers, Abijah and John, from Lincoln, Massachusetts, about 1790, settled on Lot #48, just below Bartlett's Pond.

ABIJAH MONROE was the inn-keeper for many years. He came with his brothers about 1790, and was the first inn-keeper in the town. His excellent tavern was near Sanders Corner, on Lot #47 on what was the main highway from Portland to Farmington.

JOHN MONROE, the third brother, settled on Lot #39, next east from his brother Abel.

JAMES NORTON, one of Sylvester's sons, lived in several

places in town, but from 1801 until his death, lived on the Wm. G. Griffith farm.

RANSOM NORTON, brother to James, was a Baptist minister. He settled on the I. T. Monroe place, at North Livermore. He owned the Lot on which the village of North Livermore is located; and, in 1848, deeded the land on which the old church (burned in 1847) stood to the town as a common.

SYLVESTER NORTON, of Edgartown, Martha's Vineyard, came to Port Royal with his three sons, Ransom, James and Zebulon, in 1789. He had been with General Wolfe at the storming of Quebec. He was one of Wolfe's bodyguard; and helped carry the wounded General from the field.

ZEBULON NORTON, youngest of Sylvester's sons, was only 12 years of age when the family moved to Maine.

SAMUEL SAWIN, of Watertown, Massachusetts, was a Revolutionary soldier, who came here in 1788 and settled on the Josiah Adkins farm.

JOHN WALKER was a Revolutionary War veteran, and one of Arnold's men on his expedition against Quebec. He settled, in 1789, on the farm later owned by C. R. Leach.

ELISHA WILLIAMS, son of Rev. Eliphalet Williams of East Hartford, Conn., was one of the most fascinating characters among the town's founders. After graduating from Yale in 1775, he joined the Revolutionary forces, and, as Adjutant, was in the same boat with Washington at the crossing of the Delaware River, Dec. 24, 1776. Leutze's well known painting of that event depicts Williams, behind Washington, holding onto his hat. In 1780, he married Abigail, Deacon Livermore's oldest daughter, and moved to this town in 1790. He settled, presumably, on the "ministerial" Lot #37, but later on was taxed as the owner of Lots #36 and #10.

REUBEN WING was here as early as 1785, in "Tollawalla" on the east side of the river just below Hunton's Rips. He came from Harwich, Massachusetts; and with the help and

Elisha Williams: First Livermore teacher; moderator of the first town meeting; Trustee, Brown University

Washington crossing the Delaware: Elisha Williams (Washington's aid-decamp) is the man holding' his hat (just beneath the flag).

under the direction of Deacon Livermore, he established and kept the first ferry in town.

WILLIAM WING came here prior to 1788, and built the house which for many years was owned by J. H. Farrington and called "Rocky Brook" farm.

DANIEL HOLMAN came from Massachusetts in 1789, and settled on the farm later owned by William Bryant. He was a Revolutionary soldier and one of the Minute Men who marched to Concord April 19, 1775.

Also listed among the "heads of families" residing in the town in 1789 were:

JOHN MONK

OTIS ROBINSON

RANDALL

Arrivals in 1790:

HENRY BOND, of Watertown, was the son of Colonel William Bond, who was acting Colonel at the battle of Bunker Hill. He was Colonel of the 25th Regiment in the Continental Army, and went with it to New York and to Canada. He died in service, Aug. 31, 1776. His son, Henry, accompanied him to New York and to Canada, and was with him when he died. Henry came to Livermore in 1790, having previously purchased land there and a half interest in the first grist and saw mills.

SAMUEL CHASE, of Tisbury, Martha's Vineyard, was another 1790 settler. He bought of Zebedee Delano the farm midway between Gibbs Mills and Loney Corner, on the easterly side of Long Pond.

THOMAS CHASE, son of Samuel, came here in 1790 with his father. He lived on his father's place, and it is probable that he cleared most of the land and built the house. He was in the War of the Revolution, and served aboard a privateer which was captured off the English coast. After 23 months as a prisoner, he was exchanged and sent to France, where he enlisted again and shipped aboard the "Alliance" under John Paul Jones.

SARSON CHASE, also a son of Samuel; he and his brother,

TRISTRAM, settled on Lot #53, west of Long Pond.

TRISTRAM CHASE, Captain, with his brother Sarson, as mentioned above made their "pitch" on the west side of Long Pond, near the south end.

THOMAS COOLIDGE came from Cambridge, Massachusetts, and settled, in 1790, on Lot #74, known later as the Columbus Alden farm.

JOSEPH COOLIDGE, of Waltham, moved with his family in June 1790, in company with his relative, Thomas Coolidge; and took up a farm near the Livermore line, in that part of Jay which is now Canton; but his associations are largely with the former town, where several of his children settled. His father was killed at Lexington-Concord April 19, 1775, and he himself was a Revolutionary soldier, member of the 14th Regiment of the Continental Army.

JONATHAN GODING, of Waltham, Massachusetts, moved here in 1790, and had a farm north of the Corner, where he had a nursery and introduced many choice varieties of apples and pears. His father, Jonathan C. Goding, was a Revolutionary soldier, who built a log house across the line in Jay, but is buried in the Goding yard in Livermore.

GENERAL DAVID LEARNED came from Oxford, Massachusetts, and settled on Lot #50, in 1790. He was the first trader in town, and his store stood south of the Norlands church. He also built a sawmill at the outlet of Bartlett's pond.

ELIPHALET ROWELL married Abigail Smith, daughter of Elisha Smith, and was killed in a "drive of trees" just east of where the fairgrounds were, in Livermore Falls, in 1803. He lived on the Charles Day farm.

The names listed represent sixty families. There were doubtless some others before 1791; but, as they had not taken title to land, or otherwise appeared in 1790 records, we have no knowledge of them until a later date. In any case, to all intents and purposes, these sixty families are the real founders of the town which, by 1791, was firmly established, and com-

THE LIVERMORE HOUSE

THE PARSONAGE
NORTH LIVERMORE

prised over 200 individuals. Though still called "Port Royal," the town was also referred to at this time as "Liverton." By today's standards, however, it was not much of a "town." The only traveled ways were not much more than spotted trails, passable for a man on horseback, but not for a vehicle. The first "highway" was not accepted until 1795, although two ferries across the Androscoggin, Hillman's ferry and the one operated by Reuben Wing at Tollawalla (Strickland), were in use.

Every individual was primarily a farmer, raising his own food, of which the staples were potatoes and corn; keeping cows for milk and for beef; raising usually a few pigs and hens. Sheep were kept mainly for the wool, and clothes were made from the homespun wool or flax, although hides were used for breeches, vests, caps and mittens. There was no store, or trader, prior to 1791; so each family was forced to be self-sufficient, and such items as they could not produce - articles of iron, arms, powder, etc. - were brought with them when they settled, or obtained rarely from the outside settlements, at a considerable cost in time and expense.

A number of individuals had some particular skill, which they practiced on the side, exchanging their work for products they could use, for very little actual money was in use. David Morse was a carpenter and "house joiner"; Jonathan Morse was a blacksmith, to whom Paul Coffin refers in his journals as, "my friend Morse, the excellent blacksmith." Sylvester Norton and Sarson Chase, as well as the before mentioned Thomas Fish, were shoe makers. Otis Robinson was also a blacksmith, while Thomas Chase was the town's first cabinet maker. Zebedee Rose was another skilled carpenter.

The settlers customarily helped each other by joining forces in a "bee" for raising house or barn frames, and for felling trees. With these exceptions of joint effort, and, of course, the grist and saw mill on Long Pond outlet, which served the whole community, Port Royal of 1790 consisted of self-sufficient family units, scattered on the west side of the

THE BOARDMAN HOUSE

WILLIAM BRETTUN'S HOUSE

river mostly to the east of a line from Sylvester (Turner) over Lovewell's (Waters) Hill, between Long and Round ponds, to Phips' Canada (Jay); while on the East side of the river, they were mainly to the west of a line from Moose Hill to Tollawalla (Strickland). The majority of the habitations were still log houses, one end of which was usually a huge fireplace burning 4 ft. logs, for heating, cooking and lighting, whose hearth was the real center of family life. They were connected to their neighbors, and to the horseways leading to Sylvester and to Pondtown, by spotted trails or paths. Deacon Livermore had, of course, completed his fine dwelling some years before 1790, which is still standing today, and still notable for size and beauty even by today's standards. As might be expected, his home was the real town headquarters, and the gathering place of early assemblies.

Life was far from easy in those days, and the town was only a collection of clearings in what was still a primeval wilderness. Jabez Delano, for instance, with two others (probably his brothers, Zebedee and James) each having an axe, had crossed the river below the "rips," at the old Wing ferry, and taking their course up-river toward Deacon Livermore's treed a half grown bear. They had no gun with them, so two of them cut the tree down; Jabez placed himself favorably, and when the tree fell he "seized the bear by the heels and swung him over his head till he got to a tree and knocked his brains out."

The same Jabez Delano met a large bull moose on the east side of Fish Meadow, about twenty rods east of the road across the meadow, when he was hunting for partridges. Luckily he had a ball in his pocket, and, rolling it into his gun, shot the moose dead on the spot, just as the moose was about to "charge" him.

Moose Hill, at the northeast corner of the town, got its name from the fact that, in 1787, Deacon Livermore shot a moose there with his own hand.

The before-mentioned Joseph Coolidge moved across the line into Jay in the year 1790. Since there was a scarcity of provisions that year and, in consequence, much suffering, he went to seek corn at Deacon Livermore's. The deacon told him that he had no corn, and that the best he could do was to furnish him with money and a horse to ride to the Kennebec, where it was understood corn might be purchased. Thus armed, Mr. Coolidge set out. Returning with his corn on the horse's back, he reached the Androscoggin River late at night, but the boat was on the west side, and the ferryman lived (at Deacon Livermore's) so far away that he could not raise him. At this moment a heavy shower came up, and Mr. Coolidge, tying his horse and removing the corn from his back, peeled a hemlock tree, placed the bark over the corn, plunged into the river, swam it, found the boat, crossed with it, took his horse

and corn aboard, recrossed the river, and proceeded on' to his home, which he reached at two o'clock in the morning. Arriving at home wet and hungry for he had not eaten since the previous morning - he aroused his wife, and she made him a "Johnny cake," which he said was the sweetest food he ever ate.

The family of Zebedee Delano was, at one time, reduced to such extremities that they "subsisted on boiled beech leaves for some days."

Without either doctor or dentist, they of course had to rely on home remedies when faced with serious accident or illness, such as Major Fish recorded in his journal when William Foster cut his leg above the knee, when felling trees; or Mr. Wellington "was taken not well, and violently seized with paine in the head," and carried to a settler's cabin. That such serious accidents were fairly common, particularly from falling trees, or collapsing house and barn frames, is evident from the record.

Jonathan Morse, the blacksmith, had got a barn frame raised, when a neighbor, Mrs. Eben Keith, called to see Mrs. Morse one afternoon. Both these women had nursing children. After chatting a while in the house, they went out to see the new barn frame, taking their infants with them. They sat down on the sill of the barn, when a sudden strong gust of wind brought the frame down upon them, and Mrs. Morse was killed where she sat, though the infant in her arms escaped with minor injuries, as did the other two.

Eliphalet Rowell and John Winter were both killed by falling trees, when engaged in a "drive of trees" just to the east of where Livermore Shoe Company's factory stands.

In the next five years, 1791-1795, the population of Port Royal nearly doubled, there being nearly 400 persons in the latter year. Among the most prominent of the men arriving in those years were:

SAMUEL ATWOOD, from Berkley, Massachusetts, who settled at Brettuns Mills about 1795. An active, intelligent man, he was often employed as one of the town officers.

EPHRAIM CHILD, who came from Waltham, Massachusetts, about 1794, and purchased from Samuel Livermore a lot of land bounded on the South by Lot 53, Easterly by Long Pond, Northerly by the "Last Division," Westerly by Round Pond and land of Amos Livermore.

JOHN FULLER settled first in Winthrop in 1773, but at the urging of his sons, Abram and Isaac, moved to Livermore in 1795. He later purchased the lot and mill privilege at Richmond's Mills.

ISAAC FULLER, who came with his father, John, was a Revolutionary soldier. He kept the ferry at the Intervale for many years, until he sold it to Tristram Hillman, and bought a farm near East Livermore station.

ABRAM FULLER, the other son who came with his father and brother, settled on the East side of the river, near the ferry (on the place later occupied by H. W. Bailey).

DANIEL HOLMAN came from Worcester County before 1793 (probably about 1789). He was a Revolutionary soldier, and one of the "Minute Men" who marched to Concord, April 19, 1775. He cleared and occupied a farm about a mile S.W. of No. Livermore Corner, which his son, Abner, afterwards owned and occupied - the place later known as the William Bryant farm.

AMOS LIVERMORE was a brother to the wives of Samuel Benjamin and Ephraim Childs. He came to Livermore in 1795, and first lived on the farm afterwards owned by Spencer Godding.

EBENEZER PITTS moved to Livermore from Ware, Massachusetts, in 1791, and occupied until his death the farm at N. Livermore Corner afterward owned by his grandson, Ebenezer Pitts.

HASTINGS STRICKLAND, a son of Rev. John Strickland of Turner, came here in 1795. He had a large farm, extensive orchard and cider mill, on the main road, about half a mile south of Monroe's tavern.

Not only was the place becoming much more populated in these five years, but it was taking on many of the characteristics of a real town, in place of the isolated individual units; though still a largely self-contained community, with a minimum of communication with the outside world, because of the lack of roads and difficulty of travel.

General David Learned opened the first store in 1791, south of where the Norlands church now stands. He also built a sawmill at the outlet of Bartlett's Pond. In the same year, as before mentioned, Deacon Livermore built the first mill on the Androscoggin at Rockomeka (Livermore Falls). On Aug. 7, 1793, the first church in town was organized - the First Baptist Church of Livermore - with seventeen original members, viz., Daniel Holman, Peletiah Gibbs, Isaac Lovewell, Elisha Williams, Otis Robinson, Henry Bond, James Delano, Zebedee Delano, Thomas Wyman, Peter Godding, David Reed, Anna Gibbs, Hannah Robinson, Mary Delano, Susanna Wyman, Grace Delano, Catherine Walker.

The inhabitants voted, on Sept. 4, 1793, to build a "Meet-

Sarah Livermore - 1770-1847
daughter of Deacon Elijah Livermore; ancestor of the Treat family

ing House" on Lot No. 36, the "Ministry Lot." This, of course, was to be non-denominational, for use of the whole town. A "Tree Felling Bee" was held to clear the lot; but in the process Isaiah Manley and David Handy were killed by the fall of a large tree. This was accepted as a premonition, and the project abandoned.

Prior to 1793, the town had no physician, but in that year they determined it was necessary to have one, and efforts were made to find a man of good character and ability in his profession, and induce him to make his home in the new town. Among the candidates who presented themselves were Dr. Cyrus Hamlin, of Harvard, Massachusetts, and another whose name is not recorded, but who was favored by Deacon Livermore at the citizens' meeting called to make decision on their choice. The majority favored Dr. Hamlin; and he afterwards paid off the Deacon for his error in judgement by, a year or two later, marrying his daughter.

The action of this meeting was followed by the preparation of a paper by the Rev. Sylvanus Boardman, the Baptist minister, which was signed by some of the principal inhabitants, and of which the following is a copy:

"Whereas the town of Livermore is destitute of a physician, and as the inhabitants are subject to great inconveniences on account of the distance they have to travel in order to procure one, and being informed by Dr. Hamlin that he contemplates settling in said town, and wishes to know the minds of the people in this respect, we, the subscribers, hereby testify that it is agreeable to our wishes that he should settle with us, and that we will contribute all that we can, consistently, to the encouragement so far as his prudent conduct and skill in his profession shall commend him to our esteem.

SLYVANUS BOARDMAN
RANSOM NORTON
WILLIAM HURD
ISAAC LIVERMORE"

Livermore, Sept. 1, 1795.

Also, in this year, was taken the first step toward providing

Deacon Livermore's "corner chair"

highways in the town. It had been voted, in Sept., 1793, to lay
out a road from Turner to Phips' Canada (Jay), from Deacon
True's, over Lovewell's (Water's) Hill, between the two ponds,
to the north line of the town. In 1795, this road was accepted,
and it was further voted "to run the roads straight from one end
to the other as the land will admit, without any regard to

individuals." Anyone familiar with the town will realize that the vote was complied with. This first road was for many years "the main road," and route of the Portland to Farmington stage-coaches.

It was in 1795 that the town became legally incorporated by Act of the Massachusetts General Court, passed February 28, 1795, and approved by Samuel Adams, Governor.

The organization meeting was held at Deacon Livermore's house, on April 13, 1795, with Elisha Williams acting as Moderator; and the following were elected as the first Town Officials:

Clerk and Treasurer, Samuel Hillman;

Selectmen, David Learned,

> Sylvanus Boardman,
> Peletiah Gibbs;

Surveyors of Roads, James Norton, Elisha Smith, William Lindsay, David Morse, Samuel Sawin, Reuben Wing, Abram Fuller;

Surveyors of Lumber, Thomas Chase, David Morse,
> Elijah Stevens;

Sealer of Wts. & Measures, Ransom Norton;

Fence Viewers, Thomas Chase, Isaac Lovewell;

Hog Reaves, Elijah Stevens, Abijah Monroe;

Pound Keeper, James Delano.

One of the first concerns of the new town was for its schools; and on August 10, 1795, Elisha Williams, Samuel Benjamin and Ransom Norton were appointed a committee to divide the town into school districts. It was also voted at this meeting to raise 30 pounds for support of roads, and 40 pounds for support of schools. It was voted to warn of town-meetings by posting notification at the dwelling house of Reuben Wing, at the Ferry, and at the three mills of the town.

Following its incorporation, the town's population increased rapidly. The Rev. Paul Coffin, a traveling missionary, who visited the place in 1798, records in his diary that Livermore contained 130 families (over 600 people) and adds, "there were in this place six pairs of twins under 5 years." In that year he visited Deacon Livermore and his son, "who had fifty cattle, many sheep and horses, a house large and high, of four rooms and two chimneys, and four barns and four sheds."

Most of the residents had replaced the log cabins with substantial frame dwellings, some of which are still standing, notably that of Deacon Livermore.

Beside the Main Road on the East side of the river, built in 1795, several other roads, on both sides of the river, were built and in use by 1798, though only the "Main Road" on the West side of the river, from Turner to Jay, was apparently suited for wheeled vehicles.

The center of the community at that time was, roughly, a triangular section from Fuller's (Hillman's) Ferry, northwest to and including the two ponds, Long and Round; and southwest from the Ferry to the Monroe places below Bartlett's Pond.

It is noteworthy that, as early as 1798, a vote was passed giving consent to a division of the town by which "the east side of the river would be set off into a town by itself." This of course was not effected until nearly half a century later; but evidently those on the East side were already experiencing the difficulty which led to eventual separation, namely, the lack of voice in town affairs. The town meetings being held in the spring, when ice breaking up in the river made crossing, either over the ice or on the ferry, dangerous if not impossible, those east of the river were unable to participate in the meetings, which were held on the west side.

The town's first representative in the General Court of the Commonwealth was Deacon Livermore, he being unanimously elected May 9, 1799. It is recorded that, when the time came for his departure to occupy this position he made the journey on horseback, wearing a cocked hat, shad-bellied waistcoat, ruffled shirt, and knee-breeches.

Legally incorporated as "Livermore," the town no longer was referred to as "Port Royal"; and, as it entered the new century, it did so as a firmly established and going community. Three ferries, Fuller's, Benjamin's and Wing's, were in regular use; three mills, at Livermore Falls, Gibb's Mills and Bartlett's

Pond outlet, were in steady operation; General Learned's store was doing a substantial business; Monroe's tavern was already famous; the town had an outstanding physician in Dr. Hamlin; and, in 1799, the Baptists had built their first church building, known as "The Church on the Rock," on Loney's Ledge; and at least two schoolhouses had been built.

An early historian says, "The town was fortunate in having for its founder a man so able and so wise, of so much financial strength and weight of character as Deacon Livermore. He was truly the father of the town, and his name is held in honor and veneration by its people. And he was fortunate in the character of the most of his associate proprietors and co-workers.

"Under the influence of such men, the settlers who were early attracted to the town were generally men of good character and of some pecuniary ability. Few towns in the State, probably, owe more to the character of the first settlers than this town. Many of them had been officers or soldiers in the war of the Revolution, and were active, earnest men, bent upon making their way in the world."

These settlers were, with the few exceptions noted, native New Englanders of the third to sixth generation in this country, vastly different from the rather poor and unprepared persons with whom Popham, Gilbert and others attempted to start colonies. These New Englanders, mostly from the vicinity of Waltham and Watertown, Massachusetts, had no illusions as to the hardships they would face, and were fully competent to meet them. Furthermore, they were by no means poor; some of them, such as General Learned, Major Fish, Colonel Bond, Captain Haines, Lieutenant Benjamin, and others, were men of substantial means. Deacon Livermore, at the time of his death, owned 1,120 acres of land, $10,000 in money, as well as extensive holdings of livestock and personal property.

Even more unusual for that time was the educational level of the Port Royal people. Two of Deacon Livermore's brothers were graduates of Princeton (Nassua Hall); his son-in-law, Elisha Williams, was a Yale graduate, as was Reverend John Strickland, father of Hastings. The several physicians who served the town were well educated men; and one of the first corporate actions of the settlers was to provide for schools. Another indication is the town's circulating library, which was kept at Dr. Bradford's; and was used by the people of the towi, until its small collection of classics, such as *Vicar of Wakefield, Pilgrim's Progress,* and *Robinson Crusoe* was dog-eared and falling apart.

Although these people were brought up in the strict Congregational faith, in communities where it was virtually a "State Church," to which everyone had to contribute whether a member or not, and many of the settlers, like Deacon Livermore, had been deacons or officers in the Congregational church, they nevertheless did not establish that church here. The first established church was the Baptist, of whom the first minister was Elisha Williams, son of a Congregational Minister; while the second, ten years later, was the Methodist, to which Deacon Livermore gave his allegiance.

One cannot but speculate what induced such people, with comfortable homes in settled Massachusetts communities where there was plenty of land, to leave them, and go into the wilds of Maine. Certainly they were not seeking escape from the law, or even from creditors, for they were uniformly people of excellent standing in the communities from which they came; surely they had no false hopes about gaining easy wealth here, for the land had been carefully surveyed and they knew exactly what they faced; nor were they the kind of adventurers who staked a claim, cleared the land, sold out to permanent settlers, then moved on to new country.

Possibly the abandonment of the Congregational faith indicates a desire to get away from its rather harsh and intolerant views and rule. The best guess, however, is that the adventure of building a wholly new community, with agreeable companions, in a beautiful, fertile and untouched land, is what appealed to them and motivated them.

Deacon Livermore pretty much controlled the sale of lots,

through his acquisition of title to most of the lots from the original proprietors. It is noteworthy that he was careful to include men skilled in the various occupations which would be needed, - blacksmiths, carpenters, cabinet makers, shoemakers, tanners, etc. Even more noteworthy, however, is the compatibility and cooperation of these first settlers. For the first fifty years, at least, there seemed to be no need of constables or jails. An early writer said, concerning the first half-century, "It was a neighborhood of great social harmony. I don't remember a neighborhood quarrel."

Obviously, times have changed; but we can look back with no little satisfaction to the character of that first settlement; and, truly, "the town was fortunate in having for its founder a man so able and so wise, of so much financial strength and weight of character as Deacon Livermore."

LIVERMORE
Before the Separation

THE NINETEENTH CENTURY opened with general prosperity in the young town of Livermore. The critical and dependent stage of struggling for homes in the forests during the pioneer period had passed. Comfortable farms on productive new soil had reached a profitable level, and the lumber and fur trades had become very valuable and largely extended. Nevertheless, there was little real money in circulation; and trade was carried on mostly by barter of goods. Through the ports of Hallowell and Portland, the citizens of Livermore found a ready market for their products, and brought back the articles needed from outside.

Although lumber and furs were still profitable items in trade during these early years of the 19th century, the inhabitants of Livermore were primarily farmers. The section of Massachusetts from which the majority of the first settlers came was noted for fruit raising and dairy products; so it was quite natural that these men should devote their efforts in the new town to the same specialties - fruit (mostly apples) and dairy products, especially cheeses. In the early 1800's, we find them exporting, in addition to Indian corn and potatoes, substantial amounts of both cheeses and apples, of a quality which commanded a premium in the markets of Portland and Boston, and for which the town early became famous.

Practically every settler had a few apple trees on his place, to provide fruit for his own use, and material for the making of cider. By 1810, however, there were eleven commercial orchards in town; and the number steadily increased.

These homesteads in the early 1800's were usually either the square, 2-story type (such as Deacon Livermore's, the Wadsworth house on Moose Hill, or the North Livermore Baptist parsonage) or the 1 ½ story, "Cape Cod" style (like the Boardman house). Typically, they were built on elevations, with the approach by a winding road up the hillside - a road bordered with huge maples or elms.

Florence Nelson, in her book *Lest We Forget,* describes them thus:

"Nearer the buildings were other trees, - apple, butternut or balm of Gilead, known in earlier days as "the tree of healing." The juicy buds of this tree were gathered, kept in bottles, and the juice squeezed from them into wounds. The Indians recognized this panacea and no doubt taught the white man the value of it.

"Almost caressing the house were the lilac bushes. (Today, even though found far from the haunts of men, lilac bushes are sure proof that a house once stood there.) In the summer time, there would be in bloom about the door, "ladies' delights," caraway, patches of catnip, bleeding heart, and pans running over with portulacas. A well sweep or a hand pump near the wood house, and a never failing spring nearby supplied the homestead with cool, pure, sparkling water.

"The house (if it was the 1 ½ story type) in the upper part sometimes had a finished, plastered bedroom; but more often it was all an open, unfinished attic. This was the ideal place to sleep, where one could hear the rain pattering on the roof, or Jack Frost drawing out the nails on a way-below-zero night; and, in a blizzard, see and feel the snow sifting down through the cracks in the roof.   - -

"The ceilings in all the houses were low. The floors and paneling were of broad pumpkin pine. Windows had tiny panes of glass, sometimes twenty-four or more to a window; and doors had panels built in the form of a cross to keep out evil spirits (some believed) and were known as 'Christian doors.'

"There was only one chimney, a huge one that took up a space twelve or more feet square in the center of the house. This was to accommodate all the fireplaces, which in some houses numbered many, as the main rooms all had fireplaces. In the kitchen, it also took in the long brick oven, various cupboards for ironware and kitchen implements.

"The room of great importance in the house was the kitchen. It served as pantry, dining and living room, laundry, and the place where gatherings for home entertainment were held. To the fireplace men folk brought sick and weak animals, the young lambs and chickens, to be revived by the warmth of the friendly fire; their saddles and harnesses to be thawed out in wintertime or to be greased and repaired; and the many other hand jobs that winter brought forth.

"The old kitchen fireplace was equipped with a long crane from which hung pots and large black kettles; and there were also other kettles with legs that stood on the wide brick hearth. On one side was the brick oven, wide and deep, for which wood was especially cut and fitted. When the oven was to be used, the wood was burned down and the coals pushed back, leaving the bricks hot, and ready to receive the entire Saturday's baking, - the pot of beans, brownbread, pies, white bread, Indian pudding, cakes and cookies. These were put in with a long-handled, flat shovel, made for this very purpose.

"Every kitchen had its corner cupboard in which was kept the old glass, often of Sandwich make, and beautiful sets of china, Mulberry, Chelsea and many other pieces that were the products of famous potters. Pewter mugs and porringers, that were used in the everyday living, stood here.

"On the mantel over the fireplace were the candle-sticks with their tallow dips, a mug full of lighters, or spills, made of wood or rolled paper, the snuffers to trim the wicks, and a small clock.

"The bedroom off the kitchen was grandmother's room. The spool bed was worthy of notice. Its springs were corded rope, the under mattress made of corn husks, and over it a live goose feather bed that was covered with home-woven wool blankets and a patchwork quilt.

"The front room of the house was sacred, and re-served for weddings, funerals, and the minister. In Colonial days it was known as the fore-room; but in later days it became the parlor.

"Although some of the houses were built of brick, by far the majority were constructed of wood which was readily available in abundance. Probably the most noteworthy feature of these early American homes was their uniformly excellent architecture. They might differ in size, shape, and degree of elegance; but even the humblest of them were built on simple, harmonius lines, perfectly proportioned, and with details of fanlights, side-lights, mouldings, etc., carefully and beautifully done, - things which unfortunately, cannot be said of most construction of a century later."

By this time (1800) the settlers had come to realize that, with the deep snow of Maine winters, it was a great convenience to be able to go from house to barn, to feed and water the animals, etc., entirely under cover, instead of having to shovel paths long distances through deep snow, which at times drifted in about as fast as it could be shoveled out. Consequently, most Maine homestead farms built after 1800 have the house connected to the barn by a long shed, or sheds.

The average farmer would go to market three or four times in the course of a winter. His pung, drawn by a single horse, would take a load of eight or nine hundred pounds; and the trip would usually take three days. A dressed hog, a tub or two of butter, half a dozen cheeses, a keg of cider apple-sauce, a hundred pounds of dried apples, and perhaps a few chickens or turkeys would be a typical assortment, and would make a reasonable load for a single horse to haul over a highway as uneven and snow-blocked as the farmer would expect to find.

The contents of such a pung would bring him about fifty dollars - half in cash and half in goods.

These old-time marketings were a source of fun and keen enjoyment, when a dozen neighbors would set out in company, with their train of pungs for the market town. The cold might be piercing, the winds boisterous, and the roads filled with snow drifts, but sooner or later the wayside inn, with its glowing hearthstone and ruddy landlord, was reached; the horses were carefully blanketed and fed; their drivers, who were their owners, were seated around the blazing fire, while the genial warmth of the chimney was assisted by something "comfortable" from the bar.

Most famous of the wayside inns in this section of the state was the inn of Abijah Monroe - one of four sons of Benjamin Monroe, of Lincoln, Massachusetts. Three of the brothers were given adjoining lots, just below the Bartlett's Pond, by their father, viz. - Abel Monroe was given Lot 48; John, Lot 39; and Abijah, Lot 47; while the fourth brother, Isaac, was given Lot 33, east side of river, on Jug Hill, which he later sold to F. A. Billington.

Abijah's house was built in 1790, on Lot No. 47, which is the southeast part of Bartlett's (or Sander's) Corner. It was called a "Tavern" and maintained as such by Abijah as long as he lived. He kept an excellent tavern which travelers, feeling sure of good fare, would lay their plans to reach whenever they

The mighty Androscoggin seemed to bc spewing forth a limitless supply of long logs from its upper reaches to the young industries sprouting at Livermore Falls.

Driving the logs and manhandling the long bateaus through the swift spring currents required a rugged breed.

111

could do so; and there were many travelers in those days upon what was then the great highway leading from Portland to Farmington.

One of Monroe's regular patrons was Rev. Paul Coffin, a Congregational minister, who made several "Missionary Tours" through Maine. In his diary for 1798, he makes this entry, "Aug. 30th - Invited by the wife of Abijah Monroe, put up with them for the night. He had just sprung his net on six dozen pigeons, and took them all. To take a whole flock is a common thing with him. - Aug. 31 - Returned to Monroe's and put up for the night. He and his wife are sensible and agreeable." Again, in his record for 1800, he writes, "Sept. 10 - Livermore. Mr. Munroe told me that the Baptists, who lately multiplied here, suppose religion and trade have no connection. Their religion may be pure, while they make a good bargain. - Put up with Abijah Monroe for the night."

For years Monroe's Tavern was quite a gathering place for the townspeople. The neighbors and townsfolk would congregate there to see one another, learn the news, relate what had happened, renew the past, relive the scenes and recall the events and sayings of the Revolutionary war - in which many of them had been actors. The first four lawyers who successively practiced in the town lived with Mr. Monroe, and had their office in his house, viz., a Mr. Strong from Vermont, Jonathan G. Hunton, Ezra Kingman, and Asa King.

A contemporary of his wrote that "Uncle 'Bijah kept the wayside inn, one of the old-fashioned, comfortable taverns, with a great fireplace for wood, and the cleanest sanded floor in the world. It was a treat to sit there in your comfortable kitchen chair. The ministers, the young lawyers and doctors who were waiting for something to turn up, might be found at Uncle 'Bijah's, on the pleasant summer days under the portico, or in the chimney corner in the long winter evenings."

Failing health eventually made walking difficult for Mr. Monre, so that he became accustomed, in his last years, to sit in his large arm-chair in the public room from morning until night - reading, when there was no company, some book, generally the Bible, with which he became so familiar as to be

For years, Monroe's Tavern was quite a gathering place
for the Townspeople

able to quote from any part of it with an accuracy that was phenomenal. He delighted in theological discussion; and it is related that one tilt with Rev. Jabez Woodman, a Baptist clergyman of New Gloucester, lasted from noontime dinner until the small hours of the next day, and ended in the conversion of Mr. Woodward to Mr. Monroe's way of thinking.

Abijah and his wife had no children. Both are buried in the cemetery near Robert H. Boothby's. In 1833, his tavern was moved to the "intervale," and became part of the dwelling later owned by Myron Eames.

As mentioned before, Rev. Paul Coffin quoted Abijah Monroe as saying, in 1800, "the Baptists had lately multiplied here"; and it was in 1811 that two more Baptist churches were organized - the Second Baptist Church in Livermore, and the Third Baptist Church in Livermore. The Second Baptist Church was located in the southerly part of town; and after an even century, it went out of existence in 1911. The Third Baptist Church in Livermore was situated on the east of the river, at Shy; and is now known as the First Baptist Church of Livermore Falls. A more detailed account of these organizations will be found in the Appendix; but special note should be made of the part these churches played in the establishment of what is now Colby College. Three Livermore men, Sylvanus Boardman, John Haynes, and Ransom Norton, were largely instrumental in organizing the Maine Literary & Theological Institute, later to become Colby College, primarily for the purpose of providing higher education for Baptist ministers, but not limited to that.
. All three were on its first Board of Trustees; and Boardman's son, George Dana Boardman, was the first graduate, becoming a famous missionary to Burma.

At about this same time, in 1803, the Livermore Methodist church was organized. Its first building stood on the Common at Livermore Center. It was to this church that Deacon Livermore gave his support; and a more detailed account of its history appears in the Appendix.

The Universalists held meetings in private houses, and occasionally were addressed by visiting preachers, from 1809 to 1816, in which year they voted to employ a minister, and to hold the meetings in the school house near Dr. Bradford's.

The first school house stood in the angle of the junction of the Fish Meadow Road and the Cat Corner Road, nearly opposite to the cellar of the Major Fish house, and was built in the 1790' s; and another school house (some accounts say the first) was built at about the same time at Gibbs' Mills, on the place later owned by L. L. Riggs. It was in this latter school house that Henry Bond was the teacher.

On the east side of the river, the first two school houses were located at Haines Corner and Shy; it is uncertain which was the first, but they were evidently built at about the same time, around the beginning of the last century. In the Appendix will be found a "Catalogue of Scholars," on both east and west sides, as made by Benjamin Foster, a popular and successful teacher of schools in Livermore from 1806 to 1810.

Prior to 1811, there was also a schoolhouse at Moose Hill, for it is recorded that the Third Baptist Church, organized in that year, held meetings alternately in the schoolhouse at Shy and the schoolhouse at Moose Hill.

In this first part of the 19th century, on the east side of the river, the principal settlements were at The Corner (Haines' Corner) where Francis F. Haines (son of Capt. Peter Haines), Samuel Morrison, and Samuel F. Fuller, were prosperous traders, where the first school house was built, and a Union Meeting House was located; and at Barton's Ferry (Shy), where Amos Barton carried on trade, there were several shops, and here was built the second of the early schoolhouses.

At this period, the village at Rockomeka Falls (Livermore Falls) was relatively unimportant. The saw mill and grist mill, built in 1791 by Deacon Livermore, on the Androscoggin, were operated for 'him by Aaron Wing, then later sold to Thomas Davis; and for a time the locality was known as "Davis' Mills." As late as 1813 there were only three dwellings

The Riverdrivers of 1873 break for lunch

Jam in the log drive of 1873

here - those of Samuel Richardson, who occupied Lot No.1, Thomas Davis, and Joseph Morrill. There was also one store operated by a Mr. Mills who was succeeded by Elisha Pettingill about 1815.

There were farm settlements at Moose Hill, in the vicinity of Jug Hill, and at what is now called East Livermore Campground, where Samuel Smith began operation of a saw mill in 1806. At about the same time, Mr. Leonard built and operated a saw mill in Tollawalla (Strickland), near what was later the T. D. Norris place.

As before noted, the first south-north road on the east side of the river was cleared in -1795 - little more than a track. In October, 1802, the first yoke of oxen, with wheels attached, was driven from Haines Comer to the Falls for boards, by Moses Young. The road cut out would not allow passage of a loaded team. The boards were hauled on his cart from the mill to the foot of the rapids below, there made into a raft and floated down to Fuller's (Hillman's) Ferry. In passing down the river, it being dark, his raft caught on the rocks, and he was obliged to remain on it all night.

Until after the War of 1812, settlement on the west side continued to focus around Livermore Center, where Deacon Livermore's house, the Methodist Church and western terminus of Fuller's (Hillman's) Ferry were located; and just west of it, in the Bartlett's Pond neighborhood, where Abijah Monroe kept his tavern, and General Learned had his store. The store was purchased by Artemus Leonard in 1805, and by him sold to Israel Washburn in 1809.

Livermore Village (Brettun's Mills) really began to assume importance when William H. Brettun purchased the mills and water power there, about 1810. He carried on grist and saw mills, shingle and clapboard machines, carding and fulling mills, and also established a store from which were sold large quantities of goods.

Prior to 1806, John Walker had for many years visited Portland weekly, acting as a sort of unofficial mail carrier and expressman for the town of Livermore. In 1806, Josiah Smith was appointed the first official mail carrier, covering a route through Buckfield, Hartford and Paris to Portland; and returning through New Gloucester and Turner to Livermore, making the round trip once a week. The first postmaster in town was Dr. Benjamin Prescott, whose appointment dated from April 1, 1807. Dr. Benjamin Bradford bought Prescott's house and succeeded him, both as physician and as postmaster, in August, 1809. For 15 years, this was the only post office in town.

The first Militia Company was organized in 1800, on the west side of the river, with Davis Learned as Captain, William Coolidge as Lieutenant, and Henry Sawtelle as Ensign. In 1803, a company was organized on the east side of the river, with Peter Haines as Captain, Robert Morrison as Lieutenant, and Theodore Marston as Ensign. In this same year a second company was formed on the west side, having Henry Sawtelle as Captain, James Starbird as Lieutenant, and Joseph Mills as Ensign.

The real pride of the town, however, was the company of cavalry, formed in 1809, in Livermore. Its first officers were Samuel Atwood, Captain, Isaac' Talbot, Lieutenant, and Aaron S. Barton, Cornet; while subsequent Captains included Simeon Waters, Daniel Coolidge, Alpheus Kendall, Isaac Strickland, Otis Pray, Hastings Strickland, Matthew Stone, Hezekiah Atwood, Elisha Coolidge and Rufus Hewett. An early writer says of this company, "The company was constituted for many years, in large proportion, of the intelligent and active young men of the town. It was the pride of the people. No boy or girl belonging to the town ever attended the 'general muster,' at Canton Point, and saw the 'troopers' enter the field, mounted upon the finest horses that could be procured for the occasion, and clothed in scarlet, but was proud to acknowledge that he (or she) too hailed from Livermore."

A round brick powder house with a conical roof, and plastered on the inside, was built in 1807, as a magazine for the powder and bullets furnished by the town. Although it was demolished in 1862, the foundation can still be seen on the south side of the road, easterly from Deacon Livermore's house, and in a stone wall running north and south.

In the war of 1812-14, when the State militia were called out for the defense of the sea-coast towns, two companies were called out from this town, Captain Morrison's company from the east side, and Captain Morse's company from the west side. They served about two months, in the defense of Portland, but were not engaged in any actual fighting. In the Appendix may be found the names of the men in these two companies.

A large number of Livermore men enlisted in the United States army for one year or duration of the war; and, for the most part, served in the 34th and 45th Regiments of Infantry. Of all the Livermore men engaged in that conflict, one of the most interesting was Daniel Knox, son of Stacey Knox. Daniel was a tall, slim young man who, it was said, "could outwalk 'the Wandering Jew,' or almost anybody ever heard of, - and was brave to a fault." He enlisted in the war of 1812, and was sent with the United States forces to the Canadian frontier. Whenever volunteers were called for, to undertake a dangerous expedition, Daniel Knox was always one. On the occasion of the battle on Lake Erie, when Commodore O. H. Perry wanted more men for his ships, and was permitted to call for volunteers from the land force, Daniel Knox was among the first, and was assigned to the Commodore's flagship. When that ship became disabled, during the battle, and Perry, wishing to change to another ship, called for twelve men to row him in an open boat through the thick of the battle, Daniel Knox was one of those twelve. They, of course, came under heavy fire, and the first shot hole in their boat was stopped by Perry with his own coat; while Daniel Knox plugged the second shot hole with his own jacket.

Daniel had enlisted for "duration of the war"; and did not get home for some time after the other Livermore men were back, so that the report was current that he had been killed. However, he arrived safe and sound at last; and went back to helping his father in his lumber business. About 1820, in the spring of the year, they were breaking a brow of logs on Mosquito Brook in the town of Jay; the brow gave way while Daniel was on, or in front of it; and, as the record says, "it broke him all to pieces."

A log jam forms at the second bridge (looking South).

Logs reach Livermore Falls in 1873; the young apple trees on the crest of the hill are now part of George Grua's orchard.

With the War of 1812 came hard times for the Maine towns, and Livermore was no exception. The coasting vessels had been the basis on which most Maine commerce was built, bringing in articles of necessity that were easily and cheaply obtained by the people; and carrying out many of their products to be sold at good prices in the markets of Boston and New York. The force of the Embargo imposed during the war was heavily felt, and the coasting trade was at an end. A stagnation occurred in all business; no markets could be had for home products; and the articles of necessity, so common and cheap before the War, could hardly be procured, and then only at enormous prices.

To add to the miseries of the War, came hitherto unheard of cold seasons of 1815, 1816 and 1817. In 1815 winter continued through the spring months, snow falling in the middle of May from 12 to 18 inches in depth. In April, 1816, the weather began mild, but growing steadily colder until it was like winter at month end. May was a cold month; corn was killed, replanted and again killed; buds and fruit were frozen; ice formed half an inch thick. June was still colder than May. Snow fell to the depth of 10 inches, nearly every green plant was killed, and fruit was everywhere blighted. Rev. Ransom Dunham, of Paris, as quoted in "History of Norway," said: "In 1816, June 7th, snow fell two inches. I rode from Hebron to Livermore on horseback and came near freezing. It was so cold that it killed the birds. English robins were frozen to death." July was like a winter month with snow and ice. Corn, except on some hill farms and in some moderately warm locations, was entirely killed. August was cold, ice forming half an inch thick; and what corn and green plants had been spared the previous months, were frozen. September was cold and frosty. October was colder than usual, with much ice and frost. November was cold, with sleighing. The corn and wheat of 1815 sold for seed in 1817, bringing as much as $3 per bushel; flour brought from eight to ten cents a pound.

The fall of 1817 was the beginning of better times. The deprivations caused by the War and the cold years of 1815 and 1816 had discouraged many people, and emigration took numbers of them to the new lands of the West. Those who had not migrated now reaped their reward - the crops of 1817 were bountiful; prosperity again returned; and Livermore, along with the other Androscoggin towns, grew in strength and wealth for many years.

Agriculture was a profitable employment, yet its character was steadily changing. The wheat crop, once an extensive one, was limited about 1840 by the attacks of the weevil. The culture of flax and the home manufacture of cloth was discontinued after 1840 with the building of woolen mills that made "satinets," and exchanged them for wool. This gave an impetus to sheep raising, which, before this time, had been limited to the small amount of wool needed for domestic use, and occasionally a little mutton. The largest number of sheep were raised from 1835 to 1850; and from 1840 to 1850 many importations of merinos were made, and the quality greatly improved.

Indian corn was an extensive crop until 1830-1840; but with the establishment of canning factories, the culture of sweet corn gradually replaced it. Cheese, butter and dairy products continued profitable; while apples, as they have always been, were an outstanding Livermore product.

Meanwhile, the crafts and small industries, which in the previous century had been carried on by various individuals as a side-line to farming, were fast expanding into full time occupations for a steadily increasing number of persons.

The first tannery operated, commercially was that of Jesse Stone, who maintained the tavern at North Livermore Corner; the second one was that of Alpheus Kendall, in the Bartlett's Pond neighborhood, at the beginning of the century. In 1816, John Smith established at the Falls, on the west side, a large successful tanning business, which his son, Caleb, continued after him at the same location.

Earliest of the shoemakers were Sylvester Norton at North Livermore Corner, and Sarson Chase on Lovewell's Hill. They were followed by John Sanders, near Monroe's Tavern; Samuel Harman and Thomas Lord at Livermore, Village; D. N. St. Clair and a Mr. Blake at the Falls.

Of clothiers and carders, the first probably was Joseph Horsley, located on Bog Brook, about 1800. John Fuller and John A. Kimball were engaged in this business a few years later at Fuller's (Gibbs') Mills; Ozias Bartlett had his mill at the Village as did James Hanna (from the North of Ireland); while Messrs. Stone and Pray, about the same time, did a good amount of business of this kind at the Falls.

Sarson Chase, Jr., was, for many years prior to 1830, engaged in the manufacture of carriages and sleighs. He is said to have been not only a highly skilled craftsman, but a man of fine artistic taste; so that his carriages and sleighs were in great demand from Portland to Bangor.

Thomas Chase and Samuel Boothby were excellent carpenters, who also did cabinet work; but soon after 1800 Charles Benjamin had a shop on the Intervale, doing cabinet work exclusively.

At the Falls were two shops making scythes and snaths - one operated by Samuel Park, and the other by a Mr. Holmes. Henry Aldrich came to the Village (Brettun's Mills) in 1808, to commence a similar manufacture.

Shingle and clapboard mills were usually operated in conjunction with the saw mills, and blacksmith shops were, of course, numerous in the various sections of town.

One craftsman deserving of particular note was Kilah Hall. Living in the southerly part of the town, he was occupied in making clocks. Examples of his skill and originality are still in existence, and highly prized by antique collectors. He had a son, Amasa Hall, who followed in his father's footsteps as clockmaker and jeweler. He later moved to a southern State, and eventually came back to Lewiston.

In the period following the end of the War of 1812, the centers of settlement were changing. Although Haines' Corner and Barton's Ferry (Shy) on the east of the river, and Livermore Center and Gibbs' (Fuller's) Mills on the west side did not perceptibly shrink, nevertheless the growth from then on centered at Rockomeka (Livermore) Falls on the east, and at Livermore Village (Brettun's Mills) and North Livermore Corner on the west.

At North Livermore Corner, Davis Washburn (a cousin of Israel) established a store in 1819, and had for a time, as a partner, Charles Barrell. Jefferson and Merritt Coolidge, Simeon Hersey, Palmer Elliott and Otis Thompson all went into trade there. Three lawyers moved in at "The Corner," Harry Wood in 1814, Richard Belcher in 1817, and Reuel Washburn, who was to take such an active part in town affairs, in 1818. The First Baptist Church had moved from its building on "Loney's Ledge" to a larger meeting house at North Livermore Corner in 1807, on the Common; but this building burned in 1847, and was replaced by the one standing today. In 1818 a hall was built for the accommodation of Oriental Star Lodge #21, Free & Accepted Masons, at "The Corner"; and, of course, Jesse Stone was still operating his popular tavern and his tannery. It is easy to see, therefore, that by 1820-1825 North Livermore Corner was already one of the principal villages of the town. A post office was established there in 1824, with Reuel Washburn as postmaster.

As previously mentioned, Livermore Village (Brettun's Mills) began to grow in importance with the advent of William H. Brettun in 1810, who not only purchased the mills and water power there, but also opened a large store. Henry Aldrich was already in the business of manufacturing scythes and sneaths. Thomas Wing, a well known mill-wright, was located there; and, soon after, Ozias Bartlett started a clothing and carding mill; while Samuel Harmon and Thomas Lord (a pensioner of the War of 1812) were engaged somewhat later in the business of shoe manufacture. A lawyer, Barzillai Streeter, located there sometime prior to 1840. Dr. Timothy Howe, a well educated physician, came to the Village in 1814; and later Drs. Barnard, William Drown, Albert L. Frye, J. W. Bridgham, John Ladd, and I. C. Dunham. Samuel B. Holt, Abner S. Aldrich, Barzillai Latham, Isaac and Lee Strickland, Dorillus Morison, and G. W. C. Washburn were the traders and storekeepers, in addition to William H. Brettun. The Livermore post office, which had been in the Norland neighborhood hitherto, at the time of the appointment of Isaac Strickland as postmaster in 1825 was moved to Brettun's

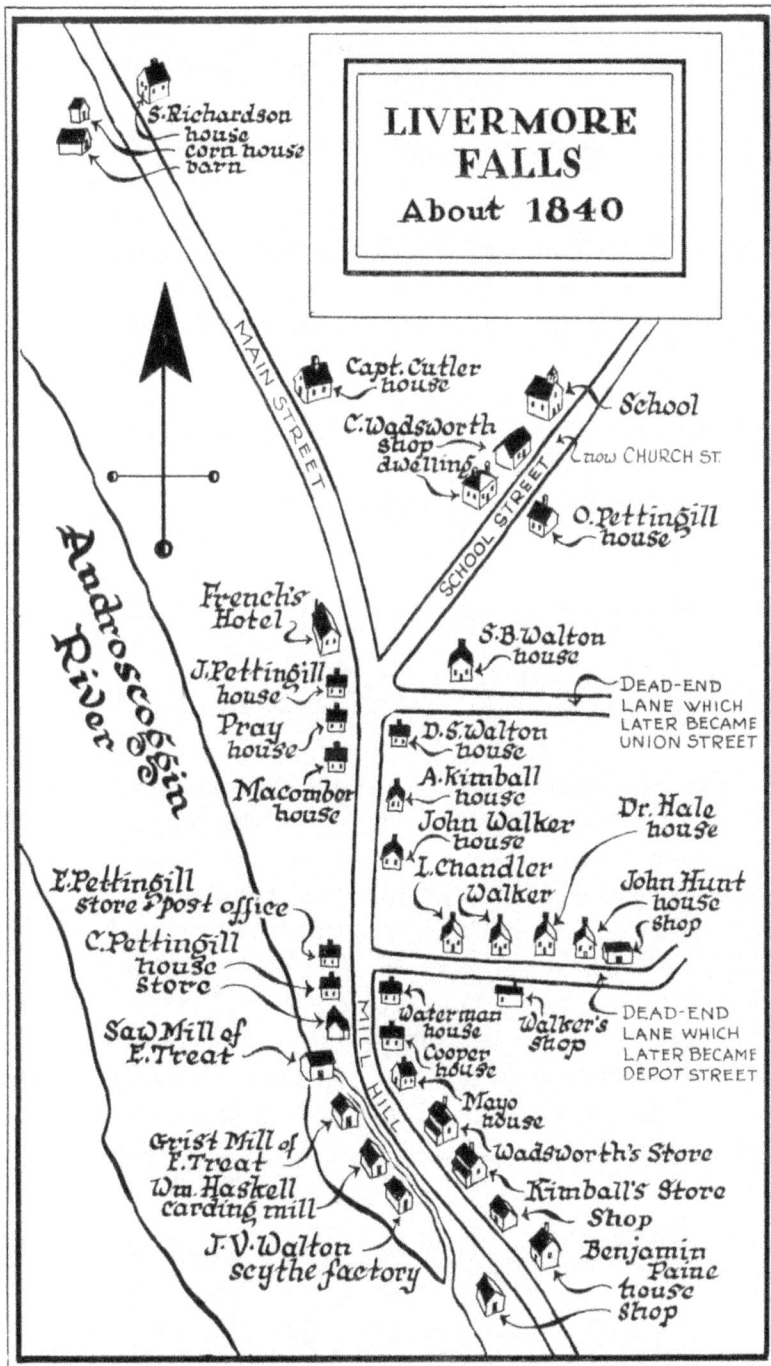

LIVERMORE
FALLS
About 1840

S. Richardson
house
corn house
barn

Capt. Cutler
house

C. Wadsworth
shop
dwelling

School

now CHURCH ST.

O. Pettingill
house

French's
Hotel

J. Pettingill
house

Pray
house

Macomber
house

S. B. Walton
house

DEAD-END
LANE WHICH
LATER BECAME
UNION STREET

D. S. Walton
house

A. Kimball
house

John Walker
house

L. Chandler
Walker

Dr. Hale
house

John Hunt
house
shop

F. Pettingill
store & post office

C. Pettingill
house
store

Saw Mill of
F. Treat

Waterman
house

Cooper
house

Walker's
shop

DEAD-END
LANE WHICH
LATER BECAME
DEPOT STREET

Mayo
house

Grist Mill of
F. Treat

Wm. Haskell
carding mill

J. V. Walton
scythe factory

Wadsworth's Store

Kimball's Store

Shop

Benjamin
Paine
house
shop

Androscoggin
River

MAIN STREET

SCHOOL STREET

MILL HILL

Mills, where it has been ever since.

On the east side of the river, from 1820-1850, the growth and development was mostly around Davis' Mills at Rockomeka Falls - sometimes referred to simply as "The Falls," and later known as "Livermore Falls."

Haines' Corner was still the important village, where Livermore's second post office, called "East Livermore" was established in 1822 with Francis F. Haines as first postmaster. The Union Meeting House, built at Haines' Corner, in 1825, for some years after 1843 was hired by the town for town meetings. Dr. Charles Millett, Dr. William B. Small, and Dr. William Carey (father of Annie Louise Carey) were all practicing physicians located there prior to 1840.

It was the new village developing around the Falls, however, which was destined to take over from the older settlements the place of prominence. Deacon Livermore's water power, saw and grist mills, which had been owned by Thomas Davis, were in 1845 purchased by Captain Ezekial Treat, a young, retired sea captain who had amassed a comfortable fortune, and whose dynamic and enterprising character was largely responsible for the growth of the young village.

The carding mill at this time was operated by William Haskell; the scythe factory by J. V. Walton; and two of three shops were located below "Mill Hill." Stores were those of Comfort Pettingill, C. Wadsworth, A. Kimball and Elisha Pettingill. William A. Evans, of Hallowell (brother of U.S. Senator George Evans) entered law practice here about 1840; and the physicians at the Falls were Dr. William Snow, from 1818; Dr. William Kelsey, prior to 1840, and who died in 1842 at the age of 34; and Dr. David Hale, beginning in 1843.

In March, 1846, occurred a freak of the river never known before or since. The water backed up over the falls, then swirled to the eastern shore and swept off nearly everything in its way. Judge Cyrus Knapp, who entered law practice here a few years afterward, described it thus:

> "The grist and saw mill of Capt. E. Treat,
> stores of C. Pettingill, A. Kimball, and C.
> Wadsworth, the carding mill of Wm. Haskell,

scythe factory of J. V. Walton, and the dwelling house of Benjamin Paine were swept from their foundations, and some of them carried a quarter of a mile and lodged against the elms that skirt the brook below the O. Lyford place. E. Pettingill's store and the Moody house, though somewhat damaged, were the only buildings left in the wake of this unnatural current. A sudden freshet breaking up the river above had brought down a huge volume of water, with ice, logs, broken bridges, and other 'impedimenta'; and when this huge drift went over the falls the unbroken ice below held it in check; but, at length, giving way with a loud report, the water sought its natural channel, leaving the ice and drift piled promiscuously in the road and flats half way or more from the foot of Mill hill to Barton's Ferry. It took a great deal of labor to make the river road passable, as the ice and drift in places were piled 40 feet high. Some of the ice did not disappear until the middle of the next July.

"As soon after this as Captain Treat could construct a saw-mill and prepare the lumber, he rebuilt the grist mill; and either the following summer, or the next, all the buildings reappeared except the scythe factory and Paine's house. Mr. Paine did not dare rebuild on the old spot, as he and his family barely escaped in the flood. He had retired the night before, apprehending no danger; but when he arose in the morning the water was so high that his family made their escape by clinging to a fence until one of his neighbors arrived with a boat. He rebuilt his house and shop up the hill, next to the Baptist church.

"At this time (1846) the business part of the place was below Mill hill, and comprised four stores, a grist and saw mill, a carding mill, a scythe factory, and two or three shops. On the west side of Main Street, north from the mills, the first structure was the Macomber house, where Ham's store now is. The house has been moved back and is the residence of Mrs. John W. Eaton (later the Alec Pomerleau/Herbert McClure residence). The next house was the Pray house near the railroad (later the R. C. Boothby house, which was replaced by the bank). There was a small house where J. Pettingill lives. The next was the hotel kept by William French, where the Basfords live (Billings Inn). Further north, the barn and corn house of S. Richardson completed the buildings on that side of the street. On the east side of the street, after passing the Richardson house south, was the Captain Cutler house (moved across the road in the fall of 1890 by G. R. Currier).

"Up Church Street, on top of the hill, was the house and shoe shop of C. Wadsworth, and a little beyond, a school house. (This was the first schoolhouse at Livermore Falls, and stood about where the Civil War cannon monument now stands.)

"On the other side of Church Street was the house of O. Pettingill, where now stands the Baptist parsonage. On the corner of Main and Union Streets was the D. S. Walton house, now owned by Comfort Pettingill; and in a lane (now Union Street) stood as now the house of S. B. Walton. Next on Main Street, below Pettingill's, was the A. Kimball house, where Cyrus Knapp now resides. The next south was the John Walker house, which became the southern part of the Bean hotel. Below this, on the Treat corner, there had been a hotel, but it was burned prior to this, and the lot was vacant.

"On the north side of the lane (now part of Depot Street) was the dwelling of L. Chandler,

Hugh Chisholm's Umbagog Mill (West side of the Androscoggin at Livermore Falls - just South of the bridge) as it appeared on completion in 1882.

Umbagog expansion under way in 1885; two machines at this mill produced 30-50 tons per day.

moved back in fall of 1890 to make way for the Odd Fellows block. The next building was the Walker house, where Mrs. Robinson now resides. The next was the Dr. hale house. Next was the house and cooper shop of John Hunt at the extreme end of the lane and close to the gully. On the south side of this lane Walker had a shop. From there to Main street was cultivated land.

"Down the hill on the east side of Main Street first was the Waterman house, long since tom down. The next was the Cooper house, now standing. One more below this, the Mayo house, still standing; and we have all there was of Livermore Falls in March, 1846, when the river, as Captain Treat used to say, 'run up the Mill hill,' and washed away its business portion."

It is apparent that early relations between the Town of Jay and Livermore were most cordial and cooperative; possibly the fact that Mr. Phips and Deacon Livermore were related had something to do with it. On August 29, 1781, a committee was appointed to confer with a committee from Phips' Canada (Jay) concerning a mill to accommodate both towns, and on June 19, 1782, it was decided to build one on the brook which is the outlet of Long and Round Ponds. Deacon Livermore contracted to do the work of construction.

April 6, 1801, it was voted that the Town of Jay, as far as the bend of the river (Riley) be annexed to Livermore evidently in response to a petition from the citizens of Jay. Apparently Livermore had a change of heart, for on the 4th of November in the same year they voted, "the bend of the river in Jay shall *not* be annexed onto this town."

A bridge across the Androscoggin was being proposed in 1802. Surprisingly, the Town of Livermore voted that, "the representatives of Livermore be instructed to oppose the proposed bridge across Androscoggin River at Davis' Mills (Livermore Falls) in Livermore, and advocate the proposed bridge at

Jay."

There were at this time several ferries linking the parts of Livermore which were separated by the river. The first was in the Tollawalla neighborhood, below the farm of Colonel Lewis Hunton, and was called WING'S FERRY. After a few years it was abandoned because it became apparent that it was not on the line of any principal highways; and FULLER'S FERRY (later known as Hillman's Ferry) took its place, con necting Haines' Corner with the Intervale at Livermore Center.

A third, called BARTON'S FERRY, opened below the Falls, at Shy; and a fourth at LIEUTENANT BENJAMIN'S. The latter was discontinued about 1835, and replaced by one in the southerly part of Tollawalla, called at first Norris', but afterwards STRICKLANDS FERRY.

In the summer and fall, these ferries afforded ready communication between the east and west sections of Livermore; in winter, crossing was even easier on the ice; but in the spring, when thaws and freshets broke up the ice, it was impossible to cross the river by either means. Since Town Meetings were customarily held in March, and on the west side (which comprised a preponderance of the population), the people on the east side felt they were not treated fairly, and started a move to make separate towns of the two sides of the river.

Agitation for separation evidently began quite early, for on Nov. 5, 1798, the town voted to consent to the division of the town, by which the "east side of the river would be set off into a town by itself." However, ten years later, on May 2, 1808, the town evidently had changed its mind for, at the meeting on that date, the set off from Livermore was refused.

Again, on August 31, 1830, it was voted to consent to the division of the Town; but nothing was done about it until September 4, 1840, when the decision was confirmed, and this time followed up by the necessary legal steps and action by the legislature in 1843 to establish "East Livermore" as a separate town under that name. Consequently, from 1844 on, the history of Livermore becomes the history of two towns, Livermore and East Livermore.

That the first half of the 19th century witnessed great changes is emphasized by a contemporary writer who, in 1867, told of Captain David Hinkley, who had just died in that year, lacking a few days of his 102nd birthday. In his article he wrote:

> "He (Hinkley) was an intelligent man and a good citizen. He voted for Washington at the first election of president under the constitution, and voted at every presidential election since. In September last (1867) he rode six miles to vote for Gov. Chamberlain, and, a few days before he died, expressed a hope that he might live to vote for Gen. Grant for president. Benjamin Franklin was in the vigor of his years, and George Washington was a young man of thirty-four, when Capt. Hinckley was born How much came to pass, how many things were done, within the limits bounded by the life of this venerable manl Will the little one of today, WHO SHALL LIVE TILL 1967, SEE AS MUCH ACCOMPLISHED WITHIN HIS TIME? WILL HE MEASURE IMPROVEMENT, PROGRESS IN SCIENCE, ART, LITERATURE, IN RELIGIOUS IDEAS, IN GOVERNMENT, IN MATERIAL HELPS, EQUAL TO THOSE WITNESSED IN THE LIFETIME OF CAPT. HINKLEY? WILL THE TURNPIKE, THE STEAMBOAT, THE RAILROAD, THE PHOTOGRAPH, THE TELEGRAPH, BE SUPERSEDED BY ACHIEVEMENTS AS MUCH GREATER THAN THEY AS THEY ARE BETTER THAN WHAT THEY DISPLACED? WILL OUR CHILDREN TRAVEL FROM LIVERMORE TO THE 'HUB' (Boston) IN HALF AN HOUR, AND FROM THE 'HUB' TO THE MOON IN HALF A DAY?"

To all, or nearly all, of his speculative questions (which the writer no doubt thought absurd) we can, of course, today answer "yes" - save only the "improvement in morals" and the "progress in religious ideas," about which, to put it mildly, there

Industrial peak of the 1800s: Umbagog Mill in foreground with the 1885
addition in process; Alvin Record's complex (dark buildings with white trim)
across the river - (sawmill, pulp mill and leatherhoard mill); and
to the right, down "Mill Hill," R. C. Boothby's grist mill and
F. S. Richmond's novelty mill and drying sheds.

Oxen hauling birch logs down "Mill Hill" - c.1880; likely destination -
Richmond's Novetly Mill

is considerable doubt.

To really understand a period beyond our own knowledge and experience, to "get the flavor of the time," it is often helpful to read the words of one who has lived it. To that end, the following is quoted from a Livermore native, who was a boy in 1820, and who wrote anonymously under the pen-name of "Uncle John":

"The first school-house in the Doctor Bradford (Norlands) district was built about the beginning of the century (1800). It was an old-fashioned, square building with a hipped roof, and was never painted; it stood on the same spot where the present school-house stands. The master's desk was on the east side of the room between two enormous fire-places, where wood was burned daily by the cord. Wood then cost nothing but hauling, and great havoc was made in its consumption. The scholars took turns in building the fires; there was some emulation as to who could keep the best fires. It might have been in the summer of 1820 or 1821 that a violent tornado took the school-house in its track and blew off a part of the roof into the field nearby, and levelled all the fences on both sides of the road. I remember to have rather enjoyed it, especially in going home through the puddles where a score of urchins had great fun, wading to their knees.

"Jane Monroe was the first school-ma'am, within my remembrance, who pointed out to the very smallest scholars the A, B, C, with a white handled penknife. She was not a relative of the two or three families of that name living in the district. Her father was a Scotchman, who came to this country with Hugh Orr, a man of considerable prominence in Bridgewater, in the old colony. She kept school four summers, to the great satisfaction of the elders and benefit of the children.

"The winter schools were very full, sometimes numbering eighty scholars or more, and among them were a good many big fellows who occupied the seats of honor, called the 'back seats.' They were not so perfect in their lessons as in feats of wrestling, snowballing, and 'washing the faces' of the boys in the snow. I forget under what reign five of these big fellows had built a desk before the fire, and had taken possession one morning before the arrival of the master, where they could kick the shins of the small fry as they were warming themselves at the fire. They had, however, but a single field day, enjoying themselves hugely under the delusion that possession was the 'nine points' in their case. When the valiant builders of desks and benches came to school next morning their demoralization was complete, finding all their carpenter work, excepting what had been used to kindle the morning fire, broken to Hinders and pitched into the middle of a four-acre lot. The heroes took to the back seats with mortification, and kept hid behind their books.

"The spelling schools, speaking schools, and debating clubs were sources of a good deal of pleasure and perhaps some profit at the time. There was considerable dramatic talent among the scholars, and the exhibitions in that line were frequent. John Monroe was enthusiastic and indefatigable in preparing for the performances and arranging the properties and scenery of the stage. Many of the old mothers, whose lives were a constant sacrifice for their children, were teased to death for carpets, blankets, curtains, and clothes lines to furnish the theatre. John, who was a good reader and prided himself on his elocution, and was the great representative of tragedy, appeared in more than one of Shakespeare's plays. His greatest achievement in this line was in the character of Marc Antony in 'Julius Caesar.' At this time the Scotch Tartan plaids were in great vogue.

John had a gay cloak (the envy of all the scholars) with big arm holes. The great point he made on the stage was in exhibiting one of the openings in the cloak to the audience, with exclamation, 'Look you here, see where ran Cassius' dagger through; see what a rent the envious Casca made!' etc. Snelling Monroe always giggled at this point.

"The reading books of the period - the *Columbian Orator, American Preceptor, Scott's Lessons,* and *Murray's English Reader* - were full of extracts from the old English comedies. These sterling old plays were well studied. Sir Charles and Lady Rackett in *Three Weeks after Marriage,* Lovegold and Lappett in the *Miser,* Boniface and Aimwell in the *Beaux Stratagem,* Lady Townley and Lady Grace in the *Provoked Husband,* Belcour and Stockwell in the *West Indian* were among the favorite pieces. Abijah Monroe, son of Uncle John, was very felicitous in reciting *Pity the Sorrows of a Poor Old Man,* and always brought down the house.

"Our entertainments were sometimes aided by Mr. Thomas Hanna, a native of Lisburn, in the north of Ireland, of good family and education, who by some curious fortune dropped right down here in the wilderness. He was known as 'The Colonel,' and had some talent as a ventriloquist. If the Colonel had a weakness it was for an occasional glass of toddy, and it was a dodge of his to decline his role of 'Killing the Calf' until a glass of old Jamaica was produced, which never failed to inspire him to his best efforts in his peculiar line. But sometimes he could be persuaded to 'Kill the Calf' for the delectation of the boys and girls who attended these exhibitions, although he knew that on such occasions he could have no dram.

"These exhibitions were not postponed on account of the weather; 'blow high, blow low, come rain, or come snow,' the attendance was prompt and full. A!bijah, John and Snelling Monroe, and all from the extreme outlying homes, came a mile and a half through the drifts, and perhaps after chopping in the woods all day. Nothing but a tremendous storm kept the girls at home.

"'Twas no uncommon thing for the boys and girls to assemble at the schoolhouse on moonlit nights for a bout at sliding down hill. There was no little rivalry about 'the speed of the sleds, and the effort to get a good start was as exciting as we see nowadays at the trotting park. The truth of history requires me to say that among all the sled owners Stedman Kendall came out the winner. Sted built the best fires, cut the most wood, could skate the fastest, and catch the most pickerel of any boy in the neighborhood.

"The Livermore Social Library was always kept at the doctor's (Bradford); the cupboards in the kitchen and parlor were the alcoves where the books were placed. The volumes were not extensive, but were select, embracing many of the standard English authors. *The Vicar of Wakefield,* the *Pilgrims Progress* and *Robinson Crusoe* were read over and over again; and the old ladies in the neighborhood never discovered to their dying day that they had been reading the best romances ever written, though they regarded novels as a delusion and a snare. 'The Arabian Nights' Entertainments' were literally 'used up.' Sterne's works were read by the old folks. The scholars used to take the library books into school to read, which with the school books before spoken of gave them a healthy literary tone.

"Capt. Pray kept the dancing school in the winter, in the old Masonic Hall over his shop. The young gentlemen were provided with sheepskin pumps from the midnight bench of John Sanders.

There was rivalry in the dancing school as well as in the sliding school. Columbus Horsley tipped the fiddle for 12 1/2 cents per capita an evening, regular, with an extra charge for nights when the school was visited by scholars from the outlying districts.

"The ball dresses of the period were not from the Lyons' looms, but were woven by the fair hands of the fair wearers themselves, and after passing through the mill of Kimball, celebrated as the best clothier and dresser in half a dozen counties, came out smooth and shining, and were very attractive to look on. Kimball was something of a gallant, and was accused of partiality to his favorites among the damsels, which he indicated by giving to them a favorite tint of coloring, much to the disgust of the homely girls.

"About this time, when Chase and Morrow were in full tide of successful experiment, and furnished all the country with better sleighs than the minds of men had ever conceived, Horace Gould kept the singing school. He had a magnificent voice and was a successful teacher.

"There was an unusually good race of men in the circle known to my boyhood. Dr. Bradford, Captain Waters, Captain Pray, Captain Kendall, Captain Leavitt, George Chandler, Jesse Kidder, Uncle John, Abijah, and Abel Monroe, Uncle Bartlett, the Coolidges, the Stricklands and the Chases were good, solid, honest, faithful, and staunch men; men of convictions and principles, with an honest purpose for every duty, and who made all reasonable sacrifices to educate their children, that their lot in life might be better than their own. They settled a new country, underwent the privations attending early settlers, worked hard, fared hard, but with industry and good management lived comfortably.

"It was a neighborhood of great social harmony. I don't remember a neighborhood quarrel. They were all politicians, to a greater or less extent, and not without ambition; they read the newspapers with interest; they discussed and criticised all questions of neighborhood, State, and country; were a trifle more conservative than their descendents, perhaps, but were intolerant of injustice, oppression, meanness, and lying. Most of them lived to old age, and died and were buried where their lives had been passed.

"I look back with a sort of mournful pleasure, not unmixed with pride, upon their useful and honest lives, and feel thankful for the lessons they imparted. May they rest in peace!"

Norlands Street

The Norlands Mansion

THE WASHBURN FAMILY OF LIVERMORE

Israel Washburn, storekeeper in that part of Livermore known as "The Norlands," and his wife, Martha Benjamin, daughter of Lieut. Samuel Benjamin, had seven sons, everyone of whom was a character of national or international importance. This one family furnished two Governors of two different States, four Representatives to Congress from four different States, one United States Senator, two Foreign Ministers, one Secretary of State, one Major General, and one Navy Captain. It is highly improbable that any family in the history of the nation has a record comparable to that, in one generation. In 1970, Norlands was designated a "National Historic Site" by the National Park Service, Department of Interior.

The Norlands Church

The Norlands Library

Israel Washburn, Jr.
Governor of Maine
U. S. Congress, 5 terms

Cadwallader Washburn
Governor of Wisconsin
Major Gen., Union Army
Washburn-Crosby Mills

Elihu Washburn
U.S Congress 9 terms
Sec. of State
Minister to France

Samuel Washbutn
Captain Union Navy
Commander of Gulf
Squadren division under
Admiral Farragut

William Drew Washburn
US Representative., MN
US Senator, Minnesota

Charles A. Washburn
Minister to Paraguay
Editor San Francisco Times

Algernon S. Washburn
President of Hallowell Bank

LIVERMORE & EAST LIVERMORE
1850 ~ 1900

HE OFTEN REPEATED STATEMENT that "all history is really biography," is nowhere better illustrated than in the history of the Towns of Livermore for the last half of the 19th century, when three men, successively, set the course and determined the fate of these towns for more than a century to come. The first was Capain Ezekiel Treat, Jr., in the years prior to the Civil War; the second was Alvin Record, in the period immediately following the war until the 1880's; and the third was Hugh Chisholm, from 1880 to the turn of the century.

Ezekiel Treat, Jr., was born in Wales, Maine, in 1804, one of six sons of Captain Ezekiel Treat, Sr., a ship owner and ship's captain, whose vessels were engaged in foreign trade. These six sons were substantial citizens in one sense at least, for their weight aggregated well over 1200 pounds. Captain Treat, Sr., moved his family to Canton, Maine, in 1814.

When young Ezekiel was 12 years of age, he packed a small bag and walked to Hallowell, the nearest port for ocean-going ships, to ship as a cabin boy on a sailing vessel. As his grandson, Harry Treat, tells it:

142

"Six years later young Ezekiel walked into the home in Canton and threw down his pack. His father, Ezekiel Sr., looked him over and said, 'You need a new pair of britches; go over to the store and get yourself a pair,' handing him some money.

"The boy said, 'All right, and while I'm gone open up this bag and see what you find.' In it was approximately $1,000 in cash that he had saved from his meager wages and from ventures in buying and selling small vessels when in different ports here and there."

He went back to sea, becoming a ship's captain while still a teenager, and following this calling until nearly 40 years of age, accumulating in the process a comfortable fortune. Then, as sailors used to express it, he "swallowed the anchor," and retired to the life of a landlubber.

In 1845, he moved to Livermore Falls, and purchased the entire water power of the Androscoggin River in East Livermore, and the land that now includes the principal business section of Livermore Falls. For some years he continued to operate the saw mill, the grist mill, and the shingle mill, as well as the mercantile firm of "E. Treat & Sons"; and built for himself a fine house at the corner of Main and Depot Streets, where the Shoppers Mall is now located.

It was about this time (1848-1850) that the Androscoggin Railroad was being organized, and construction started from Leeds Junction north. The directors were debating whether the railroad should swing easterly at Shy, and go up the Chesterville valley to Farmington, or go via Livermore Falls and Jay. Captain Treat saw immediately the tremendous importance to the town which a railroad would have, and argued to the road's directors that it MUST come here.

He did more than argue, however. Dumping in $25,000 of his own money, which in those days was the equivalent of ten or twenty times as much in today's dollars, and securing the help of Elisha Pettingill and John Smith, he built the last mile of railroad from Shy into Livermore Falls; and had the satisfaction of seeing the first locomotive steam into town in November, 1852.

For his investment, he was given stock and bonds, and

made a director of the Androscoggin Railroad. Eventually the bonds were defaulted, the company was re-organized, and the money originally invested was lost. Yet, with Biblical justice, it was in losing his fortune that he made it; for the industrial prosperity of Livermore Falls dates from the arrival of the railroad; the local business ventures boomed; the land increased greatly in value; and when Captain Treat died, about 25 years later, he left an estate amounting to much more than he had donated to the construction of the railroad.

That railroading in those days was a rugged adventure may be judged from the following extract from the diary of one who noted some of the occurrences in its beginning in this country:

"The Androscoggin branch of the Maine Central was opened to travel from Leeds Junction to Livermore Falls, in November, 1852. The rolling stock consisted of one small engine, one baggage, and two passenger cars, also a few box and flat cars. There were no snow fences, and many hard times were experienced in getting through the snow. December 29, 1853, fifteen inches of snow fell, drifting so that no trains were run, and no trains were run December 30, but one managed to get through to Livermore Falls late in the afternoon of December 31st. Again, February 23, 1854, it commenced snowing at 4 a.m., and continued all day. The train started from Leeds Junction at 10 a.m., and ran about three miles and got stuck in a drift, and as the engine was getting short of wood and water, the engineer left the cars and proceeded about two miles to Pettingill's crossing, where he filled the tender with water, carrying it in pails from the brook about ten rods. It was very cold and the men were covered with ice. As it was near night, the engineer concluded to stop there all night. The passengers, two ladies and three men, were obliged to stay in the cars two days and one night. Friday morning, the 24th, commenced shoveling out the track, and 2 p.m. got the engine down to the cars,

144

Captain Ezekiel Treat, Director of The Androscoggin Railroad Company
After 18 years sea, the Captain retired when nearly 40 years of age to operate a
store, a grist mill and a saw mill in Livermore Falls – and to promote a railroad in
which he invested $25,000.00.

and carried the ladies to Abran Wheeler's, then started toward Leeds Junction and arrived there at 12 p.m. Saturday, February 25th. They left Leeds Junction at noon and went as far as North Leeds and stopped all night. February 26th they left North Leeds at 7 a.m., arrived at Livermore Falls at noon, and did not start again until Wednesday, March 1st. March 18th the train left Leeds Junction at 11 a.m., went about one mile, got stuck and returned. March 19. - snowed all day. No trains over the road to-day. March 20. - Train left the Junction at noon and arrived at Livermore Falls at 5 p.m. March 24. - Two feet of snow fell. No trains over the road today. March 25. - Snow deep on the track. No trains to-day. March 26. - Very blustering. No trains to-day. March 27. - Very blustering. No train to-day. March 28-29-30-31. - No trains. April 1. - Train went down at 2 p.m. Sunday, April 2. - Trains made regular trips. December 9. - Very blustering last night; train left Livermore Falls on time this morning with two engines, and when near Leeds Centre ran off the track and completely wrecked both engines and baggage car. Nobody was injured. The veteran Josiah Littlefield was one of the engineers.

January 19, 1855. - Snowed hard all day. No trains run 20th. Snow-plough with one engine left the junction at 12 M., got to Livermore Falls at 10 p.m., and returned to Leeds Junction same night. February 19, 1856. - Very blustering all day. No trains on the Androscoggin Railroad to-day. January 9, 1857. - Train run off the track; nobody injured; 19th, snowed fast all day; no trains; 20th, train left Leeds Junction at 6:30 p.m. January 22. - Snowed all day; 23d, fair and colder; no trains run to-day; 24th, train got to Leeds at 9:30 p.m. During the winter of 1858 there was but little snow and trains were run regularly all winter. Commenced running to East Wilton December 21st. January 1, 1859. - Commenced snowing at 10 a.m., and continued all day. No trains up to-day. January 5.

- Train with two engines left Leeds Junction for East Wilton at 2 p.m., and went as far as Leeds Center, and thinking that it would be impossible to get through, returned to Leeds Junction. Soon after they returned, Charles Garcelon, with an engine called the "old widow," and snow-plow came down. If the up train had not returned, undoubtedly there would have been a serious accident, as there was no telegraphic line, and the up train did not know that "the widow" was coming. After "the widow" had arrived at Leeds Junction, the two engines with passenger train left Leeds at 10 p.m. February 3. - John Kauffer, engineer, burnt his mouth and throat so badly in blowing into a pet-cock which was frozen on his engine, that he died in a few hours. February 4. - Train went down at 8 p.m., and did not go up till 1 a.m., February 5th. February 10, 1860. - Stormy and blustering all day. Train arrived at Curtis Corner at 2 p.m., out of water and wood, and was obliged to haul water about twenty rods in a hogshead with a yoke of oxen. Six passengers put up at S. Brewster's for the night. The engineer, Mr. Parker, stayed in his engine all night. The other train men stopped at S. Brewster's. February 11. - Got the engine fired up and started for Leeds Junction at 1:30 p.m., and returned to Farmington that night. January 16, 1861. - Snowed fast all day. No trains to-day. January 17. - No trains run. January 18. - Train got down at 7 p.m. February 2. - Snow fell four inches last night, rained, and made a crust, and no trains were run to-day. February 8. - Was called the cold Friday; thirty degrees below at sunrise and very windy. No trains run to-day. February 9. No trains run to-day. February 21. - Cold and blustering. The morning train from Farmington got down to Leeds Junction at 5 p.m., and returned that night. February 22. - Very blustering. No trains run to-day. February 23. - No trains run. January 2, 1862. - Cold and very blustering. Train went down but did not return till

10:30 p.m., January 3d. January 22. - Snowed all day. Train went down but did not return till Sunday morning, January 26th. January 27. - Train went down at 1:30 p.m., and did not return till 1 a.m., January 30th."

In these early days of railroading, the locomotives bore names painted on their cabs, just as ships still do; but this practice was discontinued by the Maine Central RR in 1877 - since then they are known only by numbers.

The Androscoggin Railroad began operation with two locomotives, the *Livermore* and the *Leeds,* both built in 1851 by the Amoskeag Co.; and during its existence as a separate line, six more engines were built for the company, viz.: the O. *Moses* and the L. *Nichols* in 1863, by Hinckley Locomotive Works; the *Farmington* and the *Bates* in 1864, also by Hinckley Works; the *David Patten* and the *Lewiston* in 1867 and 1870, by the Manchester Co.

The line was leased to M.C.R.R. in 1871, and subsequently merged with the latter.

Although the railroad itself could hardly be called a success financially, it did bring almost immediate prosperity to the Town. There was a large and continued influx of population. George D. Lothrop purchased the Walker house on the east side of Main Street, and enlarged it for a hotel (later to become Roccomeka Hotel). French's hotel, on the west side of Main Street (more recently Billings Inn) had been owned and operated by O. Luce; but as Luce became freight master for the new railroad, the hotel was leased to R. Graffam.

The stores of A. Kimball, Comfort Pettingill and others were moved up the hill to the west side of Main Street; W. Hunton erected a store on Depot Street; S. Read moved over from North Livermore, and opened a store next to Hunton. Dr. A. R. Millett, physician, and Cyrus Knapp, attorney, both from Minot, young, unmarried, and right from school, followed the railroad into town, and opened offices. Both boarded at Lothrop's Hotel.

The Third Baptist Church of Livermore, which for 43

years had been located at Shy, moved its building in 1854 to its present location on Church St., near the new center of population.

The coming of the railroad intensified the need of a bridge between the east and west sides of the river; and in 1858 one was finally erected a little above the falls, at approximately the site of the present bridge. It was a toll bridge, of open truss construction of a rare type, called a "Haupt Truss" from Herman Haupt, who invented it in 1839. Haupt was later to gain considerable fame in the Engineer Corps of the U.S. Army during the Civil War.

Had this bridge been built a few years earlier, the town, presumably, would never have been divided.

Also, the new railroad resulted in a new Post Office in the town, in 1853, called "Stricklands Ferry," with Solomon Millett as its first Postmaster. The line was extended to North Jay in 1857 and to Farmington in 1859.

In what seems an ironic trick of fate, the first fatal accident on the road involved the builder's father. Ezekiel Treat, Sr., Captain Treat's father, who lived in Canton, was driving home from Livermore Falls. The horse he was driving had a young colt that was following on behind her. At the crossing at Jay, the mare stopped and turned to look for her colt just as the train was approaching; and in the resulting crash both horse and driver were killed.

The population of East Livermore, in the eight years following the building of the railroad, increased nearly 25%, from 890 to 1029, centering mostly about the village of Livermore Falls. It was in this period that the sons of Israel Washburn, of Livermore, began to assume importance nationally, three of them being in Congress - Israel Jr., from Maine, Elihu from Illinois, and Cadwallader from Wisconsin. In those hectic and troubled times, all three were prominent in the anti-slavery movement, and among the organizers of the new "Republican" Party. Israel, Jr., was elected Governor of Maine, and resigned his seat in the House to assume the new position in 1860.

The Civil War broke out soon after Israel, Jr., was inau-

LINCOLN & WASHBURN

This drawing shows the President-elect arriving in Washington station in the early morning hours of February 23, 1861. At his left is his friend, Congressman Elihu Washburn, of Livermore's famous family; behind him is Ward Hill Lamon and one E. J. Allen, otherwise known as "Pinkerton." Warned of an assassination planned for when the presidential train passed through Baltimore, Lincoln left the special train and came secretly from Harrisburg to Washington, accompanied only by Lamon and Pinkerton, and met only by his friend Washburn.

Lt. GENERAL GRANT RECEIVES HIS COMMISSION

General Grant entered the Cabinet room in the White House, and for the first time in his life met President Lincoln. General Halleck, to whom Grant had been a subordinate, was there; also Mr. E. B. Washburn, of Galena, member of Congress, who had been instrumental in securing Grant's appointment as Lieutenant General. (Mr. Washburn is pictured just to the right of Lincoln).

[from "Redeeming the Republic," by Chas, C. Coffin - Harper & Bros., 1890] gurated as Governor; and he gave prompt and effective support to the Union cause. Under his dynamic leadership, Maine did more than her share in the struggle. The following is taken from his proclamation issued in response to Lincoln's call for additional troops:

"Executive Department
July 4, 1862.

To The People of Maine:

An additional number of troops is required by the exigency of the public service; and, if raised immediately, it is believed by those who have the best means of knowledge that the war will be brought to a speedy and glorious issue. Of this number the President of the United States desires and expects that Maine should furnish her proportionate quota ....

I invoke of the people of this State a prompt and hearty response to this new demand upon their patriotism; and may they all unite in the work that is before them, each laboring in his own sphere, doing what he can by his example, influence and sympathy - proffering his treasure, his time, his strength, his heart, and his highest hopes to the cause of his Country.

ISRAEL WASHBURN,
JR., Governor of Maine

Of the three Washburn boys, natives of Livermore, in Congress in 1860, only Elihu, congressman from Illinois, remained after the outbreak of war. Cadwallader returned to Wisconsin to raise troops for the Union Army, and was commissioned Colonel of cavalry (later Major General). As before mentioned, Israel returned to Maine to become Governor; but Elihu, who remained in Congress, probably did the most toward winning the war. Not only was he a close friend and supporter of Lincoln; but he it was who first recognized Grant's ability, and secured for the then obscure unknown, first, a Colonel's commission; then a promotion to Brigadier General; and finally, after persuading Congress to create the rank of Lieutenant General, the appointment to command all the Union Armies.

A fourth Washburn brother, Samuel, who was previously a captain of merchant ships, offered his services to the government; and was commissioned a Captain in the Navy.

Three other men, with Livermore connections, who were nationally prominent in the Civil War era, were Hannibal Hamlin, Lieutenant-Colonel Stephen Boothby, and Major General Oliver O. Howard.

Hannibal Hamlin was the son of Livermore's first physician, Dr. Cyrus Hamlin, and grandson of Deacon Livermore. When the County of Oxford was incorporated, including Livermore, Dr. Hamlin was elected its first Clerk of Courts, which necessitated his removal to the shire town. He had moved his family to Paris Hill shortly before the birth of Hannibal, who was born August 27, 1809. As Vice-president of the United States from 1861 to 1865, and Abraham Lincoln's right hand man, Hannibal is, of course, well known.

Lieutenant Colonel Stephen A. Boothby was the son of Rev. Samuel Boothby, pastor of the Second Baptist Church of Livermore, and brother of Roswell C. Boothby who was Judge of the Livermore Falls Municipal Court and a well known musician, serving as chorister of the First Baptist Church of Livermore Falls (Third Baptist Church of Livermore) for fifty years.

Stephen graduated from Colby College in 1857; studied law and was admitted to the bar. In the Spring of 1861, he formed a partnership with Mark H. Dunnell and entered the practice of law at Portland. In the Autumn of 1861, he entered military service as First Lieutenant of Company F, First Maine Cavalry, and was promoted to Captain the following year. He remained in command of this Company until his appointment as Major in March 1863. He was again promoted to Lieutenant Colonel, in which position he was in acting command of the regiment much of the time in 1864, until his death.

The First Maine Cavalry compiled one of the proudest records in the Union Army; and Fred Humiston, in his *Echo of The Drum,* gives the following purported conversation between General Hooker and President Lincoln when the latter questioned Hooker's confidence in Stoneman's cavalry:

Lieut.-Col. Stephen A. Boothby
Among the bravest and most dashing officers of the cavalry (Civil War),
he received the wound from which he died
while leading a charge at Beaver Brook Station."

"Have you forgotten how frequently you ask, 'Whoever saw a dead cavalryman?'"

Hooker smiled complacently. "Mister President, things are different now. Did you notice the riders who led the march today? That was Averill's brigade. And did you notice the outfit in Averill's advance?"

"They looked like good men," Abe Lincoln admitted, "But as an expert on horseflesh, I was particularly impressed by their mounts. I saw a number of thoroughbreds and at least company strength in quarter-horses, by Jingo."

"That outfit was the First Maine Cavalry," Hooker said proudly. "The men are real mean fighters, and they were mounted in Maine with horses purchased in the West; Kentucky for the most part."

Or again, Hooker said, "Averill's brigade is the equal of Stuart's (Confederate General J. E. B. Stuart) riders, I'll stake my career on it."

"That is quite a gamble," Lincoln joked. "However, those boys do look good; especially that Maine regiment."

Shortly after this purported conversation between President Lincoln and General Hooker, the latter's statement was confirmed in action. The brigade, with the Second and Tenth New York cavalry in advance, ran into Hampton's brigade of cavalry and artillery, posted on an eminence near Brandy Station where General J. E. B. Stuart had his headquarters. The Second and Tenth New York regiments, being greatly outnumbered, were slowly being driven back, when the First Maine cavalry swept to the right and charged the Confederates in the flank. Although the enemy was a largely superior force, supported by artillery, the Maine men drove everything before them, two battalions sweeping around the left of Stuart's headquarters, and one around the right. They captured two of the enemy guns, nearly one hundred prisoners, and the battle flag of Hampton's brigade of cavalry.

In a similar action on July 16, 1863, Lieutenant Colonel Boothby was seriously wounded, and sent home to recover. Back in action the following year, he took part in General Sheridan's cavalry raid behind the Confederate lines, reaching within three miles of Richmond. Near Beaver Dam Station, an enemy force succeeded in getting in front of the Union cavalry; Lieutenant Colonel Boothby led companies A, D and K of the First Maine in a charge against them, in which he was severely wounded in the breast and shoulder.

When one considers those springless wagons, used as ambulances at that time, over the rough and rutted tracks that passed as roads, it is easy to understand something of the tortures suffered by the wounded in being transported from battlefield to hospital. The straw covered wagon floor was usually dripping blood from wounds that had temporary dressings torn loose by the jolting ride; and the agonies of many a sufferer were mercifully terminated by death before ever reaching the hospital.

In Boothby's case, the ride was much longer than usual, for it was far behind enemy lines that he was wounded; and he was five days in the ambulance, before he could be delivered to a Union hospital. It is little wonder that he lived only a few days after arrival, and died June 6th, 1864.

When news of his death was received in Portland, the Cumberland Bar, in special meeting, adopted resolutions expressing their sorrow and their admiration of his character. His remains were carried to Lewiston, where his father was then residing, and given a most impressive military service. Behind the caisson bearing the casket, in the procession, came the riderless horse on which he had been mounted when wounded.

The Report of the Adjutant General of the State of Maine, for the years 1864-65, says of him, "By his gallant and soldierly bearing he rapidly earned promotion, first to captain, then to major, and afterwards to lieutenant colonel. He was among the bravest and most dashing of the officers of the cavalry."

Whether it was General Hooker's praise of them, or the

outstanding record of the First Maine cavalry that impressed Lincoln, is not known; but when a District of Columbia cavalry regiment was to be formed, under orders of the War Department, it was largely on President Lincoln's recommendation that the men were recruited in Maine - eight hundred of them, in eight companies.

Major General Oliver Otis Howard was born in the adjoining town of Leeds, but was much in Livermore and East Livermore during his youth. When he entered Bowdoin College, he and Peleg Sprague Perley of Livermore roomed together, and continued as roommates during their entire college course. Perley's mother and Howard's mother had been neighbors and school friends.

The following are General Howard's words, from his autobiography:

"That winter vacation (1846), however, was a very important one to me. My roommate, Perley, lived with his parents, brothers and sisters in Livermore, which was separated from Leeds by the Androscoggin River. Among the girls, there came a young lady, visiting her relatives in the vicinity, who was a cousin of Perley. - The acquaintance ripened into a correspondence which absorbed my heart and much of my leisure during the college course. -

"The following winter (1848), I had a large district school in East Livermore, and received for my hard work $18.00 per month. .

"As I have said, in the winter vacation of 1846 I met, at her cousin's home, one who was but a girl just budding into womanhood. She arrested my attention and impressed me more deeply than I thought. - I met her during her visits to Livermore in vacations."

The young lady in question was the daughter of Alexander Black Waite who at the time was engaged in shipbuilding in Portland. He suffered a fatal accident, and his

Major General Oliver O. Howard
Livermore schoolteacher; distinguished Civil War commander at Fair Oaks, Antietam, Chancellorsville and Gettysburg; Howard University was named in his honor in recognition of his service in the education and relief of the freed slaves.

body was brought home to his father's place in Livermore for the funeral and burial. His daughter was nearly prostrated with grief; and from that time it was understood that she and Oliver Howard were engaged. They were married shortly after his graduation from West Point, to which he was appointed at the end of his college course.

In 1861 he was named Colonel to command the Third Maine Regiment. Promoted to Brigadier General for distinguished service, he was twice wounded at Fair Oaks, losing his right arm, but continued in service. He commanded his division at Antietam, and was made a Major General in 1862, commanding the Eleventh Corps at Chancellorsville, Peninsular Campaign, and at Gettysburg. President Lincoln wrote a personal letter of thanks to General Howard for his skill and bravery at Gettysburg. He commanded one of the Grand Divisions of Sherman's Army in the March to the Sea.

Following the war, he was made Chief of the Freedmen's Bureau; and, in recognition of his great service in the education and relief of the freed slaves, Howard University was named for him.

Bernice Nelke, who writes under the name of Bernice Richmond, in her book, *Right as Rain,* tells of her grandfather, Captain Soloman Nelke of Livermore, and General O. O. Howard:

"Grandpa sat down in a rocker at the head of the steps and took me in his lap. 'This is the first time,' he began, 'that you are marching in the parade and there's something I want to tell you.' The feeling in Grandpa's voice startled me. In a moment he continued, 'Now listen carefully. I think you are old enough to remember this. When you were a baby, a great general visited your grandmother and me. He was my general in the Civil War - General O. O. Howard.' Grandpa hesitated as though hunting for a way to say things. 'One day I brought him over to the little house where you were born. I said, 'General, I don't know whether you like babies or not but there is something you could do that I would appreciate very much. I would like you to hold my granddaughter in your lap. When she grows up I want to be able to tell her she had the honor of sitting on General O. O. Howard's knee.'

"Grandpa searched my face. 'He held you. And *now* I've told you.' I understood this meant a lot to Grandpa and that something unusual had happened to me. I wanted to say something that would please him, but nothing came to mind, and I said that I could not remember.

"Grandpa hugged me. 'Of course, you don't remember, child. You couldn't even sit up then. Your head wobbled, although I'll say this: you tried to look the general in the eye.'

"Grandpa rocked a moment smiling and then he went on, 'Yes, he was a great man and a good one, too. I called on him in Auburn when he was recovering from a wound. I was a young fellow then, and when I left he put a hundred-dollar bill in my hand.' -

"Grandpa put me down and said, 'Now its time for me to leave. Remember that your old grandfather arranged a great honor for you.' -

"I hung back so long after the children started that I was the last one in line. At the church (Monument Square) the ladies of the Relief Corps came in ahead of the children and I saw my mother was one of the two leaders and carried a big American flag. Further on the Sons of Veterans fell in behind the school children. Two rode on horseback on either side. Behind them came the few (veterans) still able to march - Grandpa among them. The very old soldiers with flowing white beards and canes, bringing up the rear in livery stable buggies, sat tilted sideways in their seats .

. . . I knew how Grandpa looked marching. I had watched him from the street corner the year before. It was true then that he was the only one who really marched, sternly, eyes ahead, and it was true now ... Awakened in my memory was the play, *The Drummer Boy*, which mother had taken me to the winter before. It was a very sad play and everybody cried a lot. A hungry prisoner dared to cross a line to get food, and was shot before our eyes; - hardest to bear was the scene at home after the war. It showed the empty chair where the drummer boy had sat, and now that he was dead someone in the family had the courage to rise and sing, 'We shall meet, but we shall miss him, there will be one vacant chair.' Everybody felt just awful.

"A boy in the village had been chosen each year to play the part of the drummer boy - my cousin, Percy (Cascadden), had played it the year before. But this time our dentist's daughter (Beulah Moores) was the boy. Through the drum beats I heard again what George Moulton had said to me, 'Some day, Bernice, you will play the part of the drummer boy.' As I marched near Grandpa I thought about General O. O. Howard and knew Grandpa would like very much to see me on our Town Hall stage in uniform."

This book, however, is less concerned with nationally known figures, even though they have a local connection, than it is with the two hundred thirty-three boys who went from this community into the Union army and navy. The census of 1860 showed a population of 2626 for Livermore and East Livermore. Assuming approximately an even division between the sexes, there must have been about thirteen hundred males, of which nearly 300 would have been between the ages of sixteen and thirty. Allowing for those physically unable to serve, the two hundred thirty-three who did go would be practically all of those physically able, between sixteen and thirty years of age. Fifty-five of them gave their lives - killed in action, died of wounds, died in Confederate prisons, or died from disease. No list is available of the wounded; but applying the same percentage as for all Maine troops in the Civil War, there would be over one hundred.

Of the regiments containing the most Livermore men, the 23rd Infantry included forty-one, all in Company K, of which James S. Nash of Livermore was Captain; the 8th Infantry, of which Lee Strickland of Livermore was Colonel, and Augustus Strickland, Quartermaster, numbered thirty-five, mostly in Company C whose Lieutenants were Charles F. Monroe and W. H. Timberlake, both of Livermore; and the 30th Infantry contained twenty-nine local men, largely in Company A of which William W. Noyes was lieutenant. The 1st Maine Cavalry had twenty-one men from Livermore-East Livermore;

Martha Benjamin Washburn - 1792-1861

Daughter of Lieut. Samuel Benjamin and Tabitha Livermore; wife of Israel Washburn; mother of the noted Washburn "Seven Sons."

while the famous 20th Maine Infantry (which saved the day at Gettysburg) included eighteen. The heaviest proportion of fatalities was suffered by those in the 29th Infantry - of thirteen men, six were killed; and in the 30th Infantry, which had nine killed out of twenty-nine.

Bare statistics convey only a faint idea of the tremendous impact on these towns of that tragic struggle - of the losses, human and material, of the suffering of both those who went and those who remained at home, and of the broken homes, or families left fatherless. Probably the best way to understand it is to view it from some individual's point of view; and for that purpose there follow several quotations reflecting personal reactions to those troubled years.

From an article by Nettie Mitchell in the *Livermore Falls Advertiser:*

September 14, 1961

"Perhaps the best way to begin the local recollections of this period, is to recall scenes in my mother's kitchen in my childhood. I sat, a little girl in the corner, listening absorbedly to the tales told by those who gathered there to visit my grandfather, Joseph Plant, who was wounded in the Battle of the Wilderness.

"Among those who gathered there were Hubbard Haskell, who lived on what many people round about still call 'the Hersey Record place'; Charles Crane who lived where Stanley Bamford does now; Sylvester Graves, commonly known as 'Vest,' who lived on a small farm above the 'Cold Springs,' on what is now Route 17, near 'Twelve Corners.' No vestige of that farm is left visible now, nor of the one above it where Christopher Wadsworth had a cobbler's shop, and made shoes for his wide clientele. The only reminder of this is the name 'Wadsworth Hill' given to that stretch of road.

"Vest Graves' tales always were climaxed with the

statement, 'I came out all right and the Captain gave me a pint of whiskey,' which always brought the roar of laughter and slapping of knees which he anticipated.

"Charles Black was a small, quiet man whose voice was only heard occasionally, but with telling effect.

"Others sometimes joined these, but these were the regular group who gathered there, sometimes on week days, but most often on Sunday afternoons.

"Besides their stories, I loved most to hear them sing; *Rally Round the Flag, Marching Through Georgia, The Battle Hymn of the Republic, Tenting Tonight,* and other songs; and to hear them tell of the long marches with 'Hay foot! Straw foot!' as their marking time to keep them in step.

"I remember Grandfather telling of the whine of the Minie Balls and how the Grape and Canister chains mowed down the trees around them in that last terrible battle in which he participated, the Battle of the Wilderness.

"I remember, too, his description of some of the beautiful mansions in which they were sometimes quartered; and shuddered at the terrible destruction and desecration of those homes.

"One tale of such a place always stayed with me when he told of a surgeon using a grand piano for an operation table. But it was not all grim as many -jokes and tales of comic adventure interspersed with tales of heroic daring came to life in that farmhouse kitchen on Moose Hill."

The "Charles Crane," mentioned by Mrs. Mitchell, was one of three brothers, Frank, Roscoe and Charles, who went to the front. Of the three, Charles was the only one who came back.

Although Mr. Crane was of slight build, it is said that his mother was a woman of such tremendous size that special furniture was constructed for her use; and that a stout post, topped with a heavy iron ring with a stout strap, was fastened to the floor before her chair to assist her in rising to her feet, when sitting; and that once when it became necessary for her to go into town two stout men assisted. her into the farm cart to enable her to ride there.

Still, she performed household tasks and "chores" which would stagger the average woman of today - spinning, weaving, carding wool and flax, making butter and cheese with the cumbersome implements of the day, cooking and cleaning, all the various occupations of that time, a Herculean task!

Colonel Lee Strickland raised a company in Livermore, soon after the outbreak of war, and they were organized August 23, 1861, as Company *"C,"* 8th Infantry, Maine Volunteers. Lee Strickland was elected Captain; Augustus Strickland, First Lieutenant; W. H. Timberlake, Second Lieutenant; and Charles F. Monroe, Orderly Sergeant. They met at Brettun's Mills, Livermore, on August 26th, 1861, to leave for service. Every mother, father, sister and brother were there to bid them good-bye; and the loyal men of Livermore vied with one another for the privilege of conveying them by teams to Augusta. One member of the departing company was the Sylvester Graves, of East Livermore, mentioned by Mrs. Mitchell.

Lee Strickland was elected Colonel of the regiment, but he resigned his commission four months later, because of ill health, and came home. He was a merchant, and was the only subscriber to the *Lewiston Semi-Weekly Journal* in town. Every Wednesday and Saturday evening, Robert Casey, an excellent reader, was seated in a chair on the counter, and read war news to a full house.

A letter dated "Front Royal, Va., June 23rd, 1865," written by E. C. Whittemore, of Co. E, 10th Maine, to Miss Mary Walton, describing the death of her brother, Andrew, says:

"He was shot by General Ashby at a place called Doxville, seven miles from Martinsburg on the road to Winchester. He got so tired from marching that he could go no farther, and sat down by the roadside to rest; and before he got rested enough to come on after the regiment, the Rebels were close on him and ordered him to surrender, which he refused to do. Then they fired at him, and he in turn fired at them, and continued to till General Ashby shot him, while he was in the act of loading.

"When we came from Martinsburg, the Colonel ordered us to halt, and the whole regiment went to the grave; Mr. Knox made some very good remarks and a prayer, after which the band played a funeral dirge; and afterward we fired three volleys, and left him alone."

From a letter written by Nancy Whittemore, dated "Livermore Falls, Feb. 28, 1864," the following is taken:

"Everyday adds new mourners to the list. ... Poor Dorillus Hobbs was taken prisoner at the battle of Gettysburg on the first of July, and in September got out one letter stating he was well, but suffered much before reaching there - and had very poor fare but did not complain as so many have. In December they heard he was sick, and then it was reported in the papers that he died last November. Unable to ever learn when he died, or with what disease, - much more the state of his mind, Martha is almost beside herself with grief."

Farther on in the same letter she says:

"Two regiments have just left for Texas. Among them are Levi (Ela) John Ford (as Lieutenant), William Hyde and two brothers, with Harriet's son, Wadsworth, Laforace Paine, Alva Garcelon, Wallace Noyes (as Captain), Mr. Cook, and others you would not know.

"We hear they have the small pox on board both ships, and are at quarantine off Key West, Florida.

"We still keep doing for the poor fellows. In December we sent more than a carload of vegetables from the Falls, and on the 11th of this month a Levee was attended by four hundred persons at Lane's Hall, contributing $142.00 in money to be sent to our prisoners at Richmond.

"A Company are coming to the Falls to condense milk, cider, coffee, etc., and to commence by June. It will give a new impulse to business, and I hear will employ quite a number of girls, as well as men. The Tailor's shops are lively. A Mr. Lewis takes Mr. Petrie's place. It is very sickly here this winter, Canker Rash, Lung and Typhoid fevers prevail."

Then follows a long list of dead and dying and a closing hope for welfare.

Walt Whitman, known as the "Good Gray Poet," whose *Leaves of Grass* and other publications made him famous, spent much of his time during the war years in the military hospitals, helping care for the wounded and ill; and he recalls the following incident in his *Specimen Days:*

"It is Sunday afternoon, middle of summer, hot and oppressive, and very silent through the ward. I am taking care of a critical case, now lying in a half-lethargy. Near where I sit, is a suffering rebel, from the 8th Louisiana; his name is Irving. He has been here a long time, badly wounded, and lately had his leg amputated. It is not doing very well.

"In one bed a young man, Marcus Small, Company K, 7th Maine, sick with dysentery and typhoid fever, pretty critical case. I talk with him often, he thinks he will die, looks like it indeed. I write a letter for him home to East Livermore, Maine. I let him talk to me a little, but not much. Advise him to keep very quiet. Do most of the talking myself. Stay quiet a while with him as he holds on to my hand. Talk to him in a cheering but slow, low, and measured manner. Talk about his furlough, and going home."

And from the roster of the 7th Maine Infantry:

"MARCUS SMALL, East Livermore, - Died."

Augustus D. Brown was a member of the First Maine Cavalry. At the battle of Gettysburg, he was detached from the regiment to act as orderly for one of the generals, carrying messages between the several headquarters or command posts, during the battle. On one such errand he was severly wounded so seriously in fact that the army hospital said there was no hope for his life, and shipped him home to die. However, he did recover; and for many years was an active member of Kimball Post, G.A.R.

On the occasion of the Fiftieth Anniversary of the Gettysburg battle, Mr. Brown attended the ceremonies, was taken ill, and died there. So, after all, he did die on the field where he was wounded - but fifty years later.

Ira T. Monroe, in his "History of Livermore," recounts:

"The writer (Monroe) remembers well that Charlie Wyer and Leroy Stevens were both killed in the same battle and buried where they fell, with nothing but the army blanket for a shroud. John W. Bigelow, a discharged soldier, was sent to recover and bring home the remains of these two boys.

"The funeral of Charlie was held in the old church at Livermore Center; and the choir sang at the close of the service, 'Home, Sweet Home.'"

Henry B. Rose never came in from the picket line, in the Wilderness; Nathan G. Bartlett died in Andersonville prison; Edwin T. Quimby lies buried under a beech tree on Danfusky Island, Hilton Head; and Philip H. Briggs was buried at sea.

"Milton F. Ricker was taken prisoner and confined in Andersonville until his exchange. The day after his arrival home, callers found him sitting by the window, looking out on the old familiar scenes, with his mouth filled with linen rags to soothe the stings of canker (probably scurvy) brought about by cruel treatment of the infamous General Wirts.

167

"Lieutenant Sylvan G. Shurtleff was terribly wounded at Petersburg, Virginia; and when word of it reached his mother in Livermore, she immediately started for Washington. Upon her arrival she was informed that no one, except on important business, could pass the lines; but as a last resort she sought Abraham Lincoln, who also told her that no one was allowed to pass the lines except on important business. Said Mrs. Shurtleff, 'This is important business, for my only boy is dangerously wounded, and I must go to him.'

"Characteristically, with the President, compassion overcame regulations, and on a slip of paper he wrote for the lady,

'Pass the bearer through the lines.
A. Lincoln.'"

Most of the older, present day residents of Livermore Falls will remember Henry French, who lived in the neighboring town of. Chesterville, and whose father, Joseph B. French, enlisted in 1861, in the First Maine Regiment, Mounted Artillery, and served throughout the war. The following excerpts are taken from a letter written to his father, dated "Maryland Heights, Sept. 26, 1862":

... "We had a grand chance to see the battle (Antietam) for we was all in plain sight of the contended ground but took no part in it. The reason was on account of our not having horses or men enough to man our guns

. . . "This battle is called the battle of the Antietam, it is named for the stream that separated our forces from the rebels at first. I passed over the battlefield or a part of it the second day after the fight and such a sight I

George Dana Boardman of Livermore
First graduate of Colby College; in Burma, he founded one of the greatest missions of modern times - almost singlehandedly transforming the Karen people from a despised backward race to a people with a prominent and honorable position in Burma.

never see before. I cant give you hardly eny ideas of the battlefield as it looked then. It consisted of woods, corn fields, plowed ground and grass land, now and then a fence behind. Behind one fence where the rebels layed and our men out flanked them and caim in there and fired upon them they laid dead over a hundred of them and in every shape you think. I se one fellow that was shot when he was attempting to get over the fence and thare he hung acrost the fence all shot to pieces. In another place I counted 87 in one line not more than 15 or 20 rods in length whare they probly maid a stand and tried to hold thare position. They were three deep in some places in that line and but a short distance from thare I cam acrost 27 more on a place not larger over than our setting room and so I might go on and discribe many such places. But you couldnt go but a few rods without coming acrost the dead and such looking sights you never saw for they had all turned black and a grait many of them swollen to twice thare bigness. I saw but a few of our men for they had been buried by thare friends and solgers.' I saw one fellow buring his brother as he said and another his father. That was the most solom sight to me that I see on the field .

. . . "I don't know as you can read this Father for I keep forgetting to who I was writing to. But I will try and write plainer the next time and I remain your ever loving son.

JOSEPH."

It may seem invidious to single out any particular Maine regiment for special mention, when they all, without exception, served with distinction. The Second Maine Infantry won the thanks and high praise of General McDowell at the first Bull Run (where the heroes were few), and followed through with distinction to Appomattox, where Lee's surrender was received by Maine's General Joshua Chamberlain. He asked for his old brigade (including the Twentieth Maine) to participate with him in that final ceremony. However, since Gettysburg is generally conceded to have been the decisive point of the war, and since two Maine regiments, including many Livermore men, by desperate bravery and tenacity at vital points, saved the day for the Union, it is only just to mention them.

The first was the Sixteenth Maine, which as part of the First Corps was engaged the first day of the battle, west of the town of Gettysburg along the Chambersburg Pike. The regiment had left Maine 1000 strong, a year earlier; but had taken some hard casualties in that time, and on July 1, 1863, it went into battle numbering only two hundred seventy-five men.

The First Corps, reinforced by the Eleventh Corps, was having a hard time to hold back the Confederates advancing from the west, being badly outnumbered, when Ewell's Confederate Corps appeared, advancing from the north, threatening to outflank and surround the Union troops. It was at this point that the Sixteenth Maine was ordered to the extreme right of the First Corps, and voluntarily sacrificed to enable the rest to be saved. General Robinson ordered them to advance to the indicated position and "hold it at any cost." Thus, while brigades, divisions, even two army corps were retiring, the little Sixteenth Maine was to advance alone. "You know what that means," said Colonel Tilden, as he turned to his brother officers and gave the command to move forward. Obviously that handful of men could not hold long against two army corps. For about twenty minutes the firing by this forlorn hope held up the Confederate advance, then the two long lines of gray, Ewell's men from the north and Hill's men from the south, closed on the survivors simultaneously. Ordered to surrender his .sword, Colonel Tilden drove it into the ground and broke it off at the hilt; the survivors tore the regimental flags from their staffs and ripped them into pieces which were distributed among the men.

Here it was that the "poor Dorillus Hobbs," mentioned in Nancy Whittemore's letter, as well as Nathan Bartlett, also from East Livermore, were captured and sent to prison camps from which they never returned.

Thirty-nine men managed to elude the Confederates and got back to the Union lines, but the rest of the two hundred and seventy-five were all killed, wounded, or carried off to Southern prisons - which, for most of them, was the worst kind of death sentence. The twenty minutes of time bought by their sacrifice, however, was vital in extricating the Union troops, and preventing the disaster which threatened. But these thirty-nine survivors who eluded their captors, were all that remained of the Sixteenth Maine; of which three men,

Lincoln of Illinois   **Hamlin of Maine**

Hannibal Hamlin: grandson of Deacon Livermore; son of the town's first physician;
Vice President of the United States - 1861-1865.

Lincoln & his cabinet

Hannibal Hamlin, the Vice President, who is shown standing beside Lincoln, was
the son of Livermore's first physician Dr. Cyrus Hamlin, and was a grandson of
Deacon Livermore.

Lieutenant Marshall Smith, David Hinds and James Ridley, were the only survivors from Livermore's original contingent of twelve.

The action of the Sixteenth Maine was generally lost sight of, in the magnitude of the casualties, the confusion of that great battle, and especially the fact that its brigade commander was shot through both eyes, and unable to give any report. The Twentieth Maine, on the other hand, found itself in the spotlight of history immediately, on the second day at Gettysburg, July 2, 1863; and its commander, Colonel Joshua Chamberlain, was later awarded the Congressional Medal of Honor for that day's work.

The position of the Union troops that second day was in the shape of a fishhook - Culp's Hill on their right being the barb; thence curving around by the town, and along Cemetery Ridge, as the shank, to Little Round Top as the eye of the hook. General Sickles had been ordered, with his Third Corps, to form the left of this line, and to occupy Little Round Top which dominated the whole battlefield, as the anchor of his left. Instead, he had advanced the Third Corps, in a salient, beyond the rest of the line. Before General Meade could correct this, and bring the Third Corps back into proper position, Sickles became heavily engaged with Longstreet's Confederates, and could not withdraw. Elements of the Fifth Corps were rushed to Sickles' aid.

Meanwhile, Confederate General Hood and Union General Warren discovered, at about the same time, that Little Round Top was undefended; and both recognized it at once as the key to the whole Union position. Warren, rushing down from Little Round Top, encountered Vincent's brigade of the Fifth Corps going to the aid of Sickles; and persuaded Vincent, on Warren's own responsibility, to change direction to the left and to occupy Little Round Top immediately. So Vincent's four regiments, Eighty-third Pennsylvania, Forty-fourth New York, Sixteenth Michigan, with the Twentieth Maine in the lead, narrowly won the race to the top; and took position with the Twentieth Maine on the extreme left. Hardly were they in position, when the Fourth Texas, the Fifth Texas and the Fourth Alabama struck the three regiments on the right, while the Fifteenth Alabama and the Forty-seventh Alabama, over a thousand men under command of Colonel William C. Oates, struck the less than four hundred Maine men, attempting to outflank them and roll up the Union left. For a few hours the fate of eighty thousand Union troops, and possibly the Union itself, lay in the hands of these few Maine men.

There ensued one of the most desperate and bloody hand-to-hand fights of the whole war. To meet the threat of being outflanked, Colonel Chamberlain stretched his line out nearly double, and bent the left half at right angles to meet the flanking force. Company "C," which included most of the Livermore men, was on this bent back left, and it was here that Oliver Stevens, of Livermore, was killed, and Sergeant Arad Thompson earned his promotion to Lieutenant.

The Alabama Colonel Oates afterward wrote, "I recall a circumstance which I recollect. I, with my regiment, made a rush forward from the ledge. About forty steps up the slope there is a large boulder about midway the Spur. The Maine regiment charged my line, coming right up in a hand-to-hand encounter. My regimental colors were just a step or two to the right of that boulder, and I was within ten feet. A Maine man reached to grasp the staff of the colors when Ensign Archibald stepped back and Sergeant Pat O'Connor stove his bayonet through the head of the Yankee, who fell dead. 1 witnessed the incident, which impressed me beyond the point of being forgotten."

The critical point was reached when the Maine men ran short of ammunition. They were searching among dead and wounded for cartridge boxes, but were obviously near the end. Chamberlain was under orders not to retreat at any cost; it was impossible to maintain the fire fight without ammunition; so he took the only other course possible, and ordered his men to fix bayonets and charge. The unexpected move threw the Confederates into confusion, resulting in disordered flight and in the capture of some four hundred enemy troops by the Maine men.

Again quoting the Confederate Colonel Oates, "There never were harder fighters than the Twentieth Maine men and their gallant Colonel. His skill and persistency and the great bravery of his men saved Little-Round Top and the Army of the Potomac from defeat. Great events sometimes turn on comparatively small affairs."

Again quoting Mrs. Mitchell:

"Among the tales of Civil War days were many local happenings of interest to the youngsters of seventy years ago. One such tale I remember concerned an elderly lady known as 'Aunt Liza Cole,' who lived in a farm house long since demolished, and now in the midst of the woodland behind the 'Joe Whittemore Place,' likewise abandoned, to the southward of Moose Hill Pond.

"At that time men known as 'stragglers' were not uncommon in this region. Some of these 'stragglers' were deserters from the army, some were negroes attempting to reach the Canadian border, and some were individuals who, for one reason or another, avoided the main highways and the society of their fellow men.

"It seems that, rising early one morning as was her wont, 'Aunt Liza' went to the barn to milk her cow, and found there two such rascals who had already done the milking and drank the milk.

"Incensed at this, she advanced upon them, armed with the milking stool, and commanded them to 'skedaddle and git out!' She told them they were no longer welcome 'to sleep in her hay, to milk her cow, nor to eat the grapes from her vine.' The appearance of the irate old lady seemed to be enough for the pair, as they were never seen again in this neighborhood.

"Another tale of 'stragglers' was told of a rough appearing man who entered the home of a Mrs. Hardy. He demanded a meal and a chance to rest undisturbed for a while, and became quite aggressive

175

and insisted that the little white-haired lady make the necessary provision at once, to assuage his hunger and thirst.

"The tale goes that Mrs. Hardy had a daughter, Sylvia, who was an unusually large, strong and independent young lady. Hearing the voices in the kitchen, she appeared at her mother's call; and when the rascal turned to greet 'the gal,' she appeared before his astonished eyes, fully armed with a shot-gun; and he needed no second warning when commanded to 'make tracks.'

"These are two instances of the worsting of marauders by women whose natural protectors were engaged in' the great struggle, and it seemed to be impressive when told by the fireside years later.

"The part of the women of that day has been sadly neglected, I believe, when overshadowed by the deeds of the men of the battlefield. Their labor and sacrifice were, I believe, as heroic as those deeds which are told of their sons and husbands.

"They cut their hair to sell for money for a bare existence; they dried raspberry leaves for tea; they raised sheep, sheared them, carded and spun the wool, knitted and wove it into garments for use both at home and for the soldiers to wear. They cut the hay, and harvested the crops on fields which they had plowed, harrowed, sowed and tended.

"They went into the woods and cut the fuel for their fires; they taught the children the three R's, and also the skills necessary to the day. They shod the horses and mended their harness. In short, all the labor of existence in a more laborious day than the present, fell to the lot of the women and a few decrepit males, either too old or too incapacitated to bear arms, as the country was practically stripped of all men above sixteen years of age, and many even younger. Hats off to the women of that day!"

Of the deaths of all fifty-five of the boys who never came home to Livermore, the case of Andrew Walton seems somehow the most touching. Exhausted and unable to keep up with the regiment, he was cut off by the enemy and summoned to surrender; but, alone and hopeless as he was, he chose to go down fighting rather than surrender. His regiment must have been impressed, for when they later came by that way, as one of his comrades, E. C. Whittemore, wrote to Andrew's sister, "the whole regiment went to the grave." After prayer by the Chaplain, and a dirge played by the band, "we fired three volleys - and left him alone."

Death, to them, was a commonplace thing, happening almost daily to dozens, even hundreds all around them; and to which they had of necessity become more or less hardened. The brief service and the three volleys, at Walton's grave were obviously not a tribute to his death, but rather to the indomitable spirit of a man who refused to give up.

LIVERMORE-EAST LIVERMORE MEN WHO GAVE
"The Last Full Measure of Devotion"
TO PRESERVE THE UNION

Charles H. Atwood, Company D, 32nd Inf. - died August 5, 1864

William H. Babb, Company G, 15th Maine Inf. - died in service

George W. Bean, Musician, 8th Maine Inf. - died in
      Andersonville prison

Philip H. Briggs, Company C, 8th Maine Inf. - died in service

Nathan G. Bartlett, Company C, 16th Maine Inf. -
      died in Andersonville prison

John W. Campbell, Company K, 3rd Maine Inf. died
      Sept. 16, 1861

Charles E. Cole, Sgt., Company B, 32nd Maine Inf. -
      killed July 30, 1864

M. P. *Chase,* Company F, 11th Maine Inf. - killed in action

Richard J. Cook, Company K, 30th Maine Inf. - killed in action

Adoniram L. Dyer, Company G, 4th Maine Inf. -
      killed Feb. 8, 1864, at Brandy Station

Charles Dorr, Company C, 8th Maine Inf. - died in service C.

C. *Eldridge,* 3rd Maine Inf. - killed

Eben Farrington, Corporal, Company H, 3rd Maine Inf. killed at
Gettysburg July 2, 1863

Charles D. *Fuller,* Company I, 23rd Maine Inf. - died in service

Philemon H. *Fernald,* Company G, 30th Maine Inf. -
died in service

William H. *Gordon,* Company B, 10th Maine Inf. died
July 27, 1863

A. H. S. *Garcelon,* Company A, 30th Maine Inf. - died in service

Martin Goding, 4th Bat., 1st battery Light Artillery -
died November 9, 1864

Joseph E. *Hyde,* Company A, 30th Maine Inf. died
August 26, 1864

Corydon L. *Hyde,* Company A, 30th Maine Inf. died
August 7, 1864

Charles G. *Harris,* Company G, 3rd Maine Inf. died
February 13, 1864

Clarence G. *Haskell,* Company H, 14th Maine Inf. killed
in action

David H. *Hinds,* Company C, 16th Maine Inf. died of
wounds at Gettysburg

Dorillus Hobbs, Corporal, Company C, 16th Maine Inf. -
captured at Gettysburg, died in Andersonville

Charles H. *Harrington,* Corp. Company A, 30th Maine Inf. died
July 24, 1864

John L. *Hoyt,* Company I, 29th Maine Inf. killed
in action October 19, 1864

Charles H. *Kimball,* Company I, 23rd Maine Inf. died
January 17, 1863

Volney Leavitt, Corporal, Company A, 29th Maine Inf. killed
1864

Charles Morse, Company D, 32nd Maine Inf. died June
25, 1864

Charles R. *Mitchell,* Company I, 23rd Maine Inf. died
December 26, 1862

William M. *Morrill,* Captain, Company A, 20th Maine Inf. killed

May 8, 1864

Charles F. *Monroe,* Lieutenant, Company C, 8th Maine Inf. killed
June 3, 1864 at Cold Harbor

Eliphalet C. *Morse,* Corporal, Company H, 14th Maine Inf. died of
wounds December 5, 1864

Roscoe Merrill, Company A, 30th Maine Inf. - died in service

Leonard F. *Nash,* Company A, 29th Maine Inf. -
died of wounds October 21, 1864

Joseph F. *Norris,* Company D, 32nd Maine Inf. captured, and died in
Confederate prison

Timothy B. *Niles,* Company G, 1st Maine Cavalry killed in action

L. F. *Paine,* Company I, 29th Maine Inf. - died May 8, 1864

Edwin T. *Quimby,* Company C, 8th Maine Inf. -
killed May 11, 1862 at Danfusky Island

Henry B. *Rose,* Corporal, Company D, 32nd Maine Inf. killed
June 1; 1864, in Wilderness

Henry W. *Richards,* Company E, 32nd Maine Inf. - killed 1864

George E. *Reed,* Company G, 1st Maine Cavalry -
killed in action August 25, 1864

Frank Roberts, Company A, 30th Maine Inf. -
captured, and died in Confederate prison

Jefferson T. *Stevens,* 3rd Maine Inf. - killed in action

Marcus M. *Small,* Company K, 6th Maine Inf. - died

Leroy Stevens, 8th Maine Infantry - killed

James C. *Smith,* Company I, 17th Maine Inf. - killed in action

Oliver L. *Stevens,* Company C, 20th Maine Inf. -
died of wounds at Gettysburg, July 11, 1863

Orville K. *Trask,* Company I, 23rd Maine Inf. -
died in service March 18, 1863

Llewellyn C. *Vining,* Company A, 30th Maine Inf. -
died in service

Charles L. *Wyer,* Company C, 8th Maine Inf. killed
in action

Andrew J. *Walton,* Company E, 10th Maine Inf. killed in
action

Eben C. *Whittemore,* Company E, 10th Maine Inf. died in
service

Henry A. *Wyman,* Company I, 29th Inf. - died in service

May 12, 1864
A. J. *Walton,* Company I, 29th Maine Inf. - killed in action

In a small community such as this, to take two hundred thirty-three men away for the war years, of whom fifty-five gave their lives, and nearly double that number were wounded or disabled, is a hard enough blow to the community. Unfortunately, the havoc wrought by the war did not stop there; many others, who did survive, migrated to the West, taking with them additional young men who were intrigued by their tales of the rich and level farm lands to be had there practically for the asking.

The population of the towns dropped from Twenty-six hundred to Twenty-three hundred; and did not get back to the pre-war total until 1890. The figures alone do not indicate the seriousness of the loss, for the three hundred drop was largely from the young, able-bodied men, leaving the population disproportionately the middle-aged or older, and the very young.

Extract from an article in the *Boston Herald* for December 13, 1889, which had been copied from *The Portland Press:*

"If all the sons and daughters who have left Maine to make homes in the West had gone in one time in a body, it would have been one of the most remarkable migrations in history. One by one they have been taking leave and departing for the last thirty years, so quietly that little note has been taken of their departure, except in the farmhouses that have been made lonelier by their going. Fathers and mothers have bidden adieu to sons and daughters; the State has bidden adieu to the materials of a commonwealth. The next census will show probably the exact extent of our loss; but an occasional fact crops out that gives a pretty good idea of the magnitude of the migration. One of these suggestive facts is afforded by the *Machias Republican* this week. Machias is a town of 2000 or 2200 population, not a large town by any means. Yet the *Republican* publishes a list of 125 of its former citizens who are now residents of the single city of Minneapolis. Almost a quarter of these are the names of men with families. It is fair to presume that the wives of a large proportion of these men with families were also from Machias, or at least from Maine, and deserve to be added to. the list of the 125. When a small Maine town makes such a contribution to the population of Minneapolis, it is not difficult to see where the population of Maine has gone. Every Western city of size has its Maine colony, sometimes numerous enough to form a society of the sons and daughters of Maine. Chicago has a large and influential society of this sort, including in its membership some of the most influential citizens of the city."

As indicated in the 1864 letter quoted earlier, a Company did "come to the Falls, to condense milk, cider, coffee, etc." and also to make cheese. It was known as the Rockomeka Company; and, presumably, it was producing for the Army, for it was busy during the war years; but, with coming of peace, it ceased operation. Its building, converted from a saw mill previously owned by Ezekial Treat, was sold to Alvin Record, and by him converted to a leatherboard mill.

It was at this point that Mr. Record began to assume prominence, and to take over town leadership as successor to Captain Treat. To him goes the credit for establishing the pulp and paper manufacturing business, which has been the main economic factor of the community ever since.

Alvin Record was born in Greene, Maine, on March 12, 1829. His parents moved, first to Canton, Maine; then, in 1840, when Alvin was eleven years of age, they settled in the Moose Hill area of East Livermore, where young Alvin attended school and church. The first dollar he ever earned was in picking beech-nuts on Moose Hill. The family were staunch Baptists; and Alvin, following revival services at the Moose Hill Church, was one of twenty who joined the church by baptism through a hole cut in the ice on Moose

Ship Gov. Brooks in Marseilles Harbor, 1838
Ezekiel Treat rose from a 12-year old ship's cook to captain of this brig by the time he was 18;
a fortune amassed at sea brought the railroad to Livermore Falls and contributed to the
industrialization of the town. (Ship painted by Pellegrin)

Hill Pond, ice thick enough to allow people to stand upon. One man stood with a rake to draw away the anchor ice as it formed after the opening was cut.

He learned the carpenter's' trade, at which he worked for some years; but, seeing a good opportunity, he went into trade in a small building near the foot of Mill Hill. For a while he occupied the brick building where now is Ham's Drug Store as an apothecary; but sold the business to Joseph G. Ham in 1871, and embarked upon the manufacture of "leatherboard" in a small building located on the flat below Mill Hill.

This business prospered, so in 1877 he purchased the building and water rights of the Rockomeka Company for $5500.00; constructed a dam across the river; and added a small pulp mill; while the old building of the Rockomeka Company was altered and fitted up with equipment for leatherboard manufacture. The whole involving a capital investment of $75,000.00, employing sixty men with a payroll of $1300.00 per month.

According to the *Maine Register* of 1878, in addition to Alvin Record, there were the following manufacturers in the village of Livermore Falls: E. W. Pressey, clothing; D. S. Thompson, clocks; M. E. Whitcomb, millinery; Beck & Boothby, grist mill; S. Robbins, furniture; D. N. Elliott, E. B. Hilton, harnesses; D. N. St. Clair, W. C. Walker, shoes; B. Paine, plows; Reuben Basford, shingles; B. Lane, lumber and boxes; O. A. Barker, carriages; F. Richmond, pill boxes; J. V. Young & Company, B. Jewell, shoes; Columbus Lane, saw mill; S. C. Whitney, M. N. Lambert, tailors; and Melvin Basford, tinsmith.

Ed Pressey, in his clothing factory, was employing thirty, and sales were $10,000.00.

As mentioned before, Alvin Record's general store and apothecary shop, which also contained the local post office, had been sold to Joseph G. Ham, of Portland, who moved his family here in 1873, although Mr. Record continued as Postmaster until 1885, and the post office remained in Mr. Ham's store. The exact date of sale and transfer to Mr. Ham is not known; but Mr. Record began leatherboard manufacture in 1871, and Mr. Ham moved his family here in 1873, so the conveyance was sometime between those dates. Ham's Drug Store is, today, the oldest established business in the town, and continuously in the same location for approximately one hundred years.

For a number of years, the only telephone in the town was in this store; and when, later on, other phones were installed, this became the local telephone exchange, of which Mr. Ham's three daughters, Charlotte (Mrs. Sturtevant), Grace (Mrs. Rand) and Bertha (Mrs. Hayden) were the operators. A messenger service was also provided for those not having phones. Mr. Ham used to tell many amusing things which occurred in this operation. For instance, one day he sent his young son, Arthur Ham, to deliver a phoned message, and he was gone a very long time. Mr. Ham was becoming more and more angry and worried until he happened to glance out the window at a passing funeral procession in which, much to his surprise, there was Arthur driving the hearse.

Mr. Ham closed out the "general store" part of the business, and made it wholly a drug store. For a time he also operated a hardware store at the corner of Depot and Main Streets, but sold it out after a few years. He became agent for several insurance companies, the books for which were kept by his daughter, Charlotte, (afterward Mrs. Chester Sturtevant). This business, too, still continues under the name of Sturtevant & Ham.

On the west side, in Livermore, in 1878, there were; Theodore Russell, Jr., boxes & spools; Phillips Brothers, grist mill: at Livermore Center, F. S. Richmond, wood turning; and Bigelow & Cummings, cheese factory; at North Livermore, Caleb Smith, tannery; North Livermore Cheese Company, cheeses; and Charles Alden, saw, shingle and grist mill.

Into this community, and its complex of prosperous but small industries, there was injected in 1881 an even more radical influence for change in the person of the third member of the triumverate mentioned - Hugh J. Chisholm, who was as adventurous, ambitious and capable as Mr. Record, but thought in even larger terms.

Hugh J. Chisholm was born in Chippewa, Ontario, Canada, on May 2, 1847, the fifth of ten children of Alexander and Mary Phelan Chisholm, who had migrated from Strathglass Glen, Scotland. Young Hugh, at thirteen years of age, was thrown upon his own by the accidental death of his father. He obtained employment selling newspapers and magazines on the trains running between Toronto and Detroit. The boy who held the same job, on the alternate run, was Thomas A. Edison; and the two boys became lifelong friends. While Edison went on to his world-renowned inventions, Chisholm went from the selling of papers to the manufacture of paper from wood pulp.

His first venture in the field was the organization of the Somerset Fibre Company, at Fairfield, Maine; and the production of wood fibre-ware from wood pulp. This plant burned, however, and after looking the State over for a new location for making wood pulp, he concluded that the

Androscoggin Valley offered the best combination of water, power and timber resources. In 1881 he formed the Umbagog Pulp Company at Livermore Falls, and built its plant in Livermore, directly across from Mr. Record's mills at Livermore Falls. At first a wooden structure, the Umbagog Mill was replaced in a few years by a new, substantial brick building; and its original daily capacity increased from thirty tons to fifty tons.

Naturally, the building of a mill on this site, and the addition of another dam close by that erected by Mr. Record, caused some friction between the two developments, and the relations between the two were somewhat strained. The officers of the new company were Hugh J. Chisholm, President, E. B. Dennison, Treasurer, and Daniel Bogan (father of the famed poetess, Louise Bogan) as Clerk. The Umbagog Mill had two paper machines making heavy wrapping and board papers, some of which served as stock for milk bottle caps, and some as liner material for caskets - sort of a cradle to grave operation.

Mr. Record, seeing his leadership in this area threatened, undertook construction of a second mill a short distance up the river, at Jay Bridge, where the river is divided by an island. Dams were erected on both sides of the island, and within a few months the mill was completed. Mr. Record installed two paper machines here at what was known as Jay Paper Company, of which Mr. Record was President. This company invested $100,000.00 in the Jay operation, and employed fifty men with a payroll of $1200.00 per month. Three years later another small mill was erected nearby, and another two machines added. These installations, along with a large saw mill on the island in the river, became known as "The Falmouth Mill."

Mr. Chisholm was not one to sit back and see himself outdistanced by a competitor. In 1887 he founded at Livermore Falls the Otis Falls Paper Company, capitalized at $750,000.00, with himself as its treasurer, general manager and principal owner. The Otis Falls, near the Jay-Livermore town line, was so-called from a previous owner, Oliver Otis, who operated a

185

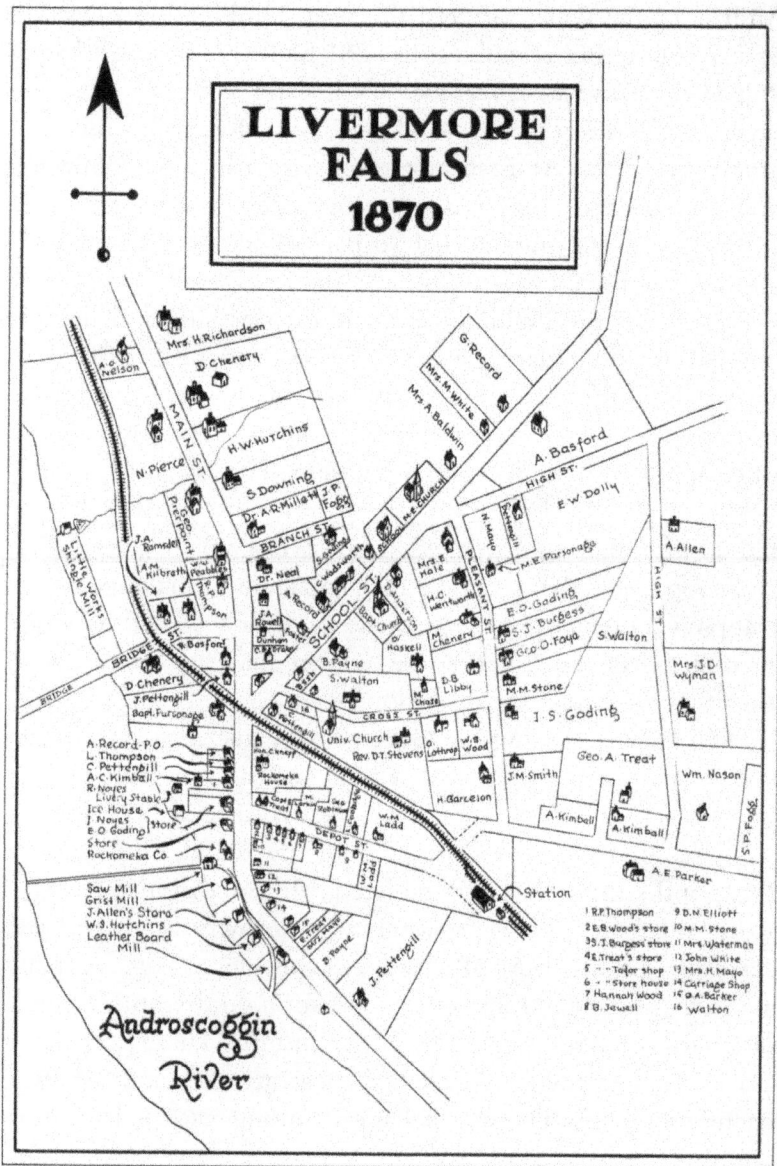

LIVERMORE FALLS 1870

Androscoggin River

A·Record·P.O
L. Thompson
C. Pettengill
A·C·Kimball
R·Noyes
Livery Stable
Ice House
J Noyes
E.O Goding | Store
Store
Rockomeka Co.

Saw Mill
Grist Mill
J.Allen's Store
W.S.Hutchins
Leather Board
Mill

1 R.P.Thompson   9 D.N.Elliott
2 E.B.Wood's store   10 M.M.Stone
3 S.J.Burgess store   11 Mrs.Waterman
4 E.Treat's store   12 John White
5 " " Tailor shop   13 Mrs.H.Mayo
6 " " Store house   14 Carriage Shop
7 Hannah Wood   15 Q.A.Barker
8 B.Jewell   16 Walton

lumber mill there.

The increasing importance to the State of this growing industry is indicated in the following extract from the *Boston
Herald,* in its issue of Friday, December 13, 1889:

"... It is manifest that the production (of wood

fibre) in this state is to be heavily increased, although in conversation with Mr. H. K. Chisholm, who is manager of the largest mechanical wood pulp mill in this state, and prominent in other branches of the industry, he informs me that the business is overdone, and that the capital invested is not securing adequate returns. He remarked that he supposed "about all the silly wood pulp cranks had now got into the business, and that henceforth there will be a let-up.

"In spite of this caveat, there does not appear to be any noticeable let-up on new enterprises; but capital is reaching into new and costlier plants than have ever been known.

"This is a great industry not confined to one section of the country, although here in Maine it has reached its highest development, and Maine is, and is to be, the leading wood pulp region, so far as quality goes. In one of the products of wood fibre - wood pulp board - Maine has now a producing capacity beyond any other state, her capacity now being 37,000 pounds per day, Michigan coming second with 20,000 pounds. The four states leading in this industry have a daily capacity for producting ordinary wood pulp as follows (in pounds):

Maine	305,000
New Hampshire	209,100
Pennsylvania	147,000
New York	891,000

"The mechanical process is away ahead of the others in volume of production and in number of plants. There are more than a dozen grinding mills, half a dozen soda ash mills and one sulphite mill in operation in Maine.

"The largest mechanical mill in Maine - The Otis Falls Company - uses 4000 horse power in driving eleven grinding machines."

The late Archie P. Richmond is an excellent spokesman for this period, the 1880's; and from his letters written in 1953 and 1954 to the *Livermore Falls Advertiser* and published by it, the following is taken:

"I will write from memory, the village as it was sixty-seven years ago (1886), and call the names of the ones who lived there and helped make Livermore Falls what it is today. As Mrs. Pool said, she had got a smart boy; he made a hog trough and two gate posts out of his own head and had some wood left. That is my case.

"Let us start at Chisholm and come down Main Street. The first dam (at Otis) was built sixty-seven years ago (1886). At that time only three houses were visible and one old barn which was cleaned out and covered with tarred paper and used for a boarding place for the help on the dam. The man who boarded the help was Mr. Barnes. Now to recall some of the others, there was Dr. Alden; next came Dr. Reynolds, then Dr. Gibbs; next was Dr. Millett, and I well remember Dr. Millett as he had a colt that he used to let out for exercise in the road, and I had a pair of red mittens my dear mother knit me. I dropped one in the road and the colt et it. I told the Doctor about it and he said it would pass through the colt and I would get it again. Sure enough, after three days of anxious waiting, the doctor got the mitten. It had gone through the colt, but was beyond any good for it was all cut up by the colt's teeth.

"As we move on (down Main Street) there was Sam Perkins who ran a grocery store. Across the road was Winfield Treat. I have often heard the business men say, 'He is one of the most honest men in town.' Next was John Rowell. He was the jeweller.

"This takes us to Bridge Street.

"Where Mel Deane is now located (Treat Library) there was a large house owned and occupied by Ensign

Goding. He used to have an apple canning factory on Pleasant Street on or near the Nazarene Church site. I well remember for there was a girl who fell into a tank of hot water and lost her life.

"Now on the South side of Bridge Street was a row of bushes which are now trees. The bushes had thorns on them; and one day, as Arthur Perkins and I were playing nearby, there was a man named Amasa Alden who had a mustang for a horse, and his wagon was a buckboard. When he got to the bushes, the mustang bolted through the thorn bushes. He got through, but the buckboard didn't, so the thorns were brading the animal in the rear. He was kicking, and the only way was for Mr. Alden to cut the traces, which he did; and the mustang lit out. I never knew where they caught him, but the way he lit out, I don't think a man in town could catch him.

"Next was a house and stable occupied by Ed Basford, now Billings Inn. The next place was Joe Pettingill's, now Dr. Rowe's. Mr. Pettingill was a one-eyed man like myself, and had long whiskers. He had an island at Shy, and used to ride on a pair of front wheels, and drove a horse whose original color was white, but had turned yellow.

"This takes us to the railroad track from Bridge Street, on the Westerly side (of Main). Now on the easterly side of Main Street, just north of the Post Office (now Frank Bailey's barber shop) was a man by the name of John Dunham. He thought he had the fastest horse in town, and told John Nash he didn't dare to start him for fear he could not hold him. John Nash told Mr. Dunham that Uncle Huff could trim him with a wheelbarrow. Mr. Huff was a man with a stiff knee.

"Next, where the Merriman Block is now, was a two-story house. I think it was moved across Church Street next to Ed Cloutier, but in front of this house

Mortgage Stock Bond issued by The Androscoggin Railroad Company

was an elm tree, not too large, and each year there used to be a man with a hand organ and a monkey and cinnamon bear. The bear would climb the tree - which we thought was wonderful.

"Now here it goes from the railroad south, where the bank is now located. There was a story and a half house and stable. It had a white picket fence around it, and was occupied by a Mr. R. C. Boothby who at the time had a grist mill at the foot of the hill. I well remember one day a long building came down the road being hauled by a pair of oxen. It was a picture salon owned by a Mr. Hayden. He set it in Mr. Boothby's yard and took pictures. I have in my home a picture of my two brothers and me, three cute little boys. Ha, Ha. Believe it or not, but we were considered the three worst devils in town. I was the only one that ever got put in the cooler. I will tell you about it later.

"Just across what is now Water Street, was only a path too rough for wagons, but it led to the old covered bridge, and a large French block that sat on the bank of the river, and I tell you it was well filled. I would not dare say how many children there were, perhaps a little less than a thousand. Next was, and is now, a drug store owned by a Mr. J. G. Ham. As they used to say, 'If the doctor can't help you, go and see Mr. Ham for he is better than any doctor in town.'

"Next came a jewelry store owned by K. John Rowell. Upstairs was a dentist by the name of Dr. Eaton, a fellow that had just as soon have pulled your tongue out as a tooth, but full of fun. One day a schoolmate by the name of Freeland Wright had a toothache. He was very saving of his money, so he called on Dr. Eaton and asked what it would cost to have a tooth out. The doctor said if it hurts, it will cost fifty cents, but if it does not hurt, it would be free. So Freeland sat down and had the tooth out, got up and was hopping around and rubbing his face. The doctor asked, 'Did it hurt?' and Freeland said, 'Not a damned bit.'

"We start next at Mr. Rowell's jewelry store. Next

The "Livermore"

Built in 1851 for the Androscoggin Railroad by Amoskeag Co., cyl 13" x 20";
drivers 5 ft. diameter; later MCRR #43, then sold to Katahdin Iron Works
c.1880, to become "B. & K.I.W. #1."

The "Leeds"

Here pictured c. 1852 at Livermore Falls' first station on Depot Street (the
Richard Brophy house and the George Grua orchard are prominent in the
background); built in 1851 by the Amoskeag Co. for Androscoggin RR;
cy. 13" x 20"; driving wheels 5 ft. diameter.

came a jewelry store owned by D. S. Thompson. One thing I remember, Mr. Thompson had a set of large scales put in front for the purpose of weighing wood, hay, and all heavy loads. The first thing to be weighed was a man by the name of Reuben Wells. He had a pound of meat, and let someone hold it. After they got his weight, he took the meat and stepped back on the scales, and he weighed just one pound more.

"Next was a brick building. The ground floor was a shoe store, the man's name was Henry Walker. Up-stairs was the printing press operated by Eugene Beck; and, if I am correct, the paper was 'The Local Express.'

"Next was a side street called Cat Alley; at the end, on the river bank, was a stable called Noyes' Stable. Next was a double store, first a grocery store owned by Mr. Sam Perkins, then a millinery store of which his wife was proprietor. This I remember: she had an old maid by the name of Lena Rowell. I was taught to sing a little song which I did not understand just what it meant. It was in the spring of the year and quite sloppy; I had on a pair of cowhide boots with copper toes, and Miss Rowell said she would give me five cents to sing to her. I did and she gave me the nickel, but did not ask for an encore - she did not even clap her hands. I am not going to put it into print, but if anyone wants to hear it, I will gladly tell it to them.

"Upstairs was a Dr. Knight. Now I will tell you all what he did for me when I was three years old. - I was troubled with my stomach a great deal, and wanted to eat most all the time. Dr. Knight said I had a tape worm, and if my mother would do as he said, he could get it, and he did. I had only soft custard to eat for twenty-four hours, and he told my mother to have a cup of strong pumpkin seed tea (ready). Oh what a taste! but the doctor came and they turned the tea down my throat. In less than fifteen minutes he had the worm, and it was thirty-nine feet long. Now this is no fish story, but about worms. The doctor took the worm for his pay.

"In the basement, under the millinery store of Mrs. Perkins, there was a meat market. Charles Cram was boss, and his wife was my Sunday School teacher. You may not think I ever went to Sunday School, but my Dad had a heavy hair brush, and I found it less painful to go to school than to tell him I was not going.

"Now as I look back sixty-three years ago, our churches were well filled, and today only half full. I wonder if there will be any churches sixty years from now; but my Dad always said, 'A Sunday well spent brings a week of content.' So just try it once in your life.

"Next came a clothing store of Venie Burbank's. I well remember my Dad gave us three boys fifty cents to spend for Christmas, and I tell you we were three millionaires. We went to Mr. Burbank's store and bought round winter caps. They were green and gray. In a short time the caps started shooting into the air and looked like dunce caps, with nothing left to cover your ears. They stretched out and were a nice fit for a half bushel basket.

"Next came a leatherboard mill owned by Alvin Record. A man by the name of Porter lost his life when one of the grinder stones burst, and piece of the stone came through the side of the mill and onto the road.

"Back towards the river Mr. Record had a saw mill; but I cannot tell much about it, as I wasn't allowed to go too near. Next was R. C. Boothby's grist mill; and the grain, such as corn and oats, came loose by the car load, and Mr. Jot Lyford hauled it from the station to the mill.

"Next was a job shop operated by a man named Alf Riggs. He did most all kinds of wood work. Next was the novelty mill owned by my uncle, F. S. Richmond, of which my Dad was foreman. He got $2.50 a day, and the help got $1.50 for 10 hours. I cannot remember all who worked, but here are a few: Steve Berry, Bert Lyford, Arthur Payne, William Pratt, Wes Luce, Stubby Townsen, Nube Kincaid, Green Kincaid and others.

"Next was a building owned by Mr. Record, but

used for a storehouse. From there down the river bank was the covered dry house where my uncle, Fred Richmond, used to dry his stock for the novelty mill. This was the last down to Shy.

"Starting (at the railroad crossing, east side of Main Street) at the Judge Knapp house, where Mrs. Kneeland's restaurant now is (since torn down for the Mall parking lot). Mrs. Knapp had two children, Cora and Pod as I knew him, but his given name was Joe. They kept cows, and used to pasture them where Knapp Street is now. The people used to go there to get milk in two quart lard pails or tin cans.

"Just across the driveway was a one-slant wood shed on the north end of the hotel. One night there was some kind of show in the hall, so Harry Goding, Albert Wilkins and I thought we would have a shed ticket, so we got on the roof and were going to look in the windows. When we got up there, someone threw a pail of water on us and they sure hit the mark. We came down, and what to do I did not know, for it was time for me to go home - and wet clothes. I thought of that hair brush, for I knew I had done wrong; and being the right time of day, for my dad most always used it after I got my pants off, and oh how it would sting. But Dad was bust (all in) and I went to bed. I don't think he knew anything about it. Let me tell you, I was more afraid of that hair brush than I am now of an atomic bomb.

"Next is the Rockomeka Hotel. A man by the name of Billy Bean was proprietor, and the Dreamland Theatre was made out of its horse stable. There was a stage route that came from Canton to Livermore Falls. The driver was Frank Stevens. He came over in the morning and stayed till night, then returned with the mail and passengers for there was no train to Canton. Mr. Stevens was quite good with his fiddle and he did like a drink of 'oh be joyful.' On this day a man by the name of Henry Hyde, commonly known as 'Father' - a

The "Farmington"
built by the Hinkley Works in 1864
for the Androscoggin RR; leased to MCRR in 1871

The "Lewiston"
built by 'Manchester Locomotive Works in 1870 for the Androscoggin RR; later
became MCRR #48; cyl I5" x 24"; driving wheels 5 ft. diameter

man who was too much of a gentleman to refuse a drink - came in. Mr. Hyde was quite pussy but very light on his feet. Mr. Stevens was playing his fiddle in the stable floor and Mr. Hyde was stepping it out. In the floor was a large scuttle to clean the waste down, and in the cellar they kept pigs. Herb Bean opened the scuttle and Mr. Hyde fell through. He called back to 'Cease the music, your old father is among the swine.' Someone sent for the constable, and at that time Veane Burbank was the officer that came. He said something to Mr. Stevens, who was a large man, and he told Mr. Burbank to go back to his store or he would put him in his vest pocket and take him home. So that was all that happened.

"The next building was a house on the corner that John Lamb lived in, but that faced Depot Street.

"Now we will go down Mill Hill, just below Mr. Fournier's store. There was a grocery store. Jim Ramsdell was the proprietor; but sold out to a man by the name of Fred Stinchfield. Next was a two story house where a man by the name of Wallingford and his family lived. I well remember Mr. Wallingford, for he had two fingers grown together on each hand. He had a boy, we used to call him 'Walliper.'

"Next was a low posted house of Miss Whitcomb's. She had a millinery store on Depot Street. Next was Keene's Foundry. Mr. and Mrs. Keene were very tall people, and at that time it was the fashion for the ladies to wear high shoes. A man from Canton, George Towle, was having a dancing school in the Billy Bean hall, and Mr. and Mrs. Keene attended. My cousin, Sam Richmond, was a pupil, and his father, my Uncle Willie, asked Sam how he made it when he had to swing with Mrs. Keene. Sam said he took hold of the tops of her shoes. Sam must have felt as if he was pretty near the foot of his class!

"Then came Albert Allen's machine shop. He got

197

his power across the road by an overhead cable. Next in line was Cale Brown's blacksmith shop where horses and oxen were shod. For the benefit of the younger people, I will tell you just the way they put shoes on oxen. They were placed in what they called slings and two wide leather straps were drawn in under them and turned up tight, so they could not lie down. There was a post at the side of each leg, and one foot at a time was strapped to the post and held there until the shoes were nailed on, as each foot had two separate shoes. After one was done, they strapped another, and so on until all four feet were shod.

"The next was Frank Millett's blacksmith shop. He shod only horses, and he had a helper by the name of Herb Soule. Next was a paint shop where Dana Bailey painted wagons and sleighs.

"As We go down the River Road (below Mill Hill) there was a house where Joe Plant lived. This takes us to the bend in the river. We used to call it 'The Willows.' The willows saw many a sad happening, for years ago, when our State of Maine had prohibition, the only way to get liquor was to send to Boston and have it come by express; but the law gave the constable the right to sign and seize it, so when they got a box, it had to go before the judge, which at that time was R. C. Boothby. He would order it spilled. The law was you should have two reliable witnesses beside the officer.

"Well, this particular time, Clair Severy was constable. He got Jot Lyford and Billy Bean to help him spill it. They said it took forty-eight hours to do the job. (Sad affair).

"Next was a driveway, towards the railroad was a set of buildings where William Pratt lived; then going toward Shy was another building; then came a road that went east to the place they call the Wing house, but my Uncle Granville Richmond lived there. There was no Park Street. A little further down was another driveway to the home of Uncle Fred Richmond. Now the home of Danny Alvino. After my uncle moved, a blacksmith by the name of Al Barker built a shop near the road. All of Park Street was a field and pasture, for many times I would find our cow under a clump of cedar trees which now stand in front of Henry Fournier's house.

"Now comes the home of a Mr. Goding, then the Luce place, which is now the home of Mrs. Olive Cram; and this takes us to the railroad crossing at Shy.

"We start on the south side of Depot Street. On the corner, what is now Henry Fournier's store, there was a hardware store of George Chandler. Next came W. A. Stuart, then a millinery store of a lady by the name of Miss Whitcomb. There was the W. S. Treat store; he sold shoes. Then next was a cottage house that David Elliott lived in. He was a cobbler, and a very small man. He and his wife used to have a disagreement at times, and David would go off and be gone a day or two. There was a low-posted house on Church Street on the lot where L. P. Brown's funeral parlor is now. A lady by the name of Aunt Benny Paine lived there. She had a large bird house which we used to call a Martin house. So this day David had been gone all night and day; and his nephew, Charles Elliott, went by the house, and his aunt, Mrs. Elliott, came out and asked if he had seen his uncle David. Charles said yes - he was up in Aunt Benny Paine's martin house!

"Next was Mr. Elliott's cobbler shop. Then came a small building where a Mr. Newman sold tobacco and also was a newsstand. He married S. S. Locklin's daughter, Effie.

"Then came the home of John Hyde. He ran a livery stable, and some of the nicest looking teams you see. Then the next place beyond the driveway was S. S. Locklin's drug store; but after the I.O.O.F. block was built, he moved across the street, and a man by the name of Joe Sharaf moved in. I can remember Mr. Sharaf before I was three years old. At that time we lived in Livermore (west side) on the Prince Hinds

MCRR Plow
One of the huge locomotives of the early twentieth century clears the tracks of snow at the Livermore Falls station.

MCRR Section Crew – c.1890
At the Depot Street station in Livermore Falls, from left: Gould, Elisha Ryder (the foreman), Knowles, and Miles.

place. Mr. Sharaf came along with a pack on his back, and my mother bought a red checkered table cloth of him. I have got it now, and it is in very good condition.

"The next store was a furniture store. A Mr. Wood was the owner, and lived in the house now occupied by W. S. Nichols. Then came Mr. Tripp's barber shop. A sign in the window – 'Shave and hair cut 15 cents:'

"Next came the harness shop of Joe Knight and everyone he met, it was 'Hello hum bug:' Then came the Riverside Hotel and a man by the name of Mr. Hacker was proprietor. In his office I saw my first phonograph. It was an Edison with cylinder records, and you had to put tubes in your ears to hear it, but it was sure wonderful then. Mr. Harker had a boy by the name of Albert, and as it goes:

Albert Hacker chews tobacca,
His father smokes a pipe.
His mother took the drummers in
And kept them over night.

"We leave the Riverside Hotel and go east to the freight yard of the Maine Central Railroad. An Indian show carne to town and set their tent in the freight yard. They were selling snake oil, bows and arrows, baskets, and so on. I will tell you what took place that night, and I think it was all planned between my Dad and Frank Warren who was constable. There was a boy by the name of Claude Hatch, and we could not come together without having a fist fight; so on this night we got at it in good shape, when Mr. Warren took us both by the collar, marched us to the "cooler" which was on the bank, put us both in the same pen, and locked the door. Now let me tell you it took the fight all out of us. Oh, how loving we were, as I was wondering what my Dad would do to me, for he had told me not to fight; and I thought of that hair brush.

"After the show was over, Mr. Warren and my Dad let us out; and oh, how pleased I was to see him. We started home, and I tell you I was one of the best boys in town. I walked right beside him, and he did not have to drag me along; but I had that hair brush in mind, for it was the right time of day to use it. But we got home and Dad never said a word about what happened. He did not have to tell me to go to bed. I went like a good' boy; but that was a great lesson for Claude and me, as two better friends never lived after that.

"Next was the long freight shed, the track, then the depot. A Mr. Sawyer was agent. Mr. Sawyer and Faun Coffin had the first bikes I ever saw. A Mr. Goding was express man then. Next, where Park Street is now, was a driveway to Will Nason's. Next came the laundry of Ed Edgecomb. All work was done by hand. The lady who did the washing was Mrs. Diamond. Next was a two story house where Frank Robbins lived. There was nothing more till we pass lower Sewall Street, then came a work shop where the Sewall Brothers used to do repair work for their houses. Next up the hill was Eugene Sewall, and just south was his brother, Howard. Then just up the hill was a house and stable where we lived; and this is all there was until you got over the hill where the butter factory was built. The man who made the butter was a Mr. Wing.

"On the north side of Depot Street, where now stands the brick building (the mall), and going east, was a two story house occupied by John Lamb, who was County Sheriff at one time. Then came two stores; one was Bartlett and Keep, but I do not know who was in the other. Then came the house, which sat on the site where the I.O.O.F. now stands, occupied by Smith Cram. It was moved back, and the I.O.O.F. Block was built in 1890; S. S. Locklin occupied one store, and the J. L. Cumming's Clothing Store was in the same block. Just across the alley was a house and Mr. Elisha Ryder lived there. Then came Jot Lyford; and this takes us to the Hilton Block where G. F. Knight's mill is now. I remember Mr. Hilton very plainly as he used to wear high heeled boots. One day, as my Dad was walking along, he said to Mr. Hilton, 'Your block is settling a little.' Mr. Hilton said, 'Let her go. I own down there as far as anyone.'

"Now we cross the railroad track, and there was a building where the engines used to take water. Just east of Pleasant Street, now occupied by Mrs. Helen Wilkins (James Reed) was the home of a Mr. Goding; then the S. S. Locklin house; then the home of Caleb Brown. On the knoll was the home of the Davenports.

"This takes us to the easterly side of High Street. from here up the hill there was only a driveway which led to a Mr. Goding's on the side of the hill. Where the home of Rossie Bailey is now was bushes, and I have picked lots of blackberries there.

"We will start on Union Street, where the park is now. Located there was a two story house where a man by the name of Mr. Pettingill lived. He had a grocery store on Main Street. Then there was a stable on the easterly side. Next was the Universalist Church; then came a large house where a man by the name of Hutchins lived (recently Chester Moore). He had two children, who lived with him. Their names were Marion and Sheldon Gill. I hope many will remember them. Next was the home of Fred Stinchfield on the corner.

"Now School Street - there were no more buildings to High Street. Now going west on School Street, only the school house (where now is the Luciano house) to the corner of Pleasant Street and Union Street, where was the home of D. S. Thompson (now Landry's). Then next was a coat shop, so-called, and a man by the name of Ed Pressy did business there. Then the home of a Mr. Walton, who was trying to invent perpetual motion. Next came the store of a

East side of Main Street in the 1870's, looking south
(from left): a comer of Drakes Store (at a spot just south of the present Foss's Jewelry Store); Union Street; C. Pettengill's house (site of the present municipal park); Railroad crossing; Judge Knapp's house; Billy Bean's "Rockomeka Hotel" (bam later became the Dreamland Theater) Capt. Treat's house; Depot Street; E. B. Wood's Store; M. M. Stone.

Church Street fire - 1875

Mr. Lothrop, which was burned in the year of 1886. I well remember, as we lived in the Millett house, and you could see across the opening at that time. The building that burned was replaced, and Ed Cloutier now occupies it.

"We start on the easterly side of Church Street where the store of Ed Cloutier is now. The next house was where Mrs. May Alden lived (since torn down). Then going up the hill to where the L. P. Brown Funeral Home now stands was a house. A lady who was known by the name of Aunt Benny Paine (lived there); but she was taken away, and a man and his wife, Mr. and Mrs. George Currier lived there. His wife was a music teacher. Next came the Baptist Church. My mother was organist and my Dad was sexton. I used to go with him Sunday morning to ring the bell and then toll it. In those days the church was well filled with worshippers, as they believed in God, and I know He will help those who trust Him.

"If I remember, the next place was the parsonage; and the next, on the corner, was the home of Henry Hyde. Then up Church Street, where the Grammar School (now Primary) is now, was an open field where Mr. Record used to stack and dry his leather board. Then came a house and stable that a Mr. Vining lived in. This is all to High Street.

"On the northerly side (of Church Street) I remember only a man by the name of Charles Lawyler; then the Methodist parsonage and the church. Across the Street a Mr. Mel Holmes lived. Then we come to the home of Dr. Pratt which was the home of Mr. Alvin Record. The stable where he kept his horses has been made into a dwelling. This is all on the street.

"We will start at the Methodist Church and go down Millett Street. At this time, 68 years ago (1885) just back north of the church was a long shed where the good people used to hitch their horses while they attended church. In those days there were more horses than there are people today, I think.

"North, on what is now Knapp Street, was only a pasture, bushes and stumps. There was a small brook, and here is the place where we boys had fun. Near the road was a bend in the brook, and the water spread out not very deep; but had a lot of frogs, and we would catch them, blow them up, and let them go. It was very amusing to see them try to go under the water, but the wind would keep them afloat a while; but after the pressure was off they would go under, but we could see where they went as little bubbles would keep coming up, and then we would catch them again. But, oh, what fun, and I bet it would be fun for you people, old or young, to see the show. We go to the pictures and all, but it does not compare to a frog game show.

"On the southerly side (of Millett Street) at the easterly end was a two story house, and a family by the name of Pomeroy lived in it. I can remember for they had a big, fat boy that they said had to have a sugar teat when he went to bed.

"Next was the home of Andrew Dain, and how I did like to get over there and get one of Mrs. Dain's molasses cookies (for she could sure make the best); and then go out on the lawn with the two boys, Charles and Jim. They would play ball with me, then tie me in the hammock and swing me over and over. As I remember, they had four children, Charles, Jim, May, and Bess. I know one of the boys played a banjo and told me when I got old enough he would teach me to play, and I am still waiting.

"Mr. Dain's house was all on that side, to the Treat house on the corner (of Main Street).

"A little more on Brettuns, Livermore. We start at the Johnnie Goding place, now occupied by Charles Ryerson. Then came the home of Ed Roberts. He had three children, as I remember, May, Bertha and George.

"Now we will turn south, towards Butter Hill. First was a Mr. Doe and a boy Harry. Then came the home of Tom Stickney. They tell the story that Tom went to work for a Mr. Atwood. He called Tom in the morning and said that breakfast was ready. Tom asked the time, and Mr. Atwood said, 'Four o'clock.' Tom told him he could stand it till morning.

"Now was the home of Andrew Brown. He was a man could not speak aloud, but his wife could. They used to keep hens and bees. I was very fond of bread and honey, so I would ask her for some, but my dad put a stop to my asking for it. I found a way to get it though, and I will tell you how.

"I had a little black dog. His name was Cuffy. I tied him up in a bag and took him in the dooryard. I would run around, call him, and, oh how he would bark. After a while Aunty Brown would come out and tell me she would give me some bread and honey to stop my dog from barking, which I was glad to do. Ever after, when I wanted bread and honey, all I had to do was get Cuffy to barking. I got my lunch, and did not have to ask for it.

"Next was the home of Bryan Strickland: then the home of a Mr. Allen. I think Arthur Wilkins now has the next place. I think Will Hall lived in it, for he had a boy by the name of Fred, who was taken away quite young. Then the home of Mr. W. Spencer, the blacksmith. Now we cross the little bridge to the home of Charles Phillips. He had two children, Earl and Flossie. Next was a large set of buildings called the Piper place. Then the store of Mr. Fuller.

"Here was something that was said, and it always makes me laugh when I think of it. There was a Mr. Nelson who lived up Canton way. He was a very moderate man, but he dropped dead. He had a hired man by the name of Rufus Cotton. I know that lots will remember him. The next day, after Mr. Nelson died, Rufus came into Mr. Fuller's store. Mr. Fuller says to Rufus, 'Well, they say Uncle Nelson has got through'; and Rufus says, 'Yes.' Mr. Fuller asked, 'Didn't he die rather quick?' and Rufus said 'Yes, he did for him.'

"Now comes the Piper novelty mill which burned,

Main Street in the 1880's
Looking North from the corner of Main, Union and Church Streets: frame building on the right is Drake's Store.

Main Street in the 1890's
Looking North: the three story brick "Merriman" block is on the site formerly occupied by Drake's Store.

I think sixty-five years ago. Then came the shoe shop, now the Grange Hall. The shoe business had gone and a Mrs. Bridgham lived in it and worked in the mill. She had two boys, Pearl and Truman. I remember her; she used to make a salve. You had to warm it up, then use it; and I tell you it would stick. You either had to whittle it off, or let it wear off. Then was the home of a Mr. Frank Francis. He had a girl by the name of Winnie. Then came the home of Mr. Welcome Fuller who ran the store. He had a girl by the name of Edna. Next was the home of Ernest Francis with a little cobbler shop. This is all to the pond bridge."

On the west side of the river, according to the *Maine Register* for 1885, the manufacturers at this time were, at Brettuns, C. F. Phillips, grist mill, G. T. Piper, novelty and wood turning, A. S. & E. F. Phillips, saw and shingle mill, Bigelow & Cummings, cheese factory, John L. Cummings, trunk factory, Lewis Leavett & Son, corn canning; and at North Livermore, Caleb Smith, tannery, North Livermore Cheese Company, William Wilson, saw mill, C. L. Wyman, carriages, Charles Alden, saw, shingle and lath mill, and E. P. Chase, saw, shingle and grist mill.

The merchants were, at Livermore, R. G. Goding, general store, Mrs. L. H. Thorne, millinery, and G. A. Gordon, apothecary; at Livermore Center, F. B. Bigelow, general store; and at North Livermore, A. W. Coolidge, general store.

Mr. Piper's wood turning mill was quite a large operation, employing fifty persons. It burned in 1883, was rebuilt, and burned again in 1888. The Bigelow & Cummings cheese factory was of great value to the farmers until it, too, burned in 1888. Mr. Cummings then moved to a site, just above the bridge at the Falls, where he built a new factory in 1890, for the manufacture of trunks and extension cases.

With the Umbagog mill already located just south of the bridge, the village at Livermore Falls began spreading across the bridge to the west side, around the two employers.

The Livermore Dairying Association was organized in 1887, with a paid up capital of $1,500.00, of which G. B. Strickland was president, G. A. Gordon, secretary, and W. F. Fuller, treasurer. This company, engaged principally in butter-making, shipped its product to the principal cities of Maine and Massachusetts.

The move of J. L. Cummings from Livermore Center to the Falls was influenced by the railroad; and soon after, for the same reason, the Richmond woodturning mill also moved to Livermore Falls. Cummings was employing fifteen, with annual production of $20,000; while Richmond was employing 80, with total annual production of $40,000.

Although the industrial growth was thus centering on the east side of the river, just across the bridge in Livermore, the west side had by far the most fertile and productive farms, whose owners were apparently quite content that the mills leave them to their established and satisfying way of life.

From *Livermore Falls News* of Nov. 28, 1885 is quoted the following:

"During the past few months twelve hundred dollars worth of oxen have been sold out of Livermore.

"Probably three thousand barrels of apples will be sold from this year's crop, making the smooth sum of thirty-nine hundred dollars. Now add the fair estimate of six tons of pork at five and one-quarter cents per pound and you have a total of $5,730.00.

"The grain crop is enormous, corn good, potatoes fair, pasturage holds out late, which will insure plenty of hay for the long winter; the streams and springs are full; wood grows as fast as we need it for home consumption;

in a word, peace and plenty prevails."

Among the leading farmers of Livermore at this time were Sewall M. Norton, Thomas M. Wyman, Irving Thompson (the largest fruit grower), Calvin Leach, Adney Goding, Seth D.

Washburn, John Sanders, Martin Keith, Edward Pratt, E. C. Fuller, Nathan Timberlake, C. F. Pike, Adney Boothby, John O. Palmer, Roswell Briggs, Dana Pollard, Samuel Nelson and William Soule.

The operations of Mr. Record and Mr. Chisholm had reversed the downward trend of population; and the fast increasing population of Livermore Falls and its adjoining neighbor, Chisholm, was creating a corresponding demand for housing. This involved not only the problem of construction, but also that of financing, since there was no bank here at that time. Both needs were met largely by two firms. Eugene and Howard Sewall, brothers who were engaged previously in the lumber trade, and the manufacture of sash, doors and blinds in Chesterville, Maine, in response to the local demand, moved here in 1880; and Gordon Brothers, Frank B. and Charles H. Gordon, who established their saw mill, with a sash, door and blind factory, across the town line, in Chisholm.

E. & H. Sewall purchased what was then a pasture, bounded approximately by the present Depot Street, Sewall Street, High School lot, and Jones' farm. They built a section of the town, called "Sewallville," with houses for rent or sale, along Sewall Street, Depot Street, and Pine Avenue. They established for the development their own private water system and sewerage system. In addition to the Sewallville project, the brothers built several other groups of four or five houses in other sections of town - on Knapp Street, Green Street, and in Chisholm. Many homes of newcomers were made possible by the Sewall brothers, by their furnishing building materials on credit, and granting construction loans.

Gordon Brothers were engaged in much the same kind of operation, but their field of operation was principally in the northern section of town - Prospect Street, Bemis Street, Otis Street, Monroe Street, and especially across the town line in Chisholm. Like the Sewall brothers, they sold houses to millworkers on a monthly payment basis.

The first bridge, built in 1858, across the Androscoggin River above the falls, was carried away by an "ice freshet" in March of 1871. Through the enterprise and capital of Caleb

The Merriman Block
Above viewed after the fire: below photographed as a restored building, minus its former third floor (and looking much as it does today).

Smith, of Livermore, a new covered bridge was built at approximately the same site the following year. This was operated as a toll bridge up until 1887, when by action of the county, the two towns, and individual contributors it was made free.

The first volunteer fire department was equipped with a "hand tub." As Mr. Richmond described it in the article quoted earlier, it required thirty-two men to operate it - in two teams of sixteen men each, the teams alternating with each other as one became tired out.

Prior to 1890, however, the town acquired a "steamer," and the Fire Company adopted the name of Atlantic Steam Fire Company. Also, to live up to their new dignity, new hats were purchased for the members, as the following quotation from the Livermore Fails *local press* of June 6, 1890, indicates:

"The Atlantic Steam Fire Company came out this week with new hats. They are very pretty, and were purchased of a New York firm.

"Early on Memorial Day morning the Atlantic Steam Fire Company run out the steamer for sport and practice, and quickly had streams on. The company appeared for the first time in their new hats which are very pretty indeed."

The following is the account of the July Fourth celebration in 1890, as written by Archie Richmond for the *Livermore Falls Advertiser:*

FOURTH OF JULY, 1890

"I well know, if this was now, they would have us up before Judge Grua; but I know if he knew the fun, he would put us on probation for twenty minutes and cancel costs of court. Hurray, boys, Fourth of July 1890. It started at 2:00 o'clock in the morning with a huge bonfire, a pile of rubbish at the junction of Main and Depot Streets. It was some fire. The church bells began to ring and the whistle at the Umbagog Mill across the river blew, and it awoke everyone. The fire department came out with a hand tub, it took thirty-two men to pump the thing. Sixteen at a time and when they got tired, the other shift took over. My Dad was one of those firemen.

"There was a man from Moose Hill by the name of Elbridge Pettingill. He heard the alarm and took his horse and came as quickly as he could, but when he saw what was going on he was rather mad, and said, 'I will never run my horse over here again if the whole darn village burns up.'

"Well, after the bonfire was over, things quieted down until 8:30 A.M., except for firecrackers and noise-makers.

"Now the street parade of horribles was to start at 8:30. They formed in line on Main Street, just north of the railroad track, and quite a tough looking bunch, white horses with red stripes painted on them, a pair of oxen and cart, hay racks all loaded with merrymakers wearing masks. I remember I got mine ripped off. I felt blue, but a Mr. Walton said I did not need any, for I looked just as bad as anyone. That made me feel good. I didn't know enough to know he was making fun of me.

"The band was going to march (ahead of) the horribles, and a man by the name of S. Nelke was to lead the parade on horseback. He had a horse owned by David Searles, very clever, but rather nervous. Mr. Nelke had on a tall, stove-pipe hat, a wooden sword at his right, purple sash on his left that came near the ground. He stood ready, waiting for the word to march. His horse stood at the corner of Mr. Ham's drug store, headed out what is now Water Street, (but then was) only a rough path that led to the old covered bridge. All was quiet when John Nash put a large firecracker beneath the horse. When it exploded, what a sight! The horse jumped ahead and Mr. Nelke's hat came off and sat upright in the road. He was headed for the bridge, the sword in the air and the purple sash flying on the other side. The horse took him into the bridge before he could stop her. Then he came back and got his hat and tried to find out who did it, but there wasn't a person that knew, not even the one that did it. Then the

214

parade started, and oh the noise! Anything - washboilers, pans, horns, trumpets - but oh, what a good time! I would love to see it once more.

"The parade started down Main Street and out Depot Street. All was fine till we got to the Riverside Hotel. There was a hammock on the piazza which hung quite close to the floor. Ralph Lyford, or as we called him, Piper, was in the hammock and someone, of course no one knew, put a cannon cracker under Piper and blew him out of the hammock. Poor Piper for several days had to stand up or lie down. When he 'walked around it would make you think of a railroad locomotive with a tender behind.'

"Well, the parade went up Pleasant Street and out Union Street. In the junction of Main, Church and Union Streets was a greased pole. A Mr. Howland, the ice man, had charge of it. A fellow by the name of Fred Smith was trying to climb it, to get the money on top. As the band went past, Mr. Howard, wearing a stove-pipe hat, stood back to. When Charles Elliott (the bass drummer) came along with the drum stick, he let it go on top of Mr. Howland's hat. It stove the top in and drove the hat down so you could see only Mr. Howland's chin. It took the skin off his nose and he had quite a job trying to pry himself out, but the band kept on going to Main Street, and the parade broke up.

"Then came a few sports in front of Billy Bean's hotel, such as potato race, bag race, three-legged race. Then came the greased pig. John Nash had the handling of that. Mr. Alvin Record had a sawdust wagon, low down with very high side boards. John got it, and went up to Sy Allen's to get an old boar hog, frame enough to weigh 500, but would not weigh half that. He had tusks two inches long sticking out of his mouth. John loaded him and covered the top so no one could see him. In front of the hotel, John started in hollering, 'Greased Pig.' All who wanted to try to catch him were to gather around, and quite a few were ready.

215

Main Street looking north from Bridge Street in the 1880's

The streets were well lined with spectators. John asked, 'Are you ready?' and opened the end board. That boar came out and let a roar out of him. Talk about an army retreating! It was a case of hog chase man, and in less time than it takes to tell it, there was hardly anyone to be seen. There was one woman, I do not know who. She screamed and yelled, 'If that thing bites me, they will pay for it.' My land, the way she was toenailing it up the street, no hog could catch her for she did sure show great speed. They drove the hog down to Mr. Record's mill yard and caught him, then carried him home.

"Now this is the end of the fun till the fireworks in the evening. But what fun we had."

Another source of local entertainment and excitement in this era, was the annual Androscoggin County Fair. This was a relatively large and ambitious undertaking, sponsored by an association of local business men and farmers, called The Androscoggin County Agricultural Society.

216

The Society in 1889 located its grounds on the large, level area at Shy, a part of which is now where the Livermore Shoe Company's buildings stand. It was known as "Evergreen Park," presumably because the Society planted all along its boundary a thick cedar hedge, some survivors of which still exist on the east side of Park Street, across from Issacson Lumber Company.

Here the Society built a "Trotting Park," which Judge Knapp, in the History of Androscoggin County, described as one of the best trotting parks in the State." Certainly it attracted competition from a wide area; and for many years the Androscoggin County Fair was reputed to be one of Maine's best fairs. Special trains were run from Lewiston and from Farmington, which stopped on the siding there at Shy, instead of the regular station. There was a large exhibition hall where farm products, fruits, canned goods, handiwork, etc. were displayed in competition for prizes. Along the north line of the park, ran a line of horse sheds for the accommodation of the "trotters" and "pacers"; while along the south end was a line of cattle sheds for the various animals entered in that competition. On the east side of the track was a large, covered grandstand, built by E. and H. Sewall, who charged admission to the stand until their cost was recovered; then gave it to the Society.

The fair ran for three days, at the last of August or first of September, and attracted the usual "fakirs" and "skin games." In the *Livermore Falls Express and Advertiser* for August 27, 1896, almost the whole front page is devoted to reporting the fair; and prominent among the exhibitors of cattle and sheep were: E. Pettingill, M. J. Wadsworth, A. M. Wing, Roy Dean, F. A. Wyman, Ward T. Moulton, S. Smith, and W. H. Allen, of Livermore Falls; Charles Knapp, and L. Morrison of East Livermore; A. F. Russell, C. W. Hutchinson, and George Monroe, of Livermore; E. H. Record, C. L. Macomber, M. L. Thompson, C. R. Thompson, and D. M. Allen of Jay; F. D. Grover, and E. W. Gould, of Beans's Corner; W. B. Crane, E. E. and C. K. Gile, of Fayette; W. B. Frost of Wayne; and A. L. French of South Chesterville. .

Poultry exhibitors were Carroll Oakes and Roy Dean of

Livermore Falls; E. J. Paige of East Livermore; H. F. Jones and M. A. Hubbard of Fayette; C. P. Swift and W. B. Frost of Wayne; while owners of prize swine were J. H. True, Fayette; F. D. Grover, Bean's Corner; E. Pettingill and Phillip Ham, of Livermore Falls.

Commenting on the Fair that year, *The Express and Advertiser* had this to say -

"A large crowd to whom the Merry-go-round was a new feature hovered around and disposed of their nickles with a speed that was astonishing. -

"The entries of stock this year compare favorably with any preceeding year. Most of the stalls are full.

"A noticeable improvement is the removal of the cattle sheds to the south end of the track. Another improvement is the addition built onto the exhibition hall for the poultry exhibits.

"In former years the water supply has not satisfied the demand, but this -year four wells have been driven, and visitors cannot reasonably complain of thirst.

"In the afternoon, two scraps of excitement broke the monotony. One of the venders of beer threatened to turn two young men upside down and telescope them because they didn't pay for their beer. A great deal of amusement arose out of the case. On every corner and at every turn were people arguing the silver question. The Association was well pleased with the day's returns."

The second bridge across the Androscoggin at Livermore Falls, opened to traffic in 1872, as a toll bridge, and made free in 1887, was a covered bridge; so snow had to be hauled into it in winter, to make it passable for sleighs. It suffered the same fate as its predecessor, for in the flood of 1896, it, too, was carried away.

It was immediately replaced by construction, in the following year, of a third bridge. No chances were taken on this one of repeating the disasters which occurred with the first two for

Union Street c. 1870
The house to the right of the Universalist Church (then having a spire) was
occupied by the White family.

this was a steel suspension bridge, placed high above the river's normal level, and leaping the full distance from bank to bank, three hundred and twenty feet, in one span. For many years the town took no little pride in "the longest one-span bridge in New England."

A weekly newspaper was started at the Falls about 1857, by John Morrill, and called *The Livermore Falls Gazette.* It was published for a time, then stopped for lack of support.

R. A. Carver began publication of the *Livermore Falls News* in 1881, and was followed by John M. S. Hunter, of Farmington, who undertook the publishing of *The Local Press* in October 1889, with E. I. Beck as Editor. Mr. Beck took over ownership April 10, 1891, at which time the paper was known as *The Livermore Falls Express and Advertiser.*

During this time the offices of the paper were located, first, above Walker's store on the west side of Main Street; second, on the second floor of the Merriman Block; third, on the second floor of the Lamb Block, on the north side of Depot Street; and fourth, on the second floor of the bank building.

Another business started in this period, and flourishing well into the next century, was the cigar manufacturing shop of Herbert L. Hersey, begun by him in 1888; and for that reason his best known brand was called "The '88 Cigar." For many years the first experiments of local boys with the weed of this form was via the '88 - and usually with disastrous results. Mr. Hersey had from four to six employees in his shop. Another of his well-known brands was the Norlands cigar - taking its name, of course, from the home of the famous Washburn family in Livermore.

The Portland and Rumford Falls Railway, which operated trains from Rumford Junction in Auburn, through Mechanic Falls, Buckfield, and Canton to Rumford Falls, constructed a branch line from Canton to Chisholm, in 1897, which was extended to Livermore Falls in 1899. Again quoting from the letters of Archie P. Richmond to the *Livermore Falls Adoertiser,*

"In the issue of the *Adoertiser* dated March 18 (1954). I was much pleased to see the picture of the locomotive, as it took my memory back. - I remember when the P. & R. Railroad came through, for I saw the first steam shovel at work just north of Bridge Street. It was operated by steam, and as they moved ahead, they had to lay a track for it to move on. This was about 1897. Then a brick depot was built on the site where the old Toll House stood. Now the picture of the engine looks much like the one that used to pull in to the station at Livermore Falls about 4:00 p.m. The engineer's name was Foster and the conductor was a Mr. Dudley.

"Now I will tell you of a sad thing that happened one night. A boy by the name of Bug Green jumped onto the track and tried to beat the train to the crossing; but he fell down, was run over and killed."

The rapid increase in employment, which Mr. Record's and Mr. Chisholm's ventures were bringing to the town, caused a shortage of labor. The Yankee farmers, rugged individualists that they were, were loath to leave the independence of self-employment, and submit to the discipline of regular hours and orders from a boss. However, the pulp and paper industry was a natural outlet for the energies and skills of this continent's oldest and most proficient body of woodsmen - the French Canadians of neighboring Quebec, who were not slow to take advantage of the opportunity.

It was Mr. Chisholm's development at the Otis Falls, just over the town line in Jay, which really brought the influx from Quebec; and consequently they tended to settle around that locality, which soon became known as "Chisholm," from the name of the founder. These newcomers, at first, spoke very little English; they naturally kept together in a French speaking community, pretty much apart from the natives who looked with some suspicion on these "foreigners who didn't know enough to speak English." The Ste. Rose de Lima Catholic Church was established to serve these people; and they formed their own French speaking parochial school. There were stores started and operated by French Canadians -

notably the L'Heureux-Poisson Company, Napoleon L'Heureux and Arthur Poisson, proprietors, and Deshaies Market, A. J. Deshaies, proprietor; Cloutier's, Fournier's and other business establishments; a French physician, Dr. Thomas Croteau; a French lawyer, J. Z. Blouin; so that Chisholm was, in effect, a town within a town.

As time has gone on, this separatism has gradually disappeared; through attendance at the same schools, inter-marriage, and movement out of Chisholm into other sections of Livermore and Jay, the fourth and fifth generations of French ancestry are pretty much assimilated.

It should be recognized that these people brought much of value to the culture of this community. In the first place, they were deeply religious, and, therefore, law-abiding citizens; they were, almost without exception, hard-working and very thrifty, with an urge to own their own homes; their natural love of music has made them prominent in that field; and so many of them are thus talented that they have tended to dominate local bands, orchestras and choral groups.

With the advent of Edwin Riley, from Fort Edward, New York, there also came with him, or followed him here, many citizens of Irish extraction who had been trained and experienced in the pulp and paper manufacture. The population of this area, which had been almost wholly Yankee-English, began to assume a far more cosmopolitan character with the Berube, Deshaies, L'Heureux, Groleau, Pomerleau, and other French names, mingling with the Shannahan, Daly, Boyle, Kelly, Hennessey, and other names of Sons of Erin.

The increasing industrialization was bringing with it increasing problems in the handling of currency. Each new mill, of course, involved additional payrolls; and new building created growing demands for mortgage loans. Alvin Record had for some time accepted money from individuals for safekeeping; and had even negotiated loans for some of them who requested it. By 1890, he realized this service was getting too large for him to handle, along with his own affairs. John F. Lamb had for some years acted as agent for a Lewiston bank, and some banking was done by mail, with Lewiston and

Portland institutions. However, none of these methods were very safe or very convenient. Accordingly, Mr. Record, with a dozen of the most prominent businessmen in town arranged to raise $50,000.00 of capital among themselves, and to start a local banking institution.

A local young man, Chester H. Sturtevant, who had then recently graduated from Colby College and was studying law in the office of Herbert C. Whittemore, was engaged to organize and manage the new bank. In order to learn the business and fit himself for that position, he went to work for the Old Portland Trust Company in 1894.

The Maine Legislature, by special act on March 25, 1895, granted a charter to "Livermore Falls Trust & Banking Company." The formal meeting of organization was held on July 27, 1895, at which the first officers elected were: Alvin Record, president; Silas H. Niles, vice president; Joseph G. Ham, secretary; and Chester H. Sturtevant, treasurer. Mr. Sturtevant returned from Portland to do the work of organization; and the bank opened to public business on January 2, 1896. The first directors of the new institution were:

3. ALVIN RECORD, the town's then leading citizen;
4. SILAS H. NILES, proprietor of a large general store at North Jay;
5. JOSEPH G. HAM, proprietor of a drug store and insurance agent;
6. CHARLES R. LORING, manager of the Umbagog Paper Company;
7. JOHN F. LAMB, hardware dealer, and Sheriff of Androscoggin County;
6. W. W. HALL, prosperous farmer and cattle dealer;
7. EDWIN RILEY, manager of Otis Falls Pulp Company;
8. HERBERT C. WHITTEMORE, attorney and owner of a large amount of real estate;
9. HENRY D. PARKER, one of the most prosperous and successful farmers.

The west side of Main Street looking South c. 1880

From right: Ham's Apothecary; D. C. Thompson's clock shop; C. Pettingill's general store; H. Walker's shoe store; the "Noyes" block, containing S. Perkins grocery store and his wife's millinery store; Burbank's clothing store; Alvin Record's Leatherboard Mill; R. C. Boothby's grist mill.

An alley on the east side of Main (facing Water Street), 1898

Between the Rockomeka Hotel and Judge Knapp's house; Ham's Apothecary on left across Main, and Sharaf Bros. Dry Goods on the right.

The village of Livermore Falls was experiencing the problems which quite generally accompany the establishment of new centers of population - notably the questions of adequate, pure water, and of sanitary sewage disposal. The Board of Health of the Town of East Livermore (Members, C. W. Brown; C. E. Knight, M.D., Health Officer; Henry Reynolds M.D., Chairman) was concerned with these needs, as witness their report to the State Board of Health in 1887:

"Some portions of the town which are supplied with wells have water of poor quality on account of the quality of the drainage, Several nuisances have been reported to us, and all but one or two have been disposed of. In one case where the sewer drainage goes into the street there seems to be no other way of disposing of it without carrying it across other men's property, which they will not permit.

"There have been seven cases of typhoid fever, two of scarlet fever, and several of diphtheria, but no deaths from these diseases. Some of the cases of typhoid fever seemed to be due to impure water. In one family there were three or four cases of typhoid fever in which the sink drainage had polluted the well.

"We need a system of sewerage in the village."

Apparently the Town Fathers decided to tackle the other end of the problem first, and provide the village with a supply of pure water.

Attorney John Maxwell and others obtained from the State Legislature of 1897 a Charter of Livermore Falls Water Company, to lay and maintain a system of water works to supply Livermore Falls and vicinity. Then there was inserted an article in the Warrant for the Town Meeting in March, 1897, to see if the Town would vote to take over the rights and duties of the Water Company.

Some of the adverse reaction to the proposal is evident in this quotation from the *Livermore Falls Express and Advertiser* of February 25, 1897:

"There has been an Article inserted in the Town Warrant to this effect:

"To see if the Town will vote to buy the rights and interests of John H. Maxwell and others, under a Charter granted to them by our recent Legislature, to lay and maintain a system of Water Works, by which to supply the Village of Livermore Falls and vicinity with water, at a price to the fixed by a Referee, to be named by one of the Judges of the Supreme Court of the State, or take any action relative thereto.'

"This means that the Town of East Livermore is to construct a system of Water Works for Livermore Falls village, Chisholm's Mills and Jay Bridge on its own account.

... "Now let us look at the facts in the case, and let us examine them in a fair and candid manner. The water will have to come either from the ponds at North Livermore or Moose Hill. Moose Hill pond is fed by springs, has a sandy bottom" and water can be brought cheaper from that pond than from North Livermore. Therefore, let us see what it will cost, and the following is a close estimate.

Cost of excavating and laying pipe, 2 1/4: miles @ $10,000	$22,250.00
Cost of pumping station	6,000.00
Cost of stand pipe	6,000.00
Excavating and laying pipes in Livermore Falls and Chisholm's Mills	24,000.00
Total	$58,250.00

"But that is not all, Jay Bridge will also demand water, and if Jay votes for you to put the water in at Jay Bridge, you will have to do it. Also they have asked this spring for a new school house at Livermore Falls; and sooner or later the town will have to build one, - and this would be the situation that the Town would find itself,

Cost of waterworks at Livermore Falls and Chisholm's Mills	$58,250.00
Cost - to and through the streets of jay Bridge	32,000.00
Present Town Debt	9,000.00
Cost of new Schoolhouse	12,000.00
Total	$111,250.00

"The town would assume a debt which the tax-payers and their grandchildren would never see the end of. The tax rate would be so high that no industry could afford to stay within our limits."

There was evidently much opposition to the project, and so much unfavorable criticism and dire predictions regarding it that the Town refused to take over; so the private company, of which John H. Maxwell was Treasurer and General Manager, went ahead with the construction. Much to the surprise of the opposition, the water was turned on in November, 1899.

The Livermore Falls Light & Power Company was organized by Edwin Riley, the before mentioned Superintendent of the Otis Division of International Paper Company, and by attorney John H. Maxwell, who was also instrumental in forming the Livermore Falls Water Company. It was incorporated in 1899, with Edwin Riley as president, John H. Maxwell as secretary and treasurer, and Waldo Pettingill as auditor. At the same time the Newlands Company, with the same officers, was formed to hold and to deal in real estate, particularly real estate for industrial use.

The Light & Power Company obtained its power from the generators of International Paper Company at its Livermore Mill.

Three commercial establishments, whose owners were destined to play a large part in the Town's development over the next half-century, date from this period. W. A. Stuart Company operated a hardware, plumbing and heating business, established originally by John F. Lamb, about 1881. In 1887,

Rockemeka Hotel in the 1880s

The South side of Depot Street, 1870s
Here looking West to the Noyes Block, on Main Street.

William A. Stuart became connected with the business, and it continued under the name of W. A. Stuart Company.

Moore's Market was operated by Chester W. Moore, who had previously been in business with Arthur W. Nelke in the

Noyes block on Main Street. Mr. Moore bought out his partner's interest in 1897, and moved to the Lamb block of Depot Street, where he started business under the name of Moore's Market.

The Livermore Falls Clothing Company was incorporated in 1897, with S. P. Judkins as president, R. M. Goodwin as vice-president, and Z. A. Mersereau as secretary and treasurer.

Mr. Chisholm's Otis Falls Company' at first was primarily a pulp mill, though in the manufacture of paper from the pulp a beginning was made, and a small, one machine, newsprint mill was the first installation, to which was added, in 1892, a second machine. Mr. Chisholm secured the services of Mr. Edwin Riley of Fort Edward, New York, as Manager; and with his arrival, three more, making a total of eight machines - at the time, one of the largest plants of its kind in North America.

Meanwhile the Jay Paper Company was beset by ill fortune from the start. Two disastrous fires, plus the problems arising from an over-ambitious expansion program, forced them to sell out to the Otis Company, which also absorbed the Umbagog Company, so that all the pulp and paper mills of this community came under the control of Mr. Chisholm in 1896. To provide ample pulp for the eight machines at Otis, and strengthen its position in 1897, a new pulp mill was erected at Riley (named for the Manager, who had already distinguished himself.)

Chisholm was now ready to make the first moves in realizing his great ambition, the "transition from the traditional papermaking of the early newsprint mills to the modern era." It was in 1898 that Mr. Chisholm and two associates, A. N. Burbank and W. A. Russell, brought together some twenty independent owners of small properties similar to the Otis in New England and New York, and International Paper Company was born of which Mr. Chisholm became president in less than a year, and continued in that office until 1907, when he resigned to become Chairman of the Board. Observers of the industry have commented that the advent of International Paper Company marked the beginning of the modern pulp and paper industry in management and

Depot Street looking East from Main in the 1880s
Demolition on the left is making way for the three story brick Lamb block (still
on the lot, as part of the Shoppers Mall, today).

Depot Street in 1887
After completion of the Lamb block. (on left).

organization as clearly as the first sulphite woodpulp is said to
have marked its modern phase technologically.

When the Jay Paper Company was forced to sell out, and
Alvin Record to dispose of his mill properties, Judson A.

Record, his son, who had been Assistant Superintendent of the Jay company, was thrown out of a job, and on his own resources. The following year, 1897, he leased the mill, formerly owned by his father, and operated it very profitably.

However, in 1898, seeing an opportunity to buy the foundry business of J. F. Allen, he acquired ownership of it; and began the development and expansion that eventually became "Record Foundry & Machine Company." This beginning venture was located, as were most local industries, in the area just below "Mill Hill." Progress was violently interrupted by the fire of September 1898, which wiped out everything below "Mill Hill," including Record's foundry.

Judson Record, thereupon, established his foundry operations in a new location on upper Main Street, where now is situated the Chisholm Fruit Company office and warehouse. The new foundry and machine shop continued at the Main Street location for about five years, when it moved to its present location at Shy.

The worst fire disaster that had thus far befallen the village of Livermore Falls struck on September 10, 1898, and destroyed all the buildings below Mill Hill, as well as everything on the south side of Depot Street, from the Riverside Hotel to Main Street. The following description of the conflagation is quoted from the *Advertiser* of September 15, 1898:

> "The first alarm was sounded about 10:00 o'clock Saturday forenoon, at which time fire was discovered in the large saw mill, the property of International Paper Company, caused, presumably, by a hot box. Like all mills of this description, quantites of fine dust and sawdust were all through the building and the flames spread with lightning like rapidity, and in a very few minutes the entire building was a mass of roaring flames.
>
> "The fire department was quickly on the spot, but were considerably delayed in getting streams from the steamer onto the fire, as the engine had been away for

repairs and had but the day before been returned; and some little remaining work was being done on it after its arrival. - The flames had gained great headway, and soon the big leatherboard mill on Main Street, property of International Paper Company was burning. - Favored by the wind, the remaining business and resident portion of Main Street was saved.

"The hose from the Umbagog Pulp Mill, laid across the river on the dam, did excellent service, and played a prominent part in the fight to save surrounding buildings. The mills, shops, storehouses, sheds, etc., everything in fact below Goding's block were burned to the ground.

"The burning of the leatherboard mill was followed shortly by the burning of the pulp mill; and, close onto this, the grist mill operated by George Chandler, the last two named buildings also the property of International Paper Company.

"The flames with great rapidity crossed Main Street; and soon the laundry building, occupied by Alden & Reynolds, and owned by E. S. Johnson, Farmington, was in flames. The wind blew strong from the northwest at this hour, and one by one the buildings, both up and down the street, caught and burned fiercely. Next below the laundry was the home and greenhouse of George H. Fuller, which were consumed. Just below Fuller's came the White dwelling; next the home of Mrs. Charles Berry; and next in order down the street were the J. A. Record foundry; A. Allen's machine shop; C. P. Brown's blacksmith shop; F. A. Millett's machine shop, and numerous other buildings in the rear of these, occupied as carriage, repair, paint shops, store sheds, etc., - all burned to the ground. The large dwelling in back of the White dwelling was here consumed.

"Before the laundry building was consumed, the store next in line, and on the corner of Depot and

Riverside House , 1880s
Located on the South side of Depot Street; later became Riverside Hotel.

The Riverside Hotel, about 1910
Here looking very much as it did in 1967, when it was demolished.

Main Streets, caught fire, and was shortly followed by the store of W. G. Love and store of Keep & Bartlett. The corner building was occupied by Sharaf Brothers, dry goods, millinery and fancy goods; the second, a shoe store, and next, a grocery store. These three stores were owned by John F. Lamb, of Lewiston.

"Prior to this, the steamer, located south of the grist mill, was obliged to leave its position; and a stand farther down was made, between the building formerly occupied by Fred S. Richmond and the large planing mill occupied by Fred Raymond & Company, - both owned by the International Paper Company.

"All this time, as the fire was spreading along the south side of Depot Street, the remaining buildings on both sides of Main Street, below the Mill Hill, were burning fiercely, and the steamer was doing hard work and the department making a desperate fight with the odds so strongly against them, as the fire had spread over so large area. It was at this point (the Richmond building and the planing mill both ablaze) that fire had so completely surrounded the steamer and worked up under the platform on which the engine stood (that) to save the engine was the immediate action of the brave fellows who were running her; but such were the odds so quickly against them that this could not be done; and, after repeated attempts they were, to save their lives, obliged to creep any way they could, some crawling on their hands and knees for only by keeping their faces low to the ground could they breathe in the suffocating and terrible volumes of dense black smoke, one of the department crawling into the river to make his escape.

"During all this time the hand tub, manned by a resolute crew, was playing on the buildings above the hill; and it is to their heroic efforts as they kept water on the building known as the Alvin Record office, just south of Goding's block on Main Street, that the fire did not gain further headway in this direction; and favored by the wind, the remaining business and resident portion of Main Street was saved.

"At the same time, the flames were gaining terrific headway along the row of Wooden buildings on Depot Street. Next beyond the store of Keep & Bartlett comes the stores owned by W. S. Treat, the first occupied by D. A. & J. P. Alden, millinery, and residence on the second floor; and the next, a three story block, occupied on the first floor by the owner, Mr. Treat, dry and fancy goods, boots and shoes, groceries, etc., the second floor by Edd Barney as a residence, and the third floor by the Knights of Columbus as a lodge hall. These buildings burned quickly. The building owned and occupied by C. Newman as hairdressing rooms, and second floor as residence by Mr. Gifford, was the next to fall before the devouring flames.

"Next came the house and stable owned by John W. Hyde, the house occupied by C. W. Elliott and family. Here dynamite was used in attempt to blow up these buildings. The flames swept across the opening to three stores owned by F. L. Jewell, the first occupied by H. L. Hersey, cigar dealer and manufacturer, the next by E. N. Bacheller, harness store, and the other by A. J. Dain, furniture. These, like others before them, fell victims to the flames.

"Next on this side of the street was the dwelling house and stable owned by George Whittier. Here a second attempt at staying the flames was made by blowing up these buildings. The store next east, also burned, was owned by Mr. Whittier, and occupied by Miss H. Hudson, millinery and fancy goods.

"The Riverside Hotel, owned by F. A. Baker, came next. Here the fire was placed under control by the work of the Lewiston Department, which at just this time, in company with a steamer from Auburn, arrived by special train. The Lewiston steamer was placed on the river bank back of Goding's block, Main Street, and a line of hose run to the burning hotel. The Riverside stable was consumed and the house badly damaged, but the fire was stopped at this point. From the hotel wreck through to Main Street, it was a clean fire, - not a thing left standing but several tall chimneys.

"We will now take a look across onto the north side of Depot Street, where during all this time a hard and heroic fight had been going on to save the buildings, which includes numerous stores, the post office, K. of P., the Odd Fellows hall, and dwellings.

"On the corner, next of Main Street, the fight commenced. First, the dwelling owned by John F. Lamb and occupied by Mrs. M. A. Latham. This building sits in from Depot Street somewhat, and it was not so hard a fight to save it as the other buildings along that side of the street. Next in order comes the post office building, in which is also located the store of E. Edgecomb, jeweler, fruits, etc.; and the next the large brick block in which are the large stores of W. A. Stuart & Company, hardware, and the Livermore Falls Clothing Company. On the second floor, J. H. Maxwell's law office, office of Deputy Sheriff, A. F. Dwelley, store room and tin shop of W. A. Stuart & Company, and Mrs. Roux, dressmaking. On the third floor the home of Port Royal Lodge K. of P. This block and the post office building are both owned by John F. Lamb. The brick block was saved by covering the windows with long strips of zinc, and much of the front with blankets, carpeting, etc., also a force of men covered the roof. The next building, the Odd Fellow block, was saved after a hard tussle and bad scorching. The first floor was occupied by S. S. Locklin, druggist, and George H. Jacobs, clothing. The second floor by Dr. Edmond Eaton, dental rooms, and G. A. R. Hall; top floor, Odd Fellows Hall.

"The dwelling of Mrs. Robinson and Fred E. Goding come next, and these were badly scorched and the windows all smashed in, but hard work saved these houses from burning. An open space comes next, then the Hilton block, which was beyond the limits of the burned district and was not injured.

"This completes the list of buildings on the upper, or north, side of Depot Street, and extremely fortunate it is that these did not go with the others; but the efforts of the people and a favorable wind saved them."

One cannot but wonder how those new hats of Atlantic Steam Fire Company, "which are very pretty, indeed," looked as the owners came crawling out of the river, after the destruction of the steamer of which they were once so proud.

Within less than a year, on June 21st, 1899, came a second bad fire, which completed the destruction of the Town's main business section which the first fire had begun nine months before. Starting on the west side of Main Street, in a barn near the Maine Central Railroad tracks, about midnight, the fire swept rapidly down the street devouring everything in its path. Once more the local fire department responded with valiant efforts, but were completely unable to stop the conflagration which had gained such momentum. Morning dawned on a scene of utter desolation. The ashes were hardly cold from the destruction of everything on the south of Depot Street, when, in this latest misfortune, everything on the west of Main Street, and south of the little wooden bank building, was swept clean to the river, leaving only smoking ashes, tumbled brick, and the little wooden bank as a pathetic survivor.

It was a discouraging outlook; and yet, at the same time, a golden opportunity to replace all at once a village of flimsy wooden stores and factories, with new, larger and more substantial masonry structures. The *Lewiston Journal* commented, in 1899, "As one passes through Livermore Falls, he is impressed by the fine, new blocks going up to replace the old ones that were destroyed by fire. Noticeable is the large five-story building on Main Street, called the Sharaf Block, which will contain the Bank, Post Office, Opera House, Court Room, and large

The fire of 1898
It destroyed the south side of Depot Street from Main Street to the Riverside House and from the Noyes block on Main Street South to the Androscoggin.

Depot Street after the 1898 fire
South side of street yet to be rebuilt; the new one story brick Lamb block (now part of the Shoppers Mall) was completed in 1898; the snowy winter streets were rolled (rather than plowed) to accommodate the sleighs.

stores."

The *Town Register* for 1903 also noted, "These two fires were very disastrous to the place - yet the village has apparently recovered from the loss and, with the new blocks she has built, looks far better than of old."

Luckily the Merriman Block, a new, three story brick block, built by John Merriman and just completed in 1898, was above the railroad tracks, and not within the fire zone. It was a ninety by sixty-seven foot structure, and cost $18,000.00 to build. The ground floor contained four stores - Israelson & Marx, C. S. Wright (2 stores) and Joseph Caproni; the second floor was occupied one-half by the *Advertiser,* and one-half by offices; while the third floor housed the Masonic bodies.

John F. Lamb, who had been associated with William A. Stuart in the hardware and plumbing business, retained ownership of the three-story brick block on the north side of Depot Street, when he and Mr. Stuart parted company. Mr. Lamb also owned the dwelling at the north corner of Depot and Main Streets. After the fire of 1898, Mr. Lamb constructed the one-story brick block at this corner location, affording eight store locations.

John Lamb had been one of the town's most active and prominent citizens; but, in 1888, he was elected Sheriff of Androscoggin County, and moved to Auburn, Maine. Through real estate holdings and personal relations, he continued to maintain, however, an active interest in town affairs up to the time of his death.

The Spanish-American War seemed to affect the towns very little. James E. Davis, in later years a local lumber operator; Winfield Nichols, a well-known farmer in East Livermore; Charles Russell, Leon Russell, A. C. Gilbert, William Murch, and Othello Tuttle, all of Livermore Falls, were among those who served in the armed forces. Charles Russell wrote home from the Philippines some interesting accounts of his experiences in the Army there with Co. "B," 43rd Infantry Volunteers, which impress one as being not greatly different from our current experiences in Vietnam. The following quotation is from one of his letters written on Jaro Leyte Island,

November 1, 1900:

"I am with Company "B," 43rd Infantry Vols., and this is the company that has so many Maine boys in it; and they are scrappers and no mistake about it. The Insurgents have a dread of Company B, and won't stand and fight them, but run. This company has had more fighting and has killed more negroes (natives) than any one company in this regiment.

"Since I was here last time they have captured a stronghold. It was on the side of a mountain and the pathway up very steep, and all along the sides were pits in which were concealed men who jumped out and tried to cut down our men, but they were too sharp to be caught that way. For half an hour our men fought, and then charged the trenches, driving all before them. They killed eighty-four and wounded one hundred more, and captured a large lot of rifles, bolos, rice, stores, medicines, and $8,000 Mexican. A couple of days after, 1300 people came into Carigara and surrendered, - men, women, and children."

Frank T. Jackson, son of Rev. A. W. and Caroline Bigelow Jackson of Livermore, was a student at Harvard and organist at the First Unitarian Church in Cambridge. When the war broke out, he left as First Sergeant, Company "I," 6th Massachusetts Inf. Vols. He was sent to the hospital in Siboney, with an attack of mumps; and his regiment went on without him. When he recovered he asked permission to join the 9th regiment Massachusetts Inf., then leaving for the front, which request was granted. His account continues:

"I was in the trenches before Santiago two days and two nights, and I can assure you it was terrible. It rained a good deal through the nights, making the trenches very muddy. Rather an uncomfortable bed. Then in the daytime the sun was hot, the mercury ranging from 120 to 135 in the shade. The fire from

240

the sharp shooters was pretty sharp which made the men lie very close to the bottom of the trenches. With no breeze, and the hot sun pouring in upon their heads, backs and necks many of the men were overpowered. The stench from the dead mules and horses, was at times very offensive. Food and water were scarce. I lived on three crackers and a small piece of raw bacon a day. Of course I saw many men wounded and a number killed. The first few days, you see, makes you feel sick, but after a little you look with indifference upon such things. My next right hand man who was lying close beside me, was struck in the head, by a piece of shell and his head was smashed in - a casualty which was hardly noticed by the rest of the men.

"The second afternoon I was in the trenches, I was overcome by the heat, and was carried back to Siboney in an ambulance, about twelve miles. Before I recovered, I began to show signs of yellow fever. I had yellow fever in a mild form, but was unconscious some of the time. I got better rapidly, and was in Santiago just after the surrender.

"Malarial fever claimed me from that time on, dragging me down. It attacked me persistently, and do my best I could not overcome it. Malarial fever patients keep growing weaker and weaker until they finally die of exhaustion.

"The medical and Commissary department in Siboney, and everywhere on the island was very poor. Men would get sick, and then, as they had no food which a weakened stomach could digest, it was impossible to build up strength. - The transport *Santiago* finally took us off and brought us to Tampa. The voyage was one of the hardest of my experiences. There was no food except hard tack and canned beef - no medicines, no doctors, no ice and the water was nauseating."

Livermore Falls Trust and Banking Company , 1895
It was first located in this frame building on the West side of Maine Street, next
to the railway tracks - its first Treasurer (and organizer), Chester H. Sturtevant,
stands in the doorway.

The *Lewiston Journal,* at that time, reported that Mr. Jackson was at the Bigelow homestead in Livermore Center, trying to recover his health; and that "Mr. Jackson's physician has prescribed Maine air in liberal doses for him, and Mr. Jackson is taking the medicine with good results."

Frank Jackson's experiences seem to be fairly typical of the hardships borne by those who did participate in the Spanish-American War. Their worst enemies were not the Spanish, but yellow fever, malaria, and other tropical diseases, abetted by lack of food and clean water, plus inadequate medical care.

In any event, the war seemed so remote, so one-sided and quickly over, and involved so relatively few battle casualties, that it did not appear to touch the lives of Livermore's citizens as had the conflicts of 1775 and 1861.

It would almost seem that the concentration of events taking place between 1895 and 1899 was a deliberate preparation for the Twentieth Century. The destruction by flood of the old, wooden, covered bridge and its replacement by a modern steel suspension bridge; the two conflagrations which, together, swept away all of the business section as it existed before, to be succeeded by larger, substantial masonry structures; the establishment of a bank; the introduction of electric light and power; the building of a municipal water supply system; all took place in that five year period. Combined with Mr. Chisholm's organization of International Paper Company, and the large expansion of the local mills already underway, they insured that the new century would find Livermore Falls as much different from the village of ten years earlier as the latter was from that of 1800.

Along with the physical changes, a new generation of young, ambitious and able men were emerging as the new leaders, most prominent of whom, at this point, were Edwin Riley, John Maxwell, Chester Sturtevant and Judson Record. John Maxwell was treasurer and general manager of Livermore Falls Light & Power Company, treasurer and general manager of the Newlands Company, treasurer and general manager of the Livermore Falls Water Company; Chester Sturtevant, in addition to his position as treasurer and general manager of

Livermore Falls Trust & Banking Company, was treasurer of Richmond Manufacturing Company, secretary and treasurer of Record Foundry & Machine Company, and through the bank, was involved in other local enterprises; Judson Record had been engaged in the manufacture of pulp, but had gone into the foundry and machine shop which he was fast expanding into a large and profitable company; Edwin Riley was most prominent of the four; besides his position as Superintendent of International Paper Company's Otis Division, he was President of Livermore Falls Light & Power Company, Newlands Company, Livermore Falls Water Company, Richmond Manufacturing Company, Record Foundry & Machine Company, and Vicepresident of Livermore Falls Trust & Banking Company.

Alvin Record had died; Hugh Chisholm was occupied in the larger, national affairs of International Paper Company. A handful of the older leaders would continue active for a few years yet - notably, J. F. Jefferds, postmaster, Fred Richmond in the wood-turning business, Joseph G. Ham, druggist, George Chandler in the grist mill, W. A. Stuart in the hardware trade, Judge R. C. Boothby, and Sharaf Brothers in millinery and dry goods. The leadership had actually already passed to the younger generation as noted. Livermore Falls, in 1900, would present to the world not only a brand new "face"; but new faces, as directors of its destiny.

Chester Sturtevant, Treasurer of Livermore Falls Trust and Banking Co.
with his only employee, Charlotte (Lottie) Ham.

An office romance
Banker Chet paid 'compound interest' to Lottie, resulting in their 1898 marriage that
produced two sons who followed them in the profession.

CHAPTER V
LIVERMORE ~ LIVERMORE FALLS
THE TWENTIETH CENTURY

THE FIRST DECADE AND A HALF of the twentieth century seem like the "Golden Years," when Joseph Caproni had the fruit and confectionery store, at the junction of Main, Union and Church streets where the peanut roaster whistled its cheerful tune at the door; and inside, in the summer, the two huge fan-like helicopter blades, rotated slowly and almost silently, and the air was filled with delicious aromas of fruit, syrups and candy. Many of the hardest decisions of life were made there, whether to spend the hard-earned nickel for "Cherry Phosphate," ice cream, or a nose-tingling soda.

In the hot, lazy days of summer, the huge "sprinkler," drawn by two beautiful, gray work-horses, would make its rounds of the principal streets, in a rather fruitless gesture of laying the dust; but a delightful shower bath for the youngsters who followed on behind. Pursued just as regularly was the ice wagon of "Ed" French, which afforded the chips of ice so eagerly sought, whenever Ted Mosher, the ice-man, chopped off a chunk for a customer.

Those were the days when the swimming-hole at "Clay Bottom" was frequented almost daily (no one owned or even thought of a bathing suit); and when Red Water Brook, Hutchinsons Brook, and all the other streams, offered a boy more than an even chance for a good mess of trout.

In winter, the sprinkler was succeeded by the "Roller" an even larger vehicle of drum shape, hauled by teams of horses, which, instead. of plowing, packed the snow solidly in the streets to make good sleighing. Instead of Ed French's ice wagon, it was his two-horse wood sleds which attracted youthful patronage, for a boy, by taking a turn of his sled rope around an upright and riding the wood-sled's runner, could be transported to the top of "Butter-factory Hill" or the summit of upper Church Street as easily as he rides a ski-lift today. It was a thrilling ride on a "Double-runner" from the top of Butterfactory Hill or from Leon Dow's, on upper Church Street; and with a good start, on a hard packed surface, one could roar right through the Town, clear down to the lower mill. The only traffic hazards were occasional teams (largely disregarded).

Nor were winter sports limited to the youngsters only, As Lincoln Hatch recalls, in the April 3, 1952, issue of the *Advertiser:*

"When the sleighing (they used to call it good footing) was good on Main and Depot Streets, they used to race horses from the corner of Richardson Avenue and Main Street to the old railroad station (on Depot Street). John Hyde owned a black mare that he called Molly. He used to come in ahead most of the time."

It may only be that one's childhood years are always the "Golden Years"; but in this case there was more involved, since life was so different in the years before World War I, from what it has become since.

The great world beyond this continent was then very far away, and of little concern to us. It might be interesting to read or to hear about events in Europe or Asia in a detached way; but we did not actually feel any connection with them in our own lives. Like the Indians of Rockomeka before the coming of white men, we felt quite secure with the Atlantic on the east, the Pacific on the west, a friendly neighbor on the north, and only jungles, sparsely inhabited by illiterate and uncivilized natives on the south. It seemed beyond the realm of possibility that this country could ever be seriously threatened from out-side the United States; and we were, therefore, free to concen-trate our attention and our efforts to our own tight little world.

Even within the State of Maine, this community was far more isolated and self-sufficient then. Automobiles had not

West side of Main Street, about 1895
All of the buildings in view were destroyed in the fires of 1898 and 1899.

West side of Main Street, 1900
Here pictured during the reconstruction that followed the fire of 1899.

yet appeared in any great number, we were still in the "horse and buggy" days, and a trip by train to Portland or Boston was a real event; even Lewiston was a distant city, 30 miles away. Consequently, virtually all shopping was done in the local stores; and social life was limited mostly to the local communities, centering around the various churches and the fraternal orders. Since radio and television were yet unknown, all entertainment was of the "home-grown" variety, except for an occasional traveling Stock Company.

As a result of this limitation and semi-isolation, the community was far more closely knit than it is today, and everyone knew everyone else - sometimes too well. Again quoting from the letter of Lincoln Hatch,

> "I have let my mind drift back to the days just prior to the influx of automobiles, and some of the social functions. 1 think that nearly everyone was more neighborly in those days. Almost every family had a vegetable garden, and there was quite a lot of rivalry in seeing who would have the first peas. George Dyke used to be one of the first ones to reach that goal. He was one of the first ones to have an auto; and he told me that he never saw anything that would make weeds grow as fast as an automobile did."

Bicycles had come into general use some ten or twelve years before. Archie Richmond wrote of them,

> "I'll tell you about the first bikes. Faun Coffin and Charles Sawyer bought one at the same time, and 1 tell you they were built to stay. The spokes were the size of a small pencil, steel rims, and red, hard rubber tires. The handle bars were two and a half feet wide. They rode them on the sidewalk; and when you met them you had to step to the street, for if they got into any loose dirt they could not ride them. They were strong enough to mount a cannon on."

Soon after the turn of the century, the first motorcycle appeared, and Archie continues,

> "George Allen had it. 1 can well remember it, for

he had to help pedal it up a grade. Later he sold it to Everett Putnam, who was working for Hayden Beckler. What a noise it made. The fuel he used smelled worse than Will Nason's swill wagon."

Politics evidently were taken much more seriously then than now; and were of absorbing interest to practically all the town's people, affording a source of common interest and entertainment as well. The following account, from the *Lewiston Journal*, of the celebration in connection with President McKinley's election is typical of the time:

"The torchlight procession and jollification at Livermore Falls Saturday night called out the largest crowd that has thronged the streets of the village for many a day, the crowd being estimated at from two to five thousand. At about 7:30 p.m. the procession formed at the lower end of Main Street, where 227 torches were distributed among them; and, headed by Chief Marshall Fred E. Riley and the Livermore Falls Band, they marched through all the principal streets.

"As they went up Main Street, one of the prettiest sights ever seen here was presented. The residences of the newly elected representatives, J. A. Rowell, A. C. Hutchinson, J. W. Dunham, E. S. Goding, Hon. R. C. Boothby and others were brilliantly illuminated, while the beauty of the scene was intensified by fire works of all descriptions. On upper Main the decorations were fine. Among the best were the residences of James Riley and Edwin Riley. In moving up the street, past the residence of the latter gentleman, the procession had to march under an arch beautifully illuminated with electric lights amid a shower of fire works.

"At Chisholm's Mills, many residences were illuminated. Other residences in town especially noticeable were those of George Tarr, Hon. J. F. Lamb, J. A. Record, J. F. Jefferds, S. W. Burbank, George O. Eustis, E. I. Beck, Hon. C. Knapp, Mrs. A. R. Millett, J. G. Ham, and others.

The 1899 Fire (Main Street, looking west toward the river)
It destroyed all of the west side of Main Street south of Livermore Falls Trust and Banking Company (far right).

The 1899 Fire (from the bank, looking south)
The new brick block in the center background (now occupied by Fournier's Hardware Store) was constructed in 1898, after the fire of that year.

"The grounds about Mr. Ham's home were beautifully lighted up by Japanese lanterns, while the windows were artistically decorated and illuminated. The *Express and Advertiser* office was resplendent with decorations and was brilliantly illuminated, while the stores about town with handsomely decorated and illuminated windows were those of George H. Jacobs & Co., Sharaf Brothers, S. S. Locklin, W. S. Treat, James Dain, H. F. Walker, A. S. Thompson, J. G. Ham, J. F. Jefferds, etc.

"At the residence of Hon. R. C. Boothby, above large pictures of McKinley and Hobart, stood Mr. Boothby's little daughter, Miss Elo; with one hand she was waving an American flag over the heads of MeKinley and Hobart, while in the other she held five $20 gold pieces.

"There came near being a serious accident at the residence of Mr. J. G. Ham. Just after the procession had passed, Mrs. Ham, who was alone, returned into the house and found that the drapery about the picture of McKinley and Hobart had caught fire from a wax candle. It was the American flag that was burning, and pulling it onto the floor, she attempted to stamp the blaze out with her feet, when the carpet and her dress caught fire."

In contrast to the foregoing was the grief of the town at Mckinley's death on September 14, 1901, at the hands of an assassin. The local *Advertiser* commented,

"From the heights of its jubilation, - the nation is plunged into the depths of grief. - Let us remember that God doeth all things well, and that the grave wins not the victory."

A local poet, J. P. Grenier, published a tribute to the martyred president, which reads in part;

"Out on the early morning air,
Softly tolled the church bells
In their mournful sounds ...
Over the village a gloom was cast,

Bells tolled and flags half mast."

Music Hall was draped in mourning, with Rags, Rowers and pictures of the dead President and the other two leaders of the nation who had previously suffered a similar fate, Lincoln and Garfield, and here was held an impressive memorial service. The mood of the town was not greatly different from what our own times have witnessed under similar national tragedies; but was, if anything, more strongly demonstrated.

In modernizing Livermore Falls for the Twentieth Century, there were two badly needed improvements which still remained unaccomplished. As noted, in the argument on the Water Company, a new school would have to be built; for the old, white, wooden structure was bursting at the seams; and, as the Board of Health reported to the State Board in 1887, a municipal sewage disposal system was a necessity.

At the annual Town Meeting in March, 1900, it was voted to build the new High School; and a committee consisting of Edwin Riley, Chairman, R. C. Boothby, Charles W. Hyde, John L. Cummings, Joseph G. Ham, Dr. C. W. Brown, and John Merriman, was appointed to undertake the project. The plans as drawn by Architect Walter R. Furbush, of Newton, Massachusetts, were accepted; and the contract let to Nathaniel Noyes & Son, of Augusta.

The Town had already purchased "a fine, large lot centrally located in the village between Baldwin and Church Streets." The plans called for a building 84' x 84', of brick and stone, two stories high, "surmounted by a handsome bell tower and flag staff"; and accommodating 360 students.

The building was completed in spring of 1901 at a cost of $20,000.00. When it was completed, it suddenly dawned on the committee that one item had been overlooked. They had "a handsome bell tower," but no provision had been made for a bell. Hugh J. Chisholm was contacted, and as a result the school bell is a gift from him.

Dedication ceremonies were held in June, 1901, at which the principal speaker was the State Superintendent, Hon. W. W. Stetson, who remarked in his address, "The plans for a more modern and up-to-date high school building are yet to be

West side of Main Street (before the 1899 fire)
From left: Thompson's store, Ham's Apothecary; Sharaf Bros. Dry Goods (burned out of their Depot Street location the previous year); Livermore Falls Trust and Banking Company.

West side of Main Street (after the 1899 fire)
About the same view as in the previous - from left: W. F. Hutchinson and Co., George Jacobs and Co., J. G. Ham's Apothecary; in the new Sharaf Block, the Post Office, Sharaf Bros., Livermore Falls Clothing Company; and Livermore Falls Trust and Banking Company.

254

drawn." Edwin Riley, chairman of the Building Committee, presented the keys to John H. Maxwell, Chairman of the School Board.

Five years later, in March 1906, the Town took steps to meet the second urgent necessity. A committee consisting of Edwin Riley, Chairman, George O. Eustis, J. A. Record, H. C. Whittemore and I. H. Webber was named to "look into laying of sewers in Livermore Falls."

Meanwhile, the Town had concluded to do what the Water Company had proposed ten years before, to take over operation of the water system, since it was a public service which ought to be publicly owned. For this purpose the Livermore Falls Water District was brought into being through an act of the Legislature in 1907. This district took over the property of Livermore Falls Water Company at a price of $117,496.48, which figure was set by three competent and disinterested persons. On January 3, 1908, the District began actual operation of the system.

The institution of the Livermore Falls Water District recalls an incident concerning the water supply related by the late Lincoln Hatch in his 1954 letter to the *Advertiser,*

"Before the present water system was installed at the Falls, the water came from wells and springs up in the higher ground, and the most of it came through lead pipes. A young doctor by the name of Smith came to the Falls and hung out his shingle. In a short time he began to diagnose some of his patients' illnesses as lead poisoning; and then many had the lead pipe on their pumps changed to galvanized iron pipe. Stuart Company had a rushing business for a while, changing pump pipes.

"Now back to Billy Bean (proprietor of the old Rockomeka Hotel). He was taken ill, and it proved to be his last illness. Dr. Smith was called, and he gave Billy the 'once over'; then went down to the kitchen for something, and saw the water coming through a lead pipe into the barrel that held the water to be used in the hotel. He rushed up to Billy's room, and said,

'Mr. Bean, I have diagnosed your illness as lead poisoning'.

"Billy asked, 'How did I get it?'

"The Doctor said, 'By drinking water that came through a lead pipe.'

"Billy said, 'I have not drank any water for over thirty years.'"

"I have not drank any water for over thirty years"

The committee, appointed in 1906, "To look into the laying of sewer in Livermore Falls," completed its investigation, surveys, and tentative plans about two years later. Complicating its problem was not only the fact that such a system would serve only a part of the town, but also should involve parts of two towns.

The district system seemed such a convenient and practical method of handling the water problem, that it was concluded to use a similar plan to provide an adequate and modern sewerage system. The Legislature was requested to grant the necessary charter, which was accepted by vote of the Town in 1909. John Merriman, Charles Gorden, and O. L. Hardy were elected as Trustees, charged with planning and construction of the sewer system.

To provide the necessary funds, bonds of the Sewer District were issued and sold in the amount of $25,000.00, bearing interest at 4%. Twenty-two thousand feet of sewer pipe were laid as a start, in sizes ranging from eight to twenty-four inches in diameter; and extension of the system was planned as growth of the village should require.

The water supply for the town came from Moose Hill pond, about four miles distant, and was brought into town by gravity through a twelve-inch main. When the Water District took over the plant, the residences in the higher levels of the town did not have the benefits of the water service, since there was insufficient pressure to send the water to them. Naturally, there was a demand that this lack be remedied. As a result, the Water District Trustees - Messrs. A. C. Hutchinson, George W. Treat, and Isaac B. Clary - undertook construction of a 1,000-000 gallon reservoir, blasted out of solid ledge, at the summit of Baldwin Hill, which point is two hundred and fifty feet above the corner of Depot and Main streets. To fill the reservoir, an electrically operated pumping station was installed on Park Street. By 1912, the whole village was provided service; and the District was prepared to extend its mains to whatever degree might be required.

The new "Music Hall," in the Sharaf Building, was indeed an ambitious design for a small community. With its large balcony extending around three sides, it could easily seat twelve hundred people; and its vast stage reached up another story higher, to accommodate the raising and lowering of stage sets and scenery. The seats on the main floor were removable, to leave a clear floor for dancing or roller skating.

Lincoln G. Hatch, writing in the Livermore Falls *Advertiser,* April 3, 1952, had this to say,

"There were a lot of good actors at and around the Falls who used to put on some good plays in the

Rockomeka Hotel Hall. I remember taking part in several plays until I was put in the doghouse. One of the plays in which I stood before the footlights was called Comrades. It was a three act comedy drama. All went well until the middle of the first act. At that point in the play, the one who was talking skipped ahead to his lines in the middle of the second act, and the first words he spoke were my cue to enter stage carrying a gun. Well, I was 'Johnnie on the Spot,' so most of the comedy part of the play was left out. I don't think that many who were there, except the actors, knew what went on. I knew the old saying, 'The show must go on.'"

When the Rockomeka Hotel Hall was replaced by the Sharaf Building's "Music Hall" in 1900, the scope was greatly widened for local talent productions. The opening play, August 29, 1900, according to the *Advertiser,* was "Denman Thompson's beautiful play, 'The Sunshine of Paradise Alley.'" It goes on to say, "The opening night saw nearly 900 people present to enjoy the occasion. It was a grand success, and not only the people of Livermore Falls, but those for miles around, are justly proud of the handsome hall."

For some years, between 1900 and 1910, an annual event was A. F. Neil's production of *The Drummer Boy, or the Spy of Shiloh,* billed as "A military Drama in Five Acts and Six Tableaux, arranged from Incidents of the late Rebellion." Mr. Neil arrived some time in advance, picked his cast, and trained them; then put the play on usually for two or three nights. Even though it had been seen before, this never failed to pack the house; and those who witnessed it, with Birchard Clary as the Confederate General, Chester Sturtevant as the Union General, George Moulton as the heartless Confederate officer, and Percy Cascadden as the poor drummer boy, never forgot it.

Forty years later, at the time of George Moulton's death, one of the local merchants, Dana M. Carter, in speaking of George's death to George's daughter, Vivian, said, "Gorry,

Vivian, your father was an awful good man; but, do you know I never could feel the same toward him after seeing him in that play, 'The Drummer Boy,'" which perhaps gives some idea of the realism that they put into it.

A dramatic club was flourishing at this time, to take advantage of the town's unusually good facilities, members of which were James D. McEdwards, manager, Ozro Roys, Leo Moulton, Nellie Pickard, J. P. Grenier, Gladys Brown, Charles McGraw, Lorenzo P. Brown, Florence Lyford, and Grace Haskell. Among the notable productions which were long remembered were *Hazel Kirke,* featuring Myrtie Keene and George Moulton; *Evangeline,* also starring Myrtie Keene; an *Historical Pageant,* with a cast of fifty, including Bess Maxwell, Ava Holmes, Louise Sewall and Cora Waite; and the musical opera, *King Jollity,* for which special trains were run by Portland & Rumford Falls Railroad and the Maine Central.

Another popular performer of the old Music Hall days was *Prescelle, hypnotist and mind reader.* His performances were usually accompanied by *Beautiful Illustrated Songs sung by George W. Moulton.* To advertise his show, he would sometimes put a subject to sleep in a store window, and leave the person there all day.

The hypnotist's subject asleep.

An annual feature for many years was the *Chapman Concert,* promoted and directed by William R. Chapman, in connection with the Maine Music Festival. Mr. Chapman organized local choruses in many towns throughout the State, and provided music to be rehearsed for weeks in advance. Then, on the nights of the concerts, Chapman arranged to have several Metropolitan Opera stars take part, along with the Festival Chorus.

When the Music Hall was not in use for plays, concerts or other entertainments, the seats on the main floor could be removed to provide a large and excellent dance floor. There are many people today who can remember Charles Elliot and his wife, Fannie, who were the town's best dancers, and good teachers of the art.

This decade, 1901-1910, was a period of, thus far, unequalled expansion of industry. As has been previously noted, the Record Foundry which was burned out of its location below Mill Hill, had built on a new site on upper Main Street in 1899. By 1902, however, it had already outgrown its Main Street location; so Judson Record incorporated the business as Record Foundry & Machine Company, August 1, 1902, with Edwin Riley as president, Chester Sturtevant as secretary-treasurer, and himself as manager; and proceeded to erect a new brick building, measuring 225' x 60', next to the railroad at Shy. The company was capitalized at $50,000.00; and employed from thirty to fifty men in the manufacture of pulleys, blowpipes, valves, pen stocks, and castings of all kinds.

Another small factory, which had been burned out in the fire of 1898, was the box and wood novelty plant of Fred Richmond. He, too, decided to incorporate as The Richmond Manufacturing Company, with $50,000.00 of capital; and the officers of that company were Edwin Riley, president; Chester H. Sturtevant, treasurer; John H. Maxwell, secretary. This concern built a two story, brick structure, 136 x 45 feet, with a single story addition of 45 x 30 feet for a boiler house and dry shed, which was located on land adjacent to the Record Foundry at Shy. There were eighty to one hundred employees engaged in the manufacture of boxes and general wood novelty work.

It was in 1906 that New England Creamery established its plant here, which, until a few years ago, was still standing next above the Moore Fuel & Heating Company. The *Livermore Falls Advertiser,* in January, 1906, commented, "Busy times over to the new creamery. Call in and see how nicely the business is conducted under the able management of J. D. McEdward." S. M. Sewall was the assistant to James D. McEdward; and they soon built an annual business of about $200,000.00.

W. L. Darrington established the Yankee Wood Turning Company here in 1909. He erected a one story main mill, 130 x 38 feet, and a boiler and tool house 38 x 30 feet. This, too, was at Shy, along the railroad, and next below the Record Foundry. The Yankee Company turned out brush handles of all kinds, small round and square boxes, darners, tops, pin barrels, and all kinds of hard wood novelties. There were over forty employees quite steadily at work for this company.

The large, frame factory which was built by John L. Cummings, to manufacture trunks and suitcases, on the west side, in Livermore, underwent several changes in ownership and product. Following its operation by John Cummings, the manufacture of extension cases, suit cases, and trunks was carried on for a time, prior to 1910, by Cascadden & Stanchfield. Cummings had been employing fifteen, and doing a $20,000.00 annual business; but apparently Cascadden & Stanchfield were not as successful, and the business was taken over by I. G. Sharaf, under the name of Standard Suit Case Company, making light weight dress-suit cases, and cases of the cane type. Sharaf employed ten persons, and produced two hundred cases per day, using matting imported from Japan. He occupied, in this business, the entire second floor of the factory building; and, according to *The Lewiston Journal* of May 11, 1912, the business was showing constant increase.

At the same time (1909-1910) that Sharaf took over the second floor of the building, the ground floor was occupied by Livermore Falls Glove Company, a corporation under the management of Leo Baum (sales), Myer Mineberg (office), and Jacob Israelson (production). They adopted the trademark,

WORK-KING for their products of cotton, or cotton and leather gloves, which became widely known and respected. The business was highly successful, and an important economic factor in the community for over fifty years. Eventually, after Myer Mineberg had sold his interest, and Jacob Israelson had died, ownership became vested entirely in the Baum family - Leo Baum and his son, David.

Henry W. Bailey had operated a carriage and sleigh manufacturing shop at Haine's Corner; and his son, Dana W. Bailey, trained in this business by his father, came to Livermore Falls to start a similar shop of his own, below "Mill Hill," next to Frank Millett's blacksmith shop. After the great fire of 1898, Dana Bailey moved to a location just off Depot Street (where, later, Park Street would run). He built up a prosperous and increasing business, covering a large part of Western Maine; and the *Advertiser,* in September 1902, noted,

"Mr. D. W. Bailey is attending Farmington Fair this week with a fine string of carriages."

By far the most important of the expanding industries, however, was the International Paper Company which in both number of employees and size of payroll greatly exceeded all other local industries combined.

A ninth paper machine was being planned for the Otis Mill, but the existing machines were already taxing the capacity for stock and pulp production; so that the need for another source of pulp was most urgent. Consequently, it was decided to build an entirely new pulp mill at Livermore Falls, to contain twenty grinders, and to be known officially as "Livermore Mill # 11," but better known locally as the "Lower Mill."

To embark upon construction of the extent contemplated, would require a temporary labor force much larger than what was available in the immediate vicinity. The Company turned over to a Massachusetts employment agency the task of recruiting such a labor force. There were, at that period, large numbers of Italian immigrants flocking into the port of Boston; and it was from that pool of unemployed that the

The Sharaf Building under construction in 1899
The fifth and sixth story tower floors contained the staging apparatus for a large "Music Hall" on the floors below.

Sharaf "Music Hall"
The 30' x 50' stage of the Sharaf Building "Music Hall" was elaborately appointed; the main floor and balcony could seat 1200 people.

263

agency secured the required laborers. From the 1962 History of the Otis Division, International Paper Company, the following is quoted,

"Penniless, largely illiterate, and completely ignorant of the new tongue of their adopted country, these were welcome prey for the employment agency. In return for a job, the agency received a percentage of the workers' pay which, during this period, averaged 17.5 cents per hour. In addition, the Agency had control of the commissary which sat amidst a settlement of two hundred camps housing these laborers. Compelled to buy food and articles of necessity from the commissary where exorbitant prices were charged, there was usually little, and more often nothing, for these people to show after a month of work. Over five hundred were employed before construction was complete.

"The camp was well policed, and rather well disciplined through the iron rule of some five bouncers who maintained a severe discipline. The main building burned in 1908, but was not rebuilt as construction was about complete."

The *Lewiston Journal,* in January 1906, had this to say about the International Paper Company's project;

"It was known early in 1904 that the International Paper Company had voted to begin on the development of their immense water privilege at Livermore Falls; and sometime in May or June bids were called. However, the undertaking was so colossal and the specifications so difficult to figure that the several large contractors, to be on the safe side, put in such large bids that President Chisholm of the Company and his confreres wouldn't stand for it for a moment, and the undertaking came very near falling through, when Mr. Chisholm called Mr. R. D. Shanahan of Portland and Mr. John Greenleaf of Auburn into consultation. These gentlemen have done contract work before for Mr. Chisholm and I. P. Company, including masonry, wood and brick work which stands today to their everlasting credit; and the above gentlemen were persuaded to join drives, so to speak, under the firm name of "Shanahan and Greenleaf," and undertake the work laid out here by the Company, which finally commenced July 1, it marked the beginning of an era of prosperity unprecedented in the annals of Livermore Falls. What the Messrs. Shanahan and Greenleaf have accomplished since the beginning of July has never before been attempted in this State."

Main Street, 1900
E. T. Abbott's "dapple gray" found things looking quite urban by the spring of that year.

The article went on to refer to the construction of "a large winged dam twenty feet in height, one hundred ninety-three feet long, with concrete eight feet thick at the top and thirty feet thick at the bottom" - requiring over thirty thousand barrels of cement.

There were other huge walls necessary, of course, to provide the forebay to the ground-wood mill; and plans were drawn for a large sulphite mill, a new paper machine room, and a new steam plant at the Otis Mill.

At the same time, the old Umbagog Mill was torn down; some of its bricks salvaged for re-use in the new construction;

and one of its machines dismantled and taken piece by piece in horse drawn carts to the Otis Mill.

With the tremendous expansion of the International Paper Company's mills here, and the importation of workers from New York and Massachusetts, there naturally came, too, organizers of labor unions. Something of their success, and the enthusiasm they aroused, is evident in the newspapers of that period. In September, 1902, the *Advertiser* reported, "The Livermore Falls Clothing Company sold one hundred eighty uniform suits for the Papermakers Union for the Labor Day parade and gathering at Rumford Falls, Monday - the boys going up by special train."

A year later, in the *Lewiston Journal* issue of September 8, 1903, we read,

"Monday will go down in history as the first time Labor Day was ever observed at Livermore Falls by the representatives of the various labor unions; and it will probably be several years before the citizens of this community see such a big parade on our streets on Labor Day. It was variously estimated that from 1,500 to 2,000 were in line.

"At an early hour the people began to fairly pour in from the surrounding towns, and long before the arrival of the big special from Rumford Falls and from Lewiston, on the P. & R.F. Railway, the streets were just crowded wtih people. When this big train pulled into the Livermore Station, it was next to impossible to get within two hundred feet of the passenger station. The special was made up of four passenger coaches and ten flat cars on which seats had been arranged, and the *Journal* correspondent gets it from a reliable source that there were fifteen hundred people aboard - at last, guided by Marshal Fred King and his four aides mounted on handsome chargers, and headed by the Livermore Falls Band, the procession paraded through the principal streets - Behind the Livermore Falls Band came a handsomely decorated four-wheeled vehicle containing four ladies beautifully costumed with two gentlemen escorts. Next came the papers of the Chisholm mills, and following them was the beautiful bateau - containing eighteen beautiful young ladies - Next came Payne's Second Regiment band, of Auburn.

"Other features of the parade were an immense float upon which, seated in the form of a pyramid; were sixty-two young ladies - The float of the Maine and New Hampshire Granite Cutters attracted lots of attention. To attempt a description of the various uniforms worn by the many labor organizations from Brunswick, Lisbon Falls, Mechanic Falls, Rumford Falls, North Jay, Chisholm, etc., would call for too long an article."

A local rhymster celebrated the occasion in verse, which read in part,

"Then came the boys from Livermore Falls
With striped shirts and overalls.
It was not the way that they were dressed That
made folks say they looked the best, But just
because that they were led
By a veteran with a shiny head,
That glittered like a gilded dome,
No other than our own Red Tom."

After the parade, the crowd assembled at Evergreen Park for a program of races and other sports, climaxed by a baseball game between Rumford Falls, champions of Oxford County, and Lisbon Falls, champions of Androscoggin County, for the State championship.

The *Lewiston Journal* article continues,

"The Union ball at Music Hall in the evening was the crowning event of the day, and for a ball was the largest attended of any ever held here, over one hundred thirty couples taking part in the grand march which was led by Mr. & Mrs. Charles K. Campbell.

"Before the Grand March, Captain Charles Hyde gave a fancy drill with his men of Samson Company, Uniform Rank, that was greatly enjoyed by all.

267

A pleasing feature of the day was the orderliness of the
big crowd."

Mr. Edwin Riley continued as Divison Manager of all the
mills in the Otis Division of International Paper Company during this expansion, and until 1909; in which year he retired,
having completed fifteen years of tremendous accomplishment
with the Otis Division. After several temporary, interim mana-
gers, Mr. William A. Murray arrived to take over the Division in
1911. It was under his direction that the last of the Division's
eleven machines was installed, and the expansion project completed as planned.

Whether Friday the thirteenth in general is unlucky or not,
it is certain that one Friday the thirteenth - of May, 1910 was
extremely unlucky for Livermore Falls. On that day, the
"beautiful Sharaf Block, towering above every business block at
Livermore Falls, and from which the business life of the entire
community seemingly pulsated," to quote the *Lewiston Journal* of
that date, "was almost completely gutted by fire, with a loss of
$150,000.00."

The newspaper article continues,

"The fire was discovered and an alarm rung in at
about 2:45 A.M. by night policeman, G. Frank Warren,
and according to Mr. Warren, when he first discovered
the fire, the flames were just breaking thru some of the
windows of the stage dressing rooms which look out
on the north end of the block, and also from one of the
public library windows .... there was a terrific explosion
and flames broke thru the scene loft over the big stage
to Music Hall which towered as much as six stories
above the street. . . .

"The fire department responded very quickly to the
call, and in short order had nine streams playing under
a pressure of 117 pounds to the square inch; with
plenty of water back of them, the best they could do
was to keep the fire confined to the building. . .

"During the fire, a part of the wall on the northwest side of the building fell. .. At this writing, 7 :00 A.M., the wall on the north end is tottering; and, as the main line of the Maine Central Railroad track passes within a few feet of it, and is now buried beneath brick and other debris, it is probable the morning train from Farmington will be considerably delayed.

"The first story of Sharaf block contained the Post Office, J. Guy Coolidge's dry and fancy goods store, Livermore Falls Clothing Company's store, L. L. Waite's book store and news stand, and the banking rooms of the Livermore Falls Trust & Banking Company.

"On the second floor were offices occupied by J. H. Maxwell, esq., law office, Livermore Falls Light & Power *Co.,* I. B. Clary, esq., law office, Dwelley & Clary, fire insurance, Livermore Falls Lumber & Realty Company, Dr. M. D. Johnson, dentist, The Livermore Falls Public Library, the Old Man's Club, the Selectmen's office, and the Municipal Court rooms. - On this floor was also located Music Hall, with a seating capacity of 1200, and a stage thirty feet deep by fifty feet long, containing scenery that cost originally $1500 (one of the finest halls in the State).

"The third story was occupied on the front by Oriental Star Lodge, No. 21, F. & A. M.; Androscoggin R. A. Chapter; and Washburn Chapter, O. E. S. The entrance to the balcony to Music Hall was also on the third floor. Part of the fourth story was occupied as a banquet hall by the Masonic bodies.

"The town clock in the tower of the block, which cost $1200 and was a present to the town, is also a total loss ....

"Mr. I. G. Sharaf, the owner, is in Boston, and what his plans are for the future the *Journal* can only guess. That he or someone else will rebuild, using the wall now standing, but probably new above the second story, is quite probable; but that Sharaf block will ever again be reproduced here in all its grandeur and architectural beauty, no one dares hope nor expect. ..

"Already the Livermore Falls Trust & Banking

Company has engaged and moved into one of Hon. J. F. Lamb's brick stores on Main Street, just across from the Sharaf block. The Livermore Falls Clothing Company have engaged quarters on Depot Street; and this afternoon J. F. Jefferds will move the Post Office into his store on Main Street. ...

"Business, in a way, is at a standstill here today, and the citizens seem dazed at the enormity of the town's loss."

Sharaf Building, 1900
Several sidewalk superintendents watch the new granite sidewalk curbs being laid in place in 1900.

The Livermore Falls Trust & Banking Company bought the ruins of the Sharaf block, and immediately began the task of clean-up and rebuilding. It truly is an ill wind that blows no one good, and to boys of that time the ruins offered a double opportunity - a chance to earn some money cleaning bricks, and a chance to hunt for treasures such as slightly charred catcher's mitts or baseball bats with lovely smoked finish, and similar salvage buried beneath the bricks.

As rebuilt, the block on the exterior looked very much like the original building; but, of course, the original was not "reproduced in all its grandeur and architectural beauty," and most conspicuous was the absence of the famed Music Hall.

That modern marvel, the moving picture, made its local debut in a space in Hamlin Dyke's harness shop, adjoining his livery stable, which had been cleared for the purpose and equipped with a few backless benches. The patrons were largely school children; and, though the images on the screen were a somewhat blurry, brownish color; the movements of men and horses rather jerky; and the acting an exaggerated burlesque, those were negligible faults which were lost in the wonder of pictures that actually moved. Saturday afternoon matinees were jammed with youngsters who had managed to earn or to beg the few cents charged as admission fee; and who watched, enthralled, the "Cowboys and Indians" or the exploits of "Blue Beard."

It was only a few years later when D. W. Griffith's production, *The Birth Of A Nation,* appeared - seemingly the ultimate in motion picture art. The usherettes were all dressed in Civil War period costumes; special music was provided and the impact of this epic upon the audiences was certainly as great, if not greater, than that of its modern counterpart, *Gone With The Wind.*

The destruction of the Sharaf Building, and with it, the loss of Music Hall, had left the town without a theatre or public hall of sufficient size to accommodate theatrical productions, movies, or large public gatherings. When the Rockomeka Hotel was taken down in 1899-1900, to make room for the second section of the Lamb block (the first section, at corner of Depot and Main having been erected in 1898), the stable was left for a public livery stable, and so used for several years. To meet the need of the townspeople for a theatre and public hall, the old stable was rebuilt, and christened, *Dreamland Theatre.* It was a far cry from the elegance of Music Hall; but it served the town well for nearly fifty years; and, to people who remember that half century, "Dreamland"

]. G. Ham in his new shop
This fine new apothecary shop was constructed after the 1899 fire.

Livermore Falls Fire Engine, August 20, 1909
Here pictured after fighting a fire in the log pile at Jay Village.

has left many "dreams" and nostalgic memories of the Ethel May Shorey stock company, of town meetings and highschool graduations, of dances to the music of Murray's Orchestra, and of a new generation of amateur actors, including among its regulars Raymond Brown, Albert "Bill" Nason, Marie Nason, Louis C. Brown, Vivian Moulton, Beryl Foster, Albert "Freezie" Bernard, Marcia Savage, Harris "Doc" Waite, Allan "Tweed" Hyde, William and George Moulton.

Particularly long remembered were "Tweed" Hyde as the Western Sheriff, Louis Brown in the title role of *Charley's Aunt,* Harris Waite and Marcia Savage in their extraordinary song and acrobatic dance number *At The Opry House.* Productions were often enlivened by unscheduled features, such as the time one actor was fortifying himself between appearances with swigs of home brew from a flask on his hip. He was on stage, when the flask blew its stopper, which sailed in an arc over his head; but he reached out and caught it as it fell; restored it to his pocket; and continued his lines without a hitch.

Actually, George W. Moulton was not an amateur performer, but was an experienced professional member of various repertoire and stock companies throughout New England; and was engaged for most of his life in some aspect of the entertainment field. For a number of years, he traveled the Maine fair circuit each autumn in his character of "Si Hopkins," becoming well known throughout the State. Later, he managed one of the town's first motion picture theatres; and, between reels, interspersed songs illustrated with colored slides. By this time, he had acquired false teeth which sometimes gave way and dropped on the high notes, but this only added to the interest of the audience.

Another stand-by in local dramatic productions was Cora "Ma" Waite (Mrs. L. L. Waite) who was the perennial coach and character actress in the town's local talent plays.

Probably most talented and best remembered in this field, however, were Allan "Tweed" Hyde and Harris "Doc" Waite, who were usually featured together as a comedy team. Tweed was about six and a half feet tall, and built like a bean pole, while Doc was under five feet, and nearly as broad as he was tall. This contrast added greatly to their effectiveness; and their uninhibited performances were as hilarious, even to a sophisticated audience, as anything Eddie Foy or George Gobel could produce.

From the earliest days of the sport, baseball was one of the predominant interests of the citizens of Livermore-Livermore Falls. Not only were the high school teams well supported, but town teams and club teams continued the game through the summer months. It was in the years between 1910 and 1930, excluding the World War I period, that interest reached its peak; and players were sought among college stars and from semi-pro ranks in the feverish attempt to dominate the competition which generally included Rumford, Dixfield, Wilton, Farmington, Weld, and Winthrop.

There was some kind of rule that a college player, or other amateur, could not accept pay for playing, without losing his amateur standing; but this constituted no problem, since "Bill" Murray, Manager of I. P. Company, was as avid a fan as anyone; and "jobs" were provided at the Mill for the ball players. It was said that one of them spent a whole summer painting one window sash.

Some of the ball players were, of course, native talent, such as Gardiner and Andrew French, Ray Brown, and Stuart Walker. Of the hired college talent, well remembered are Frank and Harold Cobb, brothers from the University of Maine; "Card" Twaddle, also from U. of M., who later was the well known and much loved Doctor Twaddle of Central Maine General Hospital in Lewiston; George Talbot, from Bates; the U. of M. battery of Abbott and Driscoll; the Colby battery of Johnny Lanpher and "Chuck" Meader; and, from Bates, Johnny Daker and Ransom Garrett, another native son.

Among the professional and semi-pro stars who played for Livermore were the old New England League veterans, Woodcock, a pitcher; Harry Moore, of Wilton, also a pitcher; Harley Rawson, a second baseman, more noted as a wily field general; "Jake" Cannon, a New England League catcher; Alphonse La-Vallee, of Winthrop; and Elmer Pushard, an outfielder who had previously played at Wiscasset.

Two of these, Jake Cannon and Elmer Pushard, married local girls, and spent the remainder of their lives here.

Perhaps the hardest job on the circuit was that of umpire.

The incensed batter would go back to the "box."

Feelings at times ran high and fans and players, both, were apt to take exception to close "calls." However, in Martin Newberg, Livermore had the answer.

Over six feet tall, a jutting under-jaw like a bulldog, and an expression that seemed to say he could hardly wait to take a bite out of you, he was the living embodiment of that saying, "When I calls 'em, that's what they are; and until I calls 'em, they ain't nuthin." Many a time. an incensed batter would whirl around to remonstrate, but when Martin straightened up, put his hands on his hips, and glared at the would be objector, the latter meekly went back to the "box."

In his letter to the *Advertiser,* Lincoln Hatch recalls some of those times.

"Livermore Falls always had a good baseball team.
I do not remember what year it was that I had the honor
of being the President of the Association, but remember,
the head, heart, pocketbook and many other aches I had.
There were two oustanding things which were hard to get
- money and good umpires. The umpires had to be rough,
tough, and the bigger the better. I think Martin Newberg
will agree with me, because (as the saying is) he was there.
I called him Ump.

"That year the team was made up mostly of college
boys, a few local boys and one player from Buckfield - I
think his name was Harley Rawson. He played shortstop,
and had full charge of the team, and knew his baseball.

"I remember one pitcher by the name of Horan. He
was left handed, for his right hand was crippled, and he
had to have a special bat made for him. About all he could
do was to bunt the ball.

"I am going to try to tell about only two games that
stood out from the others. One was with the Portland
team. During the season, each team had won a game, and
the third game was played at the Fair Grounds during the
annual fair. There was a large crowd on hand. The
Portland club had several New England League players
with them, and one of the New England crack pitchers.
The first ball that was pitched, Frauk Cobb (who played
third base for our team) hit over the centerfielder's head
for a home run, which was the only run of the day. Horan
pitched the whole game for our team.

"The other game was played at the Falls with a
team that they called the Boston Reds. They were a
traveling team, and had been winning most of the
games that they played. At the start of the first inning,
Rawson had each player bunt, to rattle the pitcher and
infielders. Our team got two runs in the first inning,
and won the game.

"We won forty out of forty-six games played, and
spent more money in about ten weeks than was paid

the three ministers of the Baptist, Universalist and Methodist Churches for a full year."

In the five years following the Sharaf Block loss, the community suffered three more disastrous fires. The first was the Green Street fire, which occurred April 28, 1911; and which destroyed most of that street, taking houses on both sides of the street. A high wind was blowing at the time, so that burning shingles and embers were carried for some distance, and people in other parts of town were kept busy snuffing out these incipient blazes.

Next came the Livermore Falls Steam Laundry fire, which was notable not so much for the material loss, as for the death and the injuries to persons involved. The Laundry, previously owned by Arthur B. Allen, had recently been purchased by B. C. Phillips, who was operating it in 1915. Mr. Phillips and an employee, Adolph Chicoine, were opening a barrel of gasoline for use in cleaning. Two high school students, Burton Phillips and Bernal Bailey, were standing nearby, watching the operation. The men were at the rear of the Laundry building, but a door had been left open into the boiler room; and when the barrel was opened the vapor ignited resulting in a terrific explosion, and ensuing fire.

Mr. Phillips died within a few hours; the other three were horribly burned, but survived after months of hospitalization, though they carried the disfiguring scars for the remainder of their lives.

The third loss was that of a picturesque old landmark at Brettuns, the Livermore Hotel and Stable, which burned down, March 3, 1916. It had not been run as a hotel for some time, but its hall was used for dances and other gatherings. Architecturally the event was the loss of one more tie with the past, which cannot be replaced.

Burnham & Morrill Company constructed a "new, modern canning plant," which began operations the week of September 15, 1915. This plant was to process string beans principally;

The Sharaf Building - May 22, 1910

The Sharaf Building - May 22, 1910

and farmers in this vicinity planted a considerable acreage to that crop, under contract to the canning company. The company gave employment to a large number of women and girls during the short canning season. This factory was located on the west side of lower Park Street, where Isaacson Lumber Company now stands. Of those connected with its management, best known as a long-time resident of this community, an active participant in town affairs, and a boon companion on fishing trips, was the late Harry H. Knowlton, whose recent death was mourned by many.

The Mexican Border affair, of 1916, while of little significance in itself, probably did have some value in pointing up to a largely civilian, part-time soldiery, what would be involved in a sudden mobilization and large scale movement of troops. The local company of the National Guard was "Company C of the Second Maine Regiment," the largest company in the regiment, which had its headquarters in the Armory located on the second floor of the present fire and police station.

The following excerpts from the *Livermore Falls Advertiser* of 1916, tell something of that incident, which was, in a way, a preparatory prelude to the coming storm of a year later.

June 21, 1916

"The Livermore Falls Military Company, the largest company in the Regiment, is at the Armory, ready to start for the front at a moment's notice. Not since the Spanish War has the nation seen such military activity as on Monday."

June 20, 1916

"Long before the time of departure, an exceedingly large throng of people assembled at the M.C.R.R. station to witness the going away of Company C, 2nd Inf., NGSM on Thursday."

August 2, 1916

"The Livermore Falls Band gave an open air concert in front of Dreamland Theatre, Thursday evening, preceding the benefit given by the King's Daughters for our soldier boys at Laredo, Texas. Pictures of Company C, taken by photographer H. N. Allen on the day of their departure for the muster grounds at Augusta, were shown."

August 9, 1916

"There were letters from the boys at Laredo, Texas. Those writing were Sgt. Frank C. Porter, Private Arlington Tretheway, and Lieut. Frank J. Burbank."

October 11, 1916

"The Second Maine Infantry left Laredo, Texas, Saturday, en route for Augusta. There were 53 officers and 909 enlisted men who departed from Laredo on three trains, Saturday."

November 1, 1916

"Company C, Second Regiment NGSM, arrived home Wednesday afternoon, and was given a reception by the citizens of Livermore Falls which showed the boys the high regard in which they were held."

In 1900, in constructing the new grammar and high school building of which the townspeople were so proud, it was thought that the school building needs of the village were amply met for a long time to come. Yet, in a little over a decade, the schools were again over crowded, and there was much discussion as to what should be done. Some people favored an addition to the present building; while others were convinced that that was only a short term answer to a problem that had to be faced eventually, and for which a new high school building would be required.

By 1915 something had to be done; and a committee consisting of Birchard A. Clary, Herbert C. Whittemore, Esq., Hon, Edwin Riley, Frank B. Gorden and P. J. Reynolds were appointed to formulate plans and estimate costs for a new high school building. This committee, with the substitution of Frank E. Deakin for P. J. Reynolds, was continued by the annual town meeting; and made its report at a special town

Coffer Dams, 7/15/05
These dams were erected prior to the construction of International Paper Co.'s
Livermore Mill # 11 ("Lower Mill"), to house 20 grinders; Judson Record's new
foundry visible in the background.

Mill Under Construction, 11/24/05
Italian laborers were brought in to build the "Lower Mill."

meeting May 17, 1916 which was to purchase the six acre Pettingill lot on Park Street, and to spend $40,000 for the lot and building, and which was approved at that meeting.

Two attempts to reverse the decision were made by the opponents, one at a special meeting on May 31, 1916, and the other at a special meeting on June 7, 1916 - both of which were defeated by small margins of 96 to 77, and 162 to 142 - so construction proceeded on what its opponents derisively called "Fort Clary," after the committee's chairman.

The building was completed, and dedication services held October 11, 1917. Dr. Augustus O. Thomas, State Superintendent of Schools, was the principal speaker for the occasion; B. A. Clary gave the report of the building committee; J. H. Maxwell spoke on behalf of the school board; and speeches were also heard from Edwin Riley and Dr. C. R. Smith.

Dana W. Bailey, who had the carriage shop on Park Street and who used to take strings of carriages around to the various Fairs in the State, foresaw what was presaged by the appearance of the first autos. Unlike some of his competitors who continued a losing battle to the tune of "Get a horse," he very wisely joined the trend of the future; owned one of the first *Reos,-* and eventually secured the dealership for *Ford.*

The following excerpts from *Livermore Falls Advertisers* of the time indicate something of the growing trend:

December 8, 1915

"Sliding is prohibited on all streets in the village of Livermore Falls except Knapp Street, Union Street and upper hill on Church Street, near E. H. Record's.

per order,

Herbert L. Hersey

Alphonso D. Cole

Houghton H. Putnam

SELECTMEN"

March 29, 1916

"The snow disappeared so rapidly from the streets of Livermore Falls last week that several teams appeared on wheels Friday and Saturday."

March 29, 1917

Italian Camp, 5/11/07

500 Italian' immigrant laborers were housed here in a village known as "Italian Camp"; they constructed the Lower Mill on wages averaging *17 ½ cents* per hour; the iron rule of five "bouncers" maintained severe camp discipline.

"Lower Mill" Completed in 1908

"A few automobiles have come out of winter hibernation and have made an appearance on our streets which is another sign of the approach of spring."
January 26, 1916

"R. A. Wing will use an auto truck in his steadily growing business."
March 29, 1917

"The large new truck of the International Paper Company made its first appearance on the streets of the village Monday, attracting considerable attention."
April 18, 1917

"Several garages are erecting curb service pumps for gasolene, in addition to the pumps in the garage. This will enable prompt service when more than one car is waiting for gasolene, and will make it more convenient for the automobile driver."
August 2, 1917

"As a certain business man in town was driving his car up one of the streets, he noticed at a corner just ahead of him two women earnestly engaged in conversation; and as he approached and was about to pass them, he noticed a signal, given by one of the women, to stop his car. Upon inquiring what was wanted, he was asked to stop his car until they were done talking as the noise of the engine made it difficult to carry on a conversation."
November 8, 1916

"D. W. Bailey advertises that the new Ford has roomier body, higher seat back, oval mud fenders and black enamel radiator."
September 15, 1915

"Dr. G. H. Rand and Leon Emerson, agents for Androscoggin and Franklin Counties, are announcing 'THE SIX OF 16,' the greatest values the world has ever known. The car has an electric starter and generator."
January 5, 1916

"Oakland Sixes, Fours, and Eights; Speedsters,

Roadsters, and touring cars $695; $1050 and $1785 F.O.B. factory."

October 20, 1915

"All records for auto registration in Maine have been broken. The figures for the nine months ending October 1st are as follows. - regular registration 19,322, truck registrations 1,006, operators 25,014."

October 16, 1916

"The auto accident Saturday night, in which Fred Mason's car figured, nearly resulted in fatalities. Mr. Mason, accompanied by Shamrock Boyle, were returning to Livermore Falls, and when descending Jay Hill, near the cemetery, Mr. Mason attempted to apply the foot brake but made the mistake of touching his foot on the foot throttle. This caused him to lose control. The car went into the ditch, burst a tire, rolled over twice with both men pinned under the car. Both men were knocked unconscious, and when Mr. Mason came to, he crawled out and extricated Mr. Boyle, who was covered with blood. T. T. Williams happened along and brought both men to Livermore Falls. Mr. Boyle did not regain consciousness until after arriving at Livermore Falls."

Advert. - "AN EXAGGERATED REPORT"

"Contrary to the report in the daily papers, W. S. Treat and son, George, were but slightly injured in an automobile collision with an electric car, near the kite track between Portland and Old Orchard.

"W. S. Treat was riding from Portland to Old Orchard Friday with his son, George W. Treat, a Boston bond salesman, who works for a banking concern on Milk Street.

"George is said to be somewhat reckless in driving his automobile, in any event, he and the electrics were 'trying titles' when they came to a sharp turn in the highway near the kite track and Mr. Treat lost control of the machine and he saw that a side-on collision with the electrics was inevitable, when he advised his father to jump. The machine and electric car came together and the auto was slightly damaged, and W. S. Treat and son were only somewhat shaken up." From Letter of L. G. Hatch, *Advertiser,* April 3, 1952-

"- when the autos became quite plentiful there were many who bragged about how their autos would take Jay Hill on high. At that time the road over Jay Hill went straight, and over the RR track at the bottom of the hill. . . . There was talk of building the road to North Jay, as it is now. Before the change was made, I heard one man remark that he wished they would hurry the job, as it would stop the lying about going over Jay Hill in high gear."

At that period, there was still no problem in getting a horse shod in the village, for according to the *Maine Register,* there were, in 1916, eight blacksmiths still on the job; S. B. Jackman, E. H. Merrill, G. A. Clark, Edson Cox, H. R. Corkum, F. E. Merrill, Henry Feindle, and J. A. Howe.

From the *Advertiser* of May 10, 1917, we note the following item:

"There will be considerable change in the appearance of things on a portion of what was formerly known as the Richardson property, north of Monroe Street. A tract of this land had been purchased by Gorden Brothers, who will at once layout twenty house lots, and commence building cottage houses. New street locations will also be made, and the property generally improved in many ways."

This land, lying just east of Main Street and south of the Jay town line, had for years been known as "Richardson's Field"; and used as a baseball field, and a location for traveling carnivals or circuses to pitch their tents. Now, as indicated by the newspaper, it would rapidly be covered with new homes built by the Gorden Brothers, on new streets called Prospect Street, Otis Street, Bemis Street, Gagnon Street and Gorden

Street. The ball games, carnivals and circuses would have to use the Fair Grounds at Shy, or the I. P. ball ground, near the Livermore Mill.

Apparently the wood turning business was flourishing at the moment, for W. L. Darrington, Manager of the Yankee Wood Turning Company, announced that it would be necessary to put on a second, or night shift to fill the orders presently on hand, on February 1st, 1917. The other two wood turning companies, Richmond Manufacturing Company and Jay Wood Turning Company could not survive the depression which followed the financial panic beginning in the financial centers in 1907, and spreading into the grass roots of business

Record Foundry, 1909
This building was completed about 1905

in 1908 and 1909. By 1911, both the latter companies had shut down, and their plants were under foreclosure. The Richmond building, a very substantial, brick structure, was bought by Record Foundry & Machine Company, whose property it adjoined, as a storehouse for the Foundry's patterns and moulds. The Yankee company was only getting started in 1909 and 1910; so found itself in the fortunate position of inheritor of the markets of the other two, when business began to pick up again. Thus, in 1917, it had more orders than it could fill.

Overshadowing all other events at this time, of course, was the World War into which the nation was about to be plunged. As early as February 10, 1917, Lieut. Frank Burbank, who was in temporary command of Company "C," 2nd Regiment Inf., NGSM, received orders to recruit every able bodied man possible; and the first of March, 1917, he was told to have his men ready for call at one hour's notice.

President Wilson called Congress into extra session for April 2nd for the purpose of taking action in the state of war which exists between the United States and Germany. "Congress will probably," said the *Advertiser*, "be asked to declare that a state of war has existed since German submarines began conducting their most warlike operations against American commerce."

Advertiser, April 19, 1917 -
"Friday forenoon the militia call was sounded (on the fire alarm system) and Company C assembled at the Armory in charge of Lieut. F. J. Burbank. Lieut. Percy M. Bleason, the new commanding officer of Company C, reported Monday noon and assumed immediate command. Cot beds are to arrive for the men today, so that they will not have to sleep on the floors any longer."

Advertiser, May 3, 1917 -
"Some twelve to fifteen hundred patriotic citizens of Livermore Falls and vicinity were at the Maine Central Railway station, Monday morning, to witness the departure of Company C, 2nd Inf., NGSM. The militia boys were escorted from the Armory to the railroad station by the Livermore Falls Band, playing patriotic selections."

Richard Lauder and Fred Riley, 1916
Displaying one of the patented Record valves that became so widely used by
the paper industry throughout the world

Advertiser, August 23, 1917 -

"Soldiers of Camp Keyes (Augusta) left for 'destination unknown,' Sunday. In a downpour of rain that
in mid-afternoon had been forecast by a bank of leaden
clouds rising from the western horizon - conditions
that seemed gloomily in keeping with the spirit of the
occasion - the stalwart boys of 2nd Maine Regiment,

U.S.A., departed from Augusta, and received the fare-wells that for many days past, parents, brothers, sisters, and sweethearts had been steeling themselves to utter with the same brave cheerfulness shown by the boys themselves. But, while the young soldiers seemed not in the least bit downhearted, and in many cases appeared eager for the move that was to take them one step nearer to the trenches, their well wishers were less successful in the attempt to hide the feelings of sadness that the smiles of the departing infantrymen must have concealed, and there were tears that persisted in howl-ing and sobs that could not be suppressed.

"The streets of Augusta seemed strangely forlorn Sunday evening, with no young men garbed in olive drab to lend the atmosphere of youthful life which the citizens had come to feel was an inherent part of the city's existence.

"The third train, which had left the station a few minutes after 6:00 o'clock, had carried the first battalion, commanded by Major John A. Haley of Rumford, including Company A of Dexter, commanded by Captain Percy A. Hasty; Company B of Rumford, commanded by Captain Spalding Bisbee; Company D of Norway, commanded by Captain James W. Hanson; and Company C of Livermore Falls, commanded by Captain Roland G. Findlay."

It would be 1919 before the townspeople learned much of what happened to Livermore's Company C, after that rainy Sunday evening in August, 1917. Re-christened, the Second Maine Infantry became the 103rd Infantry, of the 26th (Yankee) Division. It would meet its biggest test at Chateau Thierry, in July 1918, where its battalion, ordered to take Hill 190 west of Bouresches, near Belleau, did so, but at great cost. Lieut. Burbank was the only officer left in action; Sgt. George T. Bunten, Pfc. Forrest E. Merrill, and Pvts. Arthur F. Alden and George E. Ryder were killed; and so many more wounded that Lieut. Burbank found his Company reduced to 15 men.

For that day's work, both Lieut. Burbank and Pvt. Eugene
Dube of Livermore Falls were awarded the Distinguished
Service Cross.

III III III

"At a meeting held at C. A. Bryant's, a girls' club
was formed under the name of the *Androscoggin Valley
Girls' Canning Club,* with eight members. The teacher of
the Center School, Miss Ella Gordon, was present and
assisted the girls in organizing. Officers were elected as
follows: president, Miss Olive Bryant; vice president,
Miss Ruby Deane; secretary and treasurer, Miss Ruby
Edgecomb; lecturer, Miss Sadie Bryant; local leader,
Mrs. F. A. Leavitt."

August 30, 1917, "Thursday evening the Livermore Center Boys Corn Club and the Androscoggin
Valley Girls Canning Club met at the home of
Edmond Gibbs of the West Side. Thirty-six young
people were present and listened to an address by
County Agent Harold Shaw. A hay-rack load of young
folks came from Livermore Center, and others from
different parts of town. Mr. Shaw's address was full of
helpful suggestions; and very encouraging reports were
given by the young people. Corn and other crops are
looking fine and everything indicates a big harvest. The
girls are busily engaged in canning, and each one
expects to have fifty jars of fruit and vegetables to her
credit before the close of the season."

October 25, 1917, "Seventy-five parents and
friends were present at the contest of the
Androscoggin Valley canning and garden club and the
North Androscoggin corn, poultry and potato club
held at the Leavitt Memorial Home, Saturday. At that
time, a splendid exhibit and excellent program was
given.

"The meeting was held in the large barn, which,
with its electric lights and big space made an ideal place
for the purpose. A pink nosed family of pigs of aristo-
cratic lineage that were shut off from the festivities by a

high partition managed to find a crack in the wall (like boys at a baseball game) through which they watched the proceedings, and expressed their satisfaction with appreciative grunts.

"The winners in the contest were: 1st on canning, Ruby Edgecomb; 2nd canning, Ruby Deane; 3rd canning, Helen Hinkley; 1st on dry beans, Sadie Bryant; 2nd dry beans, Dorothy Bryant; 1st on beets, May Buck; 1st on corn, Omar Gibbs; 2nd corn, Earl Abbott; 3rd on corn, Charlie Gibbs; 1st on potatoes, Forrest Deane; 1st on poultry, Kenneth Gibbs."

Food production on a somewhat larger scale is indicated by this item from the *Advertiser,* on September 13, 1917. "Clarence A. Dyer, of Livermore Falls, has raised and harvested, on his farm at New Vineyard, six tons of string beans. Mr. Dyer took pickers from here and carried them to New Vineyard by autos." Herbert Hoover was the Administrator of the U. S. Food Campaign; and his warning that the campaign was being hampered by secret German propaganda is an interesting one. According to the *Advertiser,* "Mr. Hoover reported that enemy agents were telling housewives that the government planned to seize all the fruits, preserves and other materials canned by the women. Many women have cancelled their plans to can large quantities of food. The seeds of suspicion have been sown by the Kaiser's agents all over the country. Mr. Hoover said it was one of the most insidious phases of German spy work we have yet come across."

In fact, people were quite generally suspicious of strangers - especially foreigners; and all sorts of wild stories were given credence which, in normal times, would seem absurd. This article from the local paper, under date of December 27, 1917, is typical of the times. "Rumors of German spies in town, disguised as book agents, have furnished local gossips with plenty of material to keep tongues wagging the past week.

"Deputy Sheriff Williams has gone to the bottom of all these rumors, and especially the malicious statement that there

Alvin Record: he introduced the paper industry in Livermore with his sawmill, pulp mill and leatherboard mill on the east side of the Androscoggin; he also erected the Jay Paper Company (later the Falmouth Mill) at Jay Bridge.

Hugh Chisholm: he erected Livermore's second paper mill - (The Umbagog Mill); and then the Otis Mill in Jay (village now called Chisholm). His Otis Falls Paper Company absorbed Alvin Record's Jay Paper Company and the Umbagog Mill - forming the nucleus of International Paper Company (which he founded in 1898).

were disease germs of tuberculosis and small pox in the books sold.

"In fact, the representatives of the society selling the medical books entitled *The Household Physician* are at present stopping with Mrs. Everett Ray, and are all native born, American citizens."

Meanwhile, the draft (or "Selective Service") was really beginning to hit home; and within the space of two weeks, in May 1918, the *Advertiser* reported that Oliver Chandler, Carleton Bailey, Aimee Rancourt, Larry Brooks, Harry Philoon, Arthur Phillips, Merle Chandler, Roy Mason, Azarious Beaudette, Harry Severy, Ervin Marcou, David Baum, and John Gibbs were called to Camp Devens. At the same time, the first casualties were being reported from Company "C" 103rd Inf., among whom was Sergeant John Drottar of Chisholm, listed as "severely wounded,"

The attitude of the townspeople generally, at this period, was one of patriotic enthusiasm, of high adventure, and of supreme confidence in our ability to end this thing in a hurry. The songs of that time are indicative of the spirit - *Over There, Oh How I Hate to Get Up in the Morning, K-K-K-Katy, Pack Up Your Troubles In Your Old Kit Bag, How You Gonna Keep 'em Down on the Farm,* and many others.

Except for the small clashes of 1898 and 1916, which were not really wars at all, it had been more than half a century since this country was involved in a major conflict; and the only ones who had first hand knowledge of what such a conflict might mean, were a few old Civil War veterans.

The *Livermore Falls Advertiser,* at the start of the hostilities, indicates something of the fervor:

March 29, 1917, "The occupants of the Bank Building have arranged for a flag 8 feet by 16 feet which will shortly be unrolled to the breeze from the front of the building."

April 12, 1917, "The Livermore Falls Rifle Club, a well

known local organization numbering some sixty members, have offered their services to the town as home guards, should they be needed."

April 17, 1917, "The School Board have voted to devote one hour, from 3 to 4 on a selected day, to military training. This will be compulsory for all the boys."

May 3, 1917, "The first drill of the High School cadets, under Fred Riley, was held Monday afternoon from 3 to 4 o'clock. Harold Riley is to be Acting First Sergeant."

May 31, 1917, "There is only one day for registration under the Selective Service Army Bill - that day is June 5, 1917, from 7:00 A.M. to 9:00 P.M. Every male resident of the United States who has reached his twenty-first birthday, and has not reached his 31st, must register."

Then there were the well remembered Liberty Loan drives, of which the local paper said:

June 21, 1917, "The Livermore Falls Trust & Banking Company reports this community's Liberty Bond Purchase to be $107,550, which exceeds the community's proportional part, and displays the spirit of patriotism which prevails. There were 638 subscribers to these bonds."

July 5, 1917, "If the men in every manufacturing plant do as well in proportion as the men who work at the Record Foundry Co., the Liberty Loan Bonds will be well over-subscribed. Twenty-five men, or nearly 50% of the operatives, have put in their subscriptions for the Liberty Bonds."

October 25, 1917, "The big Liberty Loan Mass Meeting, held at Dreamland Theatre Wednesday was well attended. The meeting was opened by C. H. Sturtevant, who spoke of the purpose of the meeting and impressed upon the hearers the importance of the purchase of Liberty Bonds. Music was rendered by the Livermore Falls band.

"The Rev. Mr. Blair spoke, as well as J. H. Maxwell. B. A. Clary read a poem. Then Mr. Sturtevant introduced the speaker, Congressman Wallace White, who in a ringing speech, gave a brief history of the war, and (explained) how urgent it is for everyone to buy all the Liberty Bonds possible."

April 1918, "With perhaps one exception, the Liberty Loan Parade in Livermore Falls Friday evening was the largest ever witnessed in town, and everybody was, so to speak, 'on their uppers.' Enthusiasm ran high, as the local success of the sale was a matter of great personal interest to all, both young and old. The good old town of East Livermore (now, Livermore Falls) easily went over the top, passing her quota of $52,800, and the people are still buying bonds and will continue to do so until the closing hour of the drive Saturday."

This item, under date of July 26, 1917, is reminiscent of what happened in the Civil War years.

"Help has been scarce and very high priced; and the farmer who has had to depend on whom he could pick up to help in his haying has had a rather hard time of it. The lack of help has made a large sale for farm machinery as with it more women and girls could be employed; and where heretofore many farmers have not allowed their women folks to go into the fields, this year it has been necessary, and they are to be seen on every hand driving the hay rakes, handling the hay forks, or loading the racks, in fact in nearly every kind of work in the fields."

The prospect of a food shortage was an ever present worry, because of the men being drawn off the farms by the armed forces and by the defense industries. The planting of home gardens, the organization of "canning" clubs, and similar projects to augment the food supply, were urged and encouraged by the authorities.

Livermore Falls Advertiser, May 3, 1917, "The International Paper Company's land, known as the Stinchfield farm, will be well utilized this season in the way of gardens for the employees of the company. This excellent idea

Jay Paper Company

Alvin Record went North to Jay Bridge to erect Jay Paper Company (completed 1881); it contained two machines and a pulp mill; a saw mill was erected on "the Island"; this complex later became known as the Falmouth Mill - and then was absorbed by Otis Paper Company in 1896.

THE FALMOUTH PAPER MILL. JAY BRIDGE

The Falmouth Mill - c.1895

was at the suggestion of Supt. W. Murray; and the land will be plowed, and good sized garden plots staked off for such employees who wish to cultivate them for gardens."

The ladies of the towns were busily engaged in knitting for the men in service; and the girls of Saint Rose of Lima had been active in making bandages for the American Red Cross. One of the champion knitters in town was Mrs. George Cummings, of Shy, who, in three months, knitted twelve heavy sweaters besides several dozen pairs of socks.

The work of preparing clothing to be sent to the relief of Belgian children was taken up at the home of Mrs. Fred Riley. One local matron, absorbed in her task, did not notice the proximity of her own coat to the pile of donated clothing; when the time came to go home, she discovered her coat was on the way to Europe.

The rationing of coal to householders was announced by the Fuel Administration as among the plans to prevent a threatened shortage in the coming winter of 1918. Each domestic consumer would be allowed only as much coal "as is found to be scientifically necessary to heat his house to 68 degrees."

That there were some lighter, more enjoyable interludes in these war years is noted in the article in the *Advertiser,* dated October 4, 1917. "Over a hundred accepted the invitation to the old-fashioned corn roast at Rocky Brook Farm Friday evening, coming in autos, teams and on foot. Bushels of corn and three huge fires furnished an abundant supply for all. The lane that led through the pines to the garden was lighted with lanterns; and the fires, lanterns and the Harvest Moon overhead made the cleared space like day.

"After the corn roast, the young people played games, and had a general good time. It was a very late hour when the guests bade good night to their host and hostess, and expressed regrets that a whole year must elapse before corn grows again at Rocky Brook Farm."

The advent of the Armistice in 1918 was hailed with wild enthusiasm. Now that the world had been made "safe for democracy," we should not have another war; the boys could come home now, with the satisfaction of a job well done and a final solution reached.

If the returning veterans, who had experienced actual combat, were more subdued in their reactions, and unwilling to talk about their experiences, it was generally overlooked in the period of rejoicing, or charged to some personal peculiarity.

With the exception of harassment by the long-range U-Boats, including the U-156 which sank so much shipping off the Maine coast and waited a week for ships outside Portland harbor, this continent was spared major damage from hostilities.

True, there was damage from sabotage, and one U-Boat base was located and destroyed in Maine, on an uninhabited island off Washington county; but, for the most part, this country escaped damage on its homeland. Except for shortages of various kinds, the brunt of the war was borne by the armed forces.

Sir Osbert Sitwell, in his reminiscences, gives his impressions of the U.S. in the 1920's, and what he saw in the face of America at that time:

"What I saw in the eyes of a generation ago was infinite kindness and credulity, the boundless confidence which enabled a great people to grasp the leadership of the civilized world - *And then not know what to do with it.*"

In the twenty years between World War I and World War II, this country went through a phase of reactionary isolationism; then a period of resigned acceptance of the fact that the other nations had no intentions of paying their war debts, but would be bound by considerations of self-interest; and, finally, the facing of the facts of life internationally. So that when we entered World War II, we did so with no illusions.

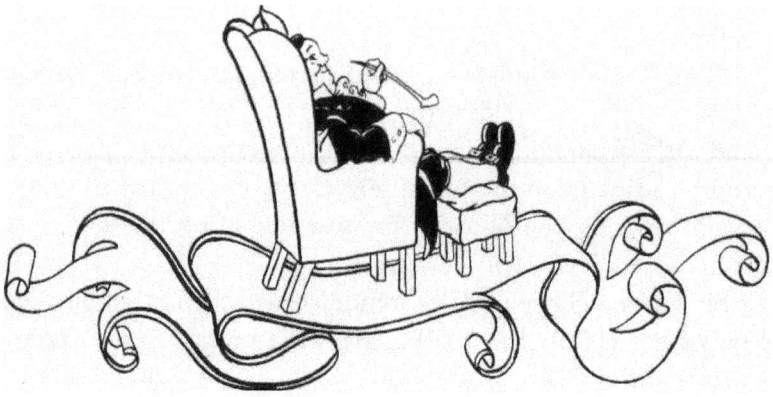

Appendix One

Town, District and State Officials, 1795-1970
Population 1795-1960

TOWN OFFICERS — Livermore 1795-1843

	Town Clerk	Selectmen
1795	Sam Hillman	David Learned, Sylvanus Boardman, Peletiah Gibbs
1796	Sam Hillman	David Learned, Sylvanus Boardman, Thomas Chace
1797	Cyrus Hamlin	David Learned, Hanes Learned, Isaac Livermore
1798	Cyrus Hamlin	Isaac Livermore, Abijah Monroe, Daniel Clark
1799	Elisha Williams	Benjamin True, David Learned, Abijah Monroe
1800	David Learned	Abijah Monroe, Nathaniel Perley, Peletiah Gibbs, Peter Hanes, Uriah Foss
1801	David Learned	Sylvanus Boardman, Nathaniel Perley, Peletiah Gibbs, Samuel Banjamin, Uriah Foss
1802	David Learned	Peletiah Gibbs, James Starbird, Nathaniel Perley, Samuel Banjamin, Jesse Stone
1803	Nathaniel Perley	David Learned, Jesse Stone, Samuel Benjamin
1804	Sarson Chase	Jesse Stone, Nathaniel Perley, Samuel Benjamin
1805	Sarson Chase	Jesse Stone, Nathaniel Perley, Simeon Waters
1806	Sarson Chase	Jesse Stone, Simeon Waters, Nathaniel Perley,
1807	Sarson Chase	Simeon Waters, Nathaniel Perley, Jacob Gibbs
1808	Sarson Chase	Nathaniel Perley, Jesse Stone, Peter Haines
1809	Simeon Waters	Nathaniel Perley, Peter Haines, Thomas Chase, Jr.
1810	Simeon Waters	Nathaniel Perley, Jesse Stone, William Morison
1811	Thomas Chase, Jr.	Nathaniel Perley, William Morison, Samuel Livermore
1812	Thomas Chase, Jr.	Nathaniel Perley, Samuel Livermore, William Morison
1813	Israel Washburn	Samuel Livermore, William Morison, Samuel Atwood
1814	Israel Washburn	Nathaniel Perley, Ebenezer Turner, Samuel Atwood
1815	Israel Washburn	Nathaniel Perley, Ebenezer Turner, Samuel Atwood
1816	Israel Washburn	Nathaniel Perley, Ebenezer Turner, Ira Thompson
1817	Simeon Waters	Jesse Stone, Peter Haines, Israel Washburn
1818	Simeon Waters	Israel Washburn, Aaron Barton, Zebulon Norton
1819	Simeon Waters	Israel Washburn, Amos Hobbs, Zebulon Norton
1820	Charles Barrell	Zebulon Norton, Amos Hobbs, Josiah Hobbs
1821	Charles Barrell	Zebulon Norton, Amos Hobbs, Josiah Hobbs
1822	Charles Barrell	Zebulon Norton, Amos Hobbs, John Leavitt
1823	Charles Barrell	Zebulon Norton, Amos Hobbs, John Leavitt
1824	Charles Barrell	Zebulon Norton, John S. Stone, John Leavitt
1825	Thomas Chase, Jr.	Zebulon Norton, Josiah Cutler, John Leavitt
1826	Thomas Chase, Jr.	Zebulon Norton, Josiah Cutler, John Leavitt
1827	Charles Barrell	Zebulon Norton, Ephraim Pray, John Leavitt

Hugh Chisholm's Otis Mill in Jay (area now called Chisholm), (c.1910)
Here shown after extensive new construction; as early as 1895, it was
recognized as one of the largest of its kind on the continent. Otis absorbed
both the Umbagog and Falmouth mills in 1896, becoming the nucleus of
International Paper Company (formed 1898).

Otis grinder room - c.1900
In 1889, a Boston paper described this facility as the "largest mechanical mill
in Maine" - (at that time 4000hp drove eleven grinding machines).

Town Clerk	Selectmen

	Town Clerk	Selectmen
1828	Charles Barrell	Zebulon Norton, Ephraim Pray, John Leavitt
1829	George Bates	Zebulon Norton, Samuel Morison, John Strickland
1830	Reuel Washburn	John Leavitt, Samuel Morison, John Strickland
1831	Reuel Washburn	Zebulon Norton, Amos Hobbs, John Strickland
1832	James Chase	Zebulon Norton, Ebenezer Turner, John Strickland
1833	Tristram Hillman	John Leavitt, Samuel Morison, John Strickland
1834	Tristram Hillman	Zebulon Norton, Amos Hobbs, John Strickland
1835	Tristram Hillman	Zebulon Norton, Samuel Morison, John Strickland
1836	Tristram Hillman	Zebulon Norton, Aaron Barton, Jr., John Strickland
1837	Tristram Hillman	John Strickland, Aaron Barton, Jr., Hezekiah Atwood
1838	Tristram Hillman	John Strickland, Aaron Barton, Jr., Hezekiah Atwood
1839	Tristram Hillman	John Strickland, Aaron Barton, Jr., Hezekiah Atwood
1840	Tristram Hillman	Hezekiah Atwood, Aaron Barton, Jr., Isaac Strickland
1841	Tristram Hillman	Hezekiah Atwood, Aaron Barton, Jr., Isaac Strickland
1842	Tristram Hillman	Hezekiah Atwood, Aaron Barton, Jr., Isaac Strickland
1843	Tristram Hillman	Hezekiah Atwood, Aaron Barton, Jr., Isaac Strickland

TOWN OFFICERS 1844-1970

Livermore / East Livermore

1844

Livermore:
Tristram Hillman, Town Clerk
Hezekiah Atwood, Selectman
Isaac Strickland, Selectman
Josiah Hobbs, Selectman

East Livermore:
A. Barton, Town Clerk
A. Barton, Selectman
D. Benjamin, Selectman
J. Ford, Selectman

1845

Livermore:
Tristram Hillman, Town Clerk
Hezekiah Atwood, Selectman
Josiah Hobbs, Selectman
Sylvester Norton, Selectman

East Livermore:
A. Barton, Town Clerk
A. Barton, Selectman
D. Benjamin, Selectman
J. Ford, Selectman

1846

Livermore:
Robert Blacker, Town Clerk
Isaac Strickland, Selectman
Matthew M. Stone, Selectman
Ulmer Perley, Selectman
(Hezekiah Atwood succeeded Mr. Strickland who moved to Turner)

East Livermore:
A. Barton, Town Clerk
D. Benjamin, Selectman
J. Ford, Selectman
J. Cutler, Selectman

1847

Livermore:
John Monroe, Jr., Town Clerk
Hezekiah Atwood, Selectman
John Strickland, Selectman
Sylvester Norton, Selectman

East Livermore:
A. Barton, Town Clerk
J. Cutler, Selectman
L. B. Young, Selectman
N. Wellington, Selectman

1848

Livermore:
Same

East Livermore:
A. Barton, Town Clerk
A. Barton, Selectman
J. Ford, Selectman
J. Lovejoy, Selectman

1849

Livermore:
John Monroe, Jr., Town Clerk
John Strickland, Selectman
Sylvester Norton, Selectman
Stephen Leavitt, Selectman

East Livermore:
Same

Same

John Monroe, Jr., Town Clerk
Sylvester Norton, Selectman
Stephen Leavitt, Selectman
Daniel Briggs, Selectman

John Munroe, Jr., Town Clerk
John Strickland, Selectman
Daniel Briggs, Selectman
Granville Childs, Selectman

John Munroe, Jr., Town Clerk
Hezekiah Atwood, Selectman
Isaac Strickland, Selectman
Tristram Hillman, Selectman

Salathiel Tilton, Town Clerk
Hezekiah Atwood, Selectman
Isaac Strickland, Selectman
Tristram Hillman, Selectman

Charles W. Fuller, Town Clerk
Tristram Hillman, Selectman
John Munroe, Jr., Selectman
Clarendon Waters, Selectman

Salathiel Tilton, Town Clerk
Isaac Strickland, Selectman
Clarendon Waters, Selectman
Stephen Leavitt, Selectman

Same

Salathiel Tilton, Town Clerk
Tristram Hillman, Selectman
Sewall M. Norton, Selectman
Cyrus Soper, Selectman

Same

Salathiel Tilton, Town Clerk
Tristram Hillman, Selectman
Cyrus Soper, Selectman
Franklin Gibbs, Selectman

Salathiel Tilton, Town Clerk
Tristram Hillman, Selectman
Cyrus Soper, Selectman
J. D. Thompson, Selectman

1850
A. Barton, Town Clerk
C. Cutler, Selectman
F. Morrill, Selectman
S. Baldwin, Selectman
1851
A. Barton, Town Clerk
J. Cutler, Selectman
J. Ford, Selectman
J. Lovejoy, Selectman
1852
A. Barton, Town Clerk
A. Barton, Selectman
J. Lovejoy, Selectman
J. Ford, Selectman
1853
Same

1854
Same

1855
A. Barton, Town Clerk
A. Barton, Selectman
J. Lovejoy, Selectman
C. S. Pray, Selectman
1856
A. Barton, Town Clerk
C. S. Pray, Selectman
H. L. Morrison, Selectman

1857
E. Kimball, Town Clerk
C. S. Pray, Selectman
J. Lovejoy, Selectman
F. F. Haines, Selectman
1858
E. Kimball, Town Clerk
C. S. Pray, Selectman
J. Lovejoy, Selectman
F. F. Haines, Selectman
1859
E. Kimball, Town Clerk
C. S. Pray, Selectman
H. L. Morrison, Selectman
J. A. Rowell, Selectman
1860
A. Barton, Town Clerk
C. S. Pray, Selectman
H. L. Morrison, Selectman
J. A. Rowell, Selectman
1861
A. Barton, Town Clerk
C. S. Pray, Selectman
H. L. Morrison, Selectman
S. Haines, Selectman

Grand Army Parade
For many years the G.A.R. was a large and potent force in town affairs.

Elaborate floats pass the Rockomeka Hotel in a parade of the 1880's.

Salathiel Tilton, Town Clerk
Lee Strickland, Selectman
Cyrus Soper, Selectman
J. D. Thompson, Selectman

Same

1863

Salathiel Tilton, Town Clerk
Cyrus Soper, Selectman
Orison Rollins, Selectman
J. B. Goding, Selectman

A. Barton, Town Clerk
C. S. Pray, Selectman
H. L. Morrison, Selectman
F. N. Billington, Selectman

1864

Salathiel Tilton, Town Clerk
Orison Rollins, Selectman
A. C. Harlow, Selectman
John White, Selectman

A. Barton, Town Clerk
W. Hunton, Selectman
S. Haines, Selectman
H. Garcelon, Selectman

1865

Same

H. Garcelon, Town Clerk
W. Hunton, Selectman
H. Garcelon, Selectman
F. N. Billington, Selectman

1866

S. F. Perley, Town Clerk
T. Hillman, Selectman
Cyrus Soper, Selectman
Sumner Soule, Selectman

H. Garcelon, Town Clerk
F. N. Billington, Selectman
J. Lovejoy, Selectman
H. Garcelon, Selectman

1867

Same

H. Garcelon, Town Clerk
H. Garcelon, Selectman
F. N. Billington, Selectman
J. Lovejoy, Selectman

1868

S. F. Perley, Town Clerk
T. Hillman, Selectman
Clarendon Waters, Selectman
John A. Hayes, Selectman

H. Garcelon, Town Clerk
H. Garcelon, Selectman
F. N. Billington, Selectman
H. L. Morrison, Selectman

1869

S. F. Perley, Town Clerk
Cyrus Soper, Selectman
John A. Hayes, Selectman
Lewis M. Wing, Selectman

H. Garcelon, Town Clerk
H. Garcelon, Selectman
C. S. Pray, Selectman
H. L. Morrison, Selectman

1870

S. F. Perley, Town Clerk
Cyrus Soper, Selectman
Henry Bradford, Selectman
Lewis M. Wing, Selectman

Same

1871

S. F. Perley, Town Clerk
Cyrus Soper, Selectman
John A. Hayes, Selectman
G. B. Strickland, Selectman

H. Garcelon, Town Clerk
E. Treat, Selectman
F. N. Billington, Selectman
H. L. Morrison, Selectman

1872

S. F. Perley, Town Clerk
Cyrus Soper, Selectman
John A. Hayes, Selectman
C. W. Fuller, Selectman

H. Garcelon, Town Clerk
E. Treat, Selectman
F. N. Billington, Selectman
H. L. Morrison, Selectman

1873

S. F. Perley, Town Clerk
Orison Rollins, Selectman
G. B. Strickland, Selectman
William H. Thompson, Selectman

Same

S. F. Perley, Town Clerk
C. W. Fuller, Selectman
William H. Thompson, Selectman
A. H. Strickland, Selectman

Same

Same

S. F. Perley, Town Clerk
Cyrus Soper, Selectman
J. D. Thompson, Selectman
E. L. Philoon, Selectman

S. F. Perley, Town Clerk
Cyrus Soper, Selectman
George T. Piper, Selectman
Millett Cummings, Selectman

Same

S. F. Perley, Town Clerk
G. B. Strickland, Selectman
E. L. Philoon, Selectman
J. N. Atwood, Selectman

S. F. Perley, Town Clerk
E. L. Philoon, Selectman
J. N. Atwood, Selectman
L. B. Thompson, Selectman

G. B. Strickland, Town Clerk
E. L. Philoon, Selectman
J. N. Atwood, Selectman
L. B. Thompson, Selectman

G. B. Strickland, Town Clerk
J. N. Atwood, Selectman
W. H. Thompson, Selectman
Sidney Boothby, Selectman

G. B. Strickland, Town Clerk
W. F. Fuller, Selectman
G. B. Strickland, Selectman
Millett Cummings, Selectman

C. E. Knight, Town Clerk
G. T. Piper, Selectman
Charles Pike, Selectman
I. T. Munroe, Selectman

Same

William N. Bennett, Town Clerk
G. T. Piper, Selectman
Charles Pike, Selectman
I. T. Munroe, Selectman

1874
E. E. Goding, Town Clerk
E. Treat, Selectman
F. N. Billington, Selectman
H. L. Morrison, Selectman
1875
E. E. Goding, Town Clerk
J. W. Eaton, Selectman
R. C. Boothby, Selectman
C. W. Brown, Selectman
1876
Same
1877
E. E. Goding, Town Clerk
J. W. Eaton, Selectman
R. C. Boothby, Selectman
N. W. Brown, Selectman
1878
Same

1879
Same
1880
E. E. Goding, Town Clerk
R. C. Boothby, Selectman
N. W. Brown, Selectman
A. M. Wing, Selectman
1881
Same

1882
E. S. Goding, Town Clerk
R. C. Boothby, Selectman
A. H. Ford, Selectman
C. B. Knapp, Selectman
1883
C. H. Gibbs, Town Clerk
R. C. Boothby, Selectman
A. H. Ford, Selectman
L. C. Wyman, Selectman
1884
Same

1885
Same

1886
Same
1887
C. H. Gibbs, Town Clerk
N. W. Brown, Selectman
A. J. Dain, Selectman
E. E. Goding, Selectman

An 1883 celebration at the corner of Depot and Main Street.

A building on Mill Hill is well decorated for this 1885 celebration.

William N. Bennett, Town Clerk
I. T. Munroe, Selectman
A. G. Timberlake, Selectman
E. Pratt, Selectman

William N. Bennett, Town Clerk
William Pratt, Selectman
William Thompson, Selectman
Calvin R. Leach, Selectman

William N. Bennett, Town Clerk
Edward Pratt, Selectman
William H. Thompson, Selectman
C. R. Leach, Selectman

Same

William N. Bennett, Town Clerk
I. T. Monroe, Selectman
C. R. Leach, Selectman
D. R. Briggs, Selectman

William N. Bennett, Town Clerk
I. T. Monroe, Selectman
D. R. Briggs, Selectman
A. F. Russell, Selectman

William N. Bennett, Town Clerk
I. T. Monroe, Selectman
A. F. Russell, Selectman
R. B. Bradford, Selectman

William N. Bennett, Town Clerk
I. T. Monroe, Selectman
C. F. Pike, Selectman
C. E. Emerson, Selectman

William N. Bennett, Town Clerk
I. T. Monroe, Selectman
C. F. Pike, Selectman
C. E. Emerson, Selectman

William N. Bennett, Town Clerk
C. L. Day, Selectman
A. G. Timberlake, Selectman
C. P. Sanders, Selectman

Same

Same

Same

1888
C. H. Gibbs, Town Clerk
E. E. Goding, Selectman
N. W. Brown, Selectman
C. B. Knapp, Selectman
1889
C. H. Gibbs, Town Clerk
Geo. R. Currier, Selectman
C. W. Brown, Selectman
A. M. Bumpus, Selectman
1890
Same

1891
C. H. Gibbs, Town Clerk
R. C. Boothby, Selectman
J. A. Rowell, Selectman
A. H. Ford, Selectman
1892
Same

1893
C. H. Gibbs, Town Clerk
R. C. Boothby, Selectman
R. N. Maxim, Selectman
George O. Eustis, Selectman
1894
C. H. Gibbs, Town Clerk
E. E. Goding, Selectman
R. N. Maxim, Selectman
George O. Eustis, Selectman
1895
Same

1896
C. H. Gibbs, Town Clerk
George O. Eustis, Selectman
R. N. Maxim, Selectman
D. C. Searles, Selectman
1897
C. W. Hyde, Town Clerk
R. C. Boothby, Selectman
Frank Billington, Selectman
A. Wilkins, Selectman
1898
C. H. Gibbs, Town Clerk
R. C. Boothby, Selectman
T. A. Billington, Selectman
A. M. Bumpus, Selectman
1899
Same
1900
C. H. Gibbs, Town Clerk
A. M. Bumpus, Selectman
George O. Eustis, Selectman

Dedication of the "Civil War Memorial" monument in 1907.

Afternoon service at the East Livermore Campground Tabernacle in 1912.

S. P. Judkins, Selectman

1901

William N. Bennett, Town Clerk
D. R. Briggs, Selectman
A. G. Timberlake, Selectman
C. P. Sanders, Selectman

Same

1902

William N. Bennett, Town Clerk
D. R. Briggs, Selectman
A. G. Timberlake, Selectman
C. P. Sanders, Selectman

C. H. Gibbs, Town Clerk
A. M. Bumpus, Selectman
F. A. Billington, Selectman
J. A. Record, Selectman

1903

William N. Bennett, Town Clerk
C. P. Sanders, Selectman
C. R. Leach, Selectman
C. F. Pike, Selectman

I. B. Clary, Town Clerk
A. M. Bumpus, Selectman
H. A. Morrison, Selectman
J. A. Record, Selectman

1904

William N. Bennett, Town Clerk
C. F. Pike, Selectman
C. R. Leach, Selectman
H. P. Berry, Selectman

I. B. Clary, Town Clerk
A. M. Bumpus, Selectman
H. A. Morrison, Selectman
H. L. Hersey, Selectman

1905

William N. Bennett, Town Clerk
I. T. Monroe, Selectman
H. L. Ayer, Selectman
S. H. Beckler, Selectman

I. B. Clary, Town Clerk
George O. Eustis, Selectman
Frank A. Billington, Selectman
H. L. Hersey, Selectman

1906

William N. Bennett, Town Clerk
I. T. Monroe, Selectman
H. L. Ayer, Selectman
C. D. Leavitt, Selectman

Same

1907

William N. Bennett, Town Clerk
H. L. Ayer, Selectman
C. D. Leavitt, Selectman
H. C. Soule, Selectman

Same

1908

William N. Bennett, Town Clerk
C. D. Leavitt, Selectman
H. C. Soule, Selectman
W. R. Soper, Selectman

Same

1909

William N. Bennett, Town Clerk
D. R. Briggs, Selectman
H. P. Berry, Selectman
W. R. Soper, Selectman

I. B. Clary, Town Clerk
George O. Eustis, Selectman
Frank A. Billington, Selectman
D. F. Blunt, Selectman

1910

William N. Bennett, Town Clerk
C. F. Pike, Selectman
H. L. Ayer, Selectman
W. R. Soper, Selectman

I. B. Clary, Town Clerk
George O. Eustis, Selectman
Frank A. Billington, Selectman
H. L. Hersey, Selectman

1911

William N. Bennett, Town Clerk
I. T. Monroe, Selectman
D. R. Briggs, Selectman
R. E. Verrill, Selectman

L. P. Brown, Town Clerk
H. L. Hersey, Selectman
A. D. Cole, Selectman
E. H. Strout, Selectman

1912

William N. Bennett, Town Clerk
I. T. Monroe, Selectman
D. R. Briggs, Selectman
J. N. Sinnett, Selectman

L. P. Brown, Town Clerk
Everett H. Strout, Selectman
Alphonso D. Cole, Selectman
Houghton H. Putnam, Selectman

311

Company "C" of the 103rd Maine National Guard Regt., just prior to its Mexican Border Campaign.

Dedication of the memorial to the World War I veterans of East Livermore - May 30, 1923

H. L. Ayer, Town Clerk
C. P. Sanders, Selectman
J. N. Sinnett, Selectman
C. F. Edgecomb, Selectman

Same

Same

H. L. Ayer, Town Clerk
J. N. Sinnett, Selectman
F. E. Adkins, Selectman
C. F. Edgecomb, Selectman

H. L. Ayer, Town Clerk
F. E. Adkins, Selectman
C. R. Babb, Selectman
C. F. Edgecomb, Selectman

H. L. Ayer, Town Clerk
F. E. Adkins, Selectman
W. S. Lovewell, Selectman
C. F. Edgecomb, Selectman

H. L. Ayer, Town Clerk
F. E. Adkins, Selectman
J. E. Richmond, Selectman
R. E. Pike, Selectman

H. L. Ayer, Town Clerk
I. T. Monroe, Selectman
H. L. Ayer, Selectman
F. S. Dow, Selectman

Olin Briggs, Town Clerk (resigned)
F. A. Sproul, Town Clerk
F. E. Adkins, Selectman
F. S. Dow, Selectman
R. S. Timberlake, Selectman

F. A. Sproul, Town Clerk
F. S. Dow, Selectman
F. E. Adkins, Selectman
R. S. Timberlake, Selectman

F. A. Sproul, Town Clerk
F. E. Adkins, Selectman
J. N. Sinnett, Selectman
U. P. Francis, Selectman

F. A. Sproul, Town Clerk
F. E. Adkins, Selectman
U. P. Francis, Selectman
L. E. Boothby, Selectman

Same

1913
Same

1914
Same

1915
L. P. Brown, Town Clerk
Herbert L. Hersey, Selectman
A. D. Cole, Selectman
H. H. Putnam, Selectman

1916
L. P. Brown, Town Clerk
Herbert L. Hersey, Selectman
A. D. Cole, Selectman
Walter B. Hood, Selectman

1917
Lorenzo P. Brown, Town Clerk
Herbert L. Hersey, Selectman
Alphonso D. Cole, Selectman
Walter B. Hood, Selectman

1918
Lorenzo P. Brown, Town Clerk
Everett H. Strout, Selectman
Samuel W. Coolidge, Selectman
Z. A. Mersereau, Selectman

1919
Lorenzo P. Brown, Town Clerk
E. H. Strout, Selectman
S. W. Coolidge, Selectman
W. H. Randall, Selectman

1920
Lorenzo P. Brown, Town Clerk
Albert F. Dwelley, Selectman
W. M. Randall, Selectman
C. M. Bailey, Selectman

1921
Willis Sewall, Town Clerk
Albert F. Dwelley, Selectman
W. M. Randall, Selectman
C. M. Bailey, Selectman

1922
H. Isma Dyke, Town Clerk
Albert F. Dwelley, Selectman
William H. Randall, Selectman
Albert Haskell, Selectman

1923
H. Isma Dyke, Town Clerk
Everett H. Strout, Selectman
Walter Ford, Selectman
George Dyke, Selectman

1924
H. Isma Dyke, Town Clerk
Everett H. Strout, Selectman
Walter E. Ford, Selectman
George W. Dyke, Selectman

1925
H. Isma Dyke, Town Clerk
Everett H. Strout, Selectman
Walter E. Ford, Selectman

For many years the Androscoggin County Agricultural Society's Androscoggin County Fair was considered one of Maine's finest. It was held for three days each year at "Evergreen Park" (where the Livermore Shoe building now stands).

Livermore Falls Cornet Band, 1866

314

F. A. Sproul, Town Clerk
U. P. Francis, Selectman
L. E. Boothby, Selectman
A. L. Sanders, Selectman

Same

F. A. Sproul, Town Clerk
F. S. Dow, Selectman
A. L. Sanders, Selectman
C. A. Bryant, Selectman

Fred E. Adkins, Town Clerk
J. N. Sennett, Selectman
A. L. Sanders, Selectman
W. M. Richmond, Selectman

Livermore

Fred A. Sproul, Town Clerk
J. N. Sennett, Selectman
A. L. Sanders, Selectman
W. M. Richmond, Selectman

Fred A. Sproul, Town Clerk
Francis S. Dow, Selectman
W. M. Richmond, Selectman
P. M. Brown, Selectman

Fred A. Sproul, Town Clerk
Francis S. Dow, Selectman
W. M. Richmond, Selectman
C. A. Jordan, Selectman

F. E. Adkins, Town Clerk
Francis S. Dow, Selectman
W. M. Richmond, Selectman
C. A. Jordan, Selectman

?

F. E. Adkins, Town Clerk
Roy E. Pike, Selectman
Francis S. Dow, Selectman
C. F. Edgecomb, Selectman

F. E. Adkins, Town Clerk
Roy E. Pike, Selectman
C. F. Edgecomb, Selectman
H. P. Berry, Selectman

F. E. Adkins, Town Clerk

George Dyke, Selectman
1926
Same

1927
H. Isma Dyke, Town Clerk
Everett H. Strout, Selectman
Walter E. Ford,
Ralph J. Riley, Selectman
1928
H. Isma Dyke, Town Clerk
Ralph J. Riley, Selectman
Walter E. Ford, Selectman
Myrle G. Davenport, Selectman
1929
H. Isma Dyke, Town Clerk
Ralph J. Riley, Selectman
A. G. Morrison, Selectman
Myrle G. Davenport, Selectman

Livermore Falls
1930
H. Isma Dyke, Town Clerk
Ralph J. Riley, Selectman
A. G. Morrison, Selectman
Myrtle Davenport, Selectman
1931
H. Isma Dyke & C. Newell Dyke,
   Town Clerks
Ralph J. Riley, Selectman
A. G. Morrison, Selectman
M. G. Davenport, Selectman
1932
C. Newell Dyke, Town Clerk
Ralph J. Riley, Selectman
A. G. Morrison, Selectman
Myrle Davenport, Selectman
1933
C. Newell Dyke, Town Clerk
Edward N. French, Selectman
Adelbert Morrison, Selectman
Myrtle G. Davenport, Selectman
1934
C. Newell Dyke, Town Clerk
Ralph J. Riley, Selectman
A. G. Morrison, Selectman
M. G. Davenport, Selectman
1935
C. Newell Dyke, Town Clerk
Ralph Riley, Selectman
Myrle Davenport, Selectman
Morris Allen, Selectman
1936
C. Newell Dyke, Town Clerk
Myrle G. Davenport, Selectman
Morris G. Allen, Selectman
Edward N. French, Selectman
1937
C. Newell Dyke, Town Clerk

Tweed Hyde's "Rube" Band, 1926

Dreamland Theater
Tweed Hyde's "Rube" Band was a favorite attraction at this theater.

Oscar Turner appointed
Town Clerk 4/10/37
C. F. Edgecomb, Selectman
Roy E. Pike, Selectman
H. P. Berry, Selectman

Oscar Turner, Town Clerk
C. F. Edgecomb, Selectman
Roy E. Pike, Selectman
N. A. Timberlake, Selectman

Oscar Turner, Town Clerk
N. A. Timberlake, Selectman
Roy E. Pike, Selectman
C. F. Edgecomb, Selectman

Same

Oscar Turner, Town Clerk
Arthur Boothby, Selectman
Roy Pike. Selectman
C. F. Edgecomb, Selectman

Same

Same

Oscar Turner, Town Clerk
Arthur Boothby. Selectman
C. F. Edgecomb, Selectman
Roy Pike, Selectman

Same

Same

Oscar Turner, Town Clerk
Dwight Lamb, Selectman
Roy Pike. Selectman
C. F. Edgecomb, Selectman

Oscar Turner, Town Clerk
C. F. Edgecomb, Selectman
Dwight Lamb, Selectman
Richard Cook, Selectman

Same

Same

Oscar Turner, Town Clerk
C. F. Edgecomb, Selectman
Dwight Lamb, Selectman
Richard Cook, Selectman

Myrle G. Davenport, Selectman
Morris G. Allen, Selectman
Edward N. French, Selectman

1938
C. Newell Dyke & Claribel H.
Gordon, Town Clerks
Myrle G. Davenport, Selectman
Morris G. Allen, Selectman
Edward N. French, Selectman
1939
Claribel H. Gordon, Town Clerk
Morris G. Allen, Selectman
Edward N. French, Selectman
Philip S. Strout, Selectman
1940
Same
1941
Same

1942
Same
1943
Claribel H. Gordon, Town Clerk
Myrle G. Davenport. Selectman
Edward N. French, Selectman
Howard H. Dyke, Selectman
1944
Claribel H. Gordon, Town Clerk
Myrle G. Davenport. Selectman
Edward N. French, Selectman
Samuel W. Coolidge, Selectman
1945
Same
1946
Same
1947
Claribel H. Gordon, Town Clerk
Myrle G. Davenport, Selectman
Samuel W. Coolidge, Selectman
William L. Kinch, Selectman
1948
Claribel H. Gordon. Town Clerk
William L. Kinch. Selectman
Louis C. Brown. Selectman
Anatole L'Heureux, Selectman
1949
Claribel H. Gordon, Town Clerk
William L. Kinch, Selectman
Samuel Coolidge, Selectman
John H. Barclay, Selectman
1950
Same
1951
Claribel H. Gordon, Town Clerk
William L. Kinch, Selectman
Harold W. Jennings, Selectman
Maurice A. Lapointe, Selectman

Livermore Falls High School, 1891

Livermore Falls School, 1891
Although not the oldest school building, this one did originally house all grades,
and was the first home of Livermore Falls High School.

Oscar Turner, Town Clerk
E. H. Beckler, Selectman
C. F. Edgecomb, Selectman
Dwight Lamb, Selectman

Same

Same

Same

Same

Same

Oscar Turner, Town Clerk
E. H. Beckler, Selectman
Dwight Lamb, Selectman
C. F. Edgecomb, Selectman

Oscar Turner, Town Clerk
Thomas Nichols, Selectman
E. H. Beckler, Selectman
C. F. Edgecomb, Selectman

Oscar Turner, Town Clerk
J. Lowell Bowles, Selectman
E. H. Beckler, Selectman
Thomas Nichols, Selectman

Same

Oscar Turner, Town Clerk
Uuno Pulkkinen, Selectman
E. H. Beckler, Selectman
J. L. Bowles, Selectman

Same

Same

Oscar Turner, Town Clerk
J. L. Bowles, Selectman
E. H. Beckler, Selectman
Uuno Pulkkinen, Selectman

1952
Same

1953
Same
1954
Same
1955
Claribel H. Gordon, Town Clerk
Claude H. Edwards, Selectman
Arthur B. Wagner, Selectman
Maurice A. LaPointe, Selectman
1956
Claribel H. Gordon, Town Clerk
Maurice A. LaPointe, Selectman
Arthur B. Wagner, Selectman
Charles Alvino, Selectman
1957
Claribel H. Gordon, Town Clerk
Walter M. Baker, Selectman
J. Merton Knowlton, Selectman
William L. Kinch, Selectman
1958
Claribel H. Gordon, Town Clerk
Walter M. Baker, Selectman
J. Merton Knowlton, Selectman
William L. Kinch, Selectman
1959
Claribel H. Gordon &
Myrle G. Davenport, Town Clerks
J. Merton Knowlton, Selectman
William L. Kinch, Selectman
Walter Baker, Selectman
1960
Marion Hood, Town Clerk
William L. Kinch, Selectman
Walter M. Baker, Selectman
J. Merton Knowlton, Selectman
1961
Same
1962
Same

1963
Marion P. Hood, Town Clerk
Graydon M. Mann, Selectman
J. Merton Knowlton, Selectman
Walter Baker, Selectman
1964
Marion P. Hood, Town Clerk
Walter M. Baker, Selectman
J. Merton Knowlton, Selectman
Gerald J. O'Hanlon, Selectman
1965
Marion P. Hood, Town Clerk
J. Merton Knowlton, Selectman
Gerald O'Hanlon, Selectman
Cameron F. Osgood, Selectman

Same

1966
Marion P. Hood, Town Clerk
Gerald O'Hanlon, Selectman
Cameron Osgood, Selectman
George Cummings, Selectman
Edward Maxwell, Selectman
James Miller, Selectman
1967
Same

Oscar Turner, Town Clerk
Uuno Pulkkinen, Selectman
J. L. Bowles, Selectman
Leslie E. Boothby, Selectman

Same

1968
Marion P. Hood, Town Clerk
George Cummings, Selectman
Gerold O'Hanlon, Selectman
James Miller, Selectman
Cameron Osgood, Selectman
Clark Souther, Selectman
1969

Same

Marion P. Hood, Town Clerk
James Miller, Selectman
Harry Moulton, Selectman
Cameron Osgood, Selectman
Clark Souther, Selectman
George Cummings, Selectman
1970

Nellie Tidswell, Town Clerk
Uuro J. Pulkkinen, Selectman
J. L. Bowles, Selectman
Leslie E. Boothby, Selectman

Marion P. Hood, Town Clerk
Clark Souther, Selectman
Cameron Osgood, Selectman
Harry Moulton, Selectman

Representatives elected to the Great and General Court of Massachusetts with the date of their election:

1799	Elijah Livermore	1812	Simeon Waters
1800	David Learned	1813	William H. Brettun
1801	David Learned	1813	Samuel Livermore
1802	Sylvanus Boardman	1814	Simeon Waters
1803	Cyrus Hamlin	1814	Israel Washburn
1804	No election	1815	Simeon Waters
1805	Voted not to send	1815	Israel Washburn
1806	Simeon Waters	1816	Simeon Waters
1807	Nathaniel Perley	1816	Ira Thompson
1808	Simeon Waters	1817	Voted not to send
1809	Simeon Waters	1818	Simeon Waters
1810	Simeon Waters	1818	Israel Washburn
1811	William H. Brettun	1819	Israel Washburn
1812	William H. Brettun		

REPRESENTATIVES TO THE LEGISLATURE OF MAINE

1820 Thomas Chase, Jr.
1821 Thomas Chase, Jr.
1822 Thomas Chase, Jr.
1823 Thomas Chase, Jr.
1824 Thomas Chase, Jr.
1825 Thomas Chase, Jr.
1826 Thomas Chase, Jr.
1827 Benjamin Bradford
1828 Benjamin Bradford
1829 Benjamin Bradford
1830 Charles Barrell
1831 William Snow
1832 Reuel Washburn
1833 Reuel Washburn
1834 Reuel Washburn
1835 Reuel Washburn
1836 Benjamin Bradford
1837 Samuel B. Holt
1838 Samuel B. Holt
1839 William Kelsey
1840 William Kelsey
1841 Reuel Washburn
1842 Samuel B. Morrison
1843 Isaac S. Daly
1844 Samuel B. Morrison
1845 Isaac S. Daly
1846 Philip Munger
1847 Benjamin Bradford
1848 James Chase
1849 William B. Small
1850 Nathaniel Norcross
1851 Nathaniel Norcross
1852 No election
1853 Livermore, Canton, Dixfield
     and Mexico as a representa-
     tive district, elected John B.
     Morrow of Dixfield
1854 E. G. Harlow of Canton
1855 T. C. Gurney of Canton
1856 Peter Trask of Mexico
1857 Orison Rollins of Livermore
1858 Calvin Stanley of Dixfield
1859 T. C. Gurney of Canton
1860 S. M. Norton of Livermore
1861 John Monroe of Livermore
1862 Livermore classed with Tur-
     ner as a representative dis-
     trict, elected:
     Solon Chase of Turner
1863 Solon Chase of Turner
1864 C. W. Fuller of Livermore
1865 D. H. Kilbreth of Livermore
1866 Philip Bradford, Turner
1867 S. G. Shurtleff

1868 Philip Bradford, Turner
1869 A. C. Pray, Livermore
1870 Z. H. Bearce of Turner
1871 James Fish of Turner
1872 Rufus Prince of Turner
1873 James A. Gary of Turner
1874 Caleb Smith, Livermore
1875 John Sanders
1877 Samuel F. Boothby
1878 James N. Atwood
1884 J. O. Palmer
1884 J. O. Palmer
1894 R. A. Ryerson
1898 R. A. Ryerson
1904 R. B. Bradford
1908 R. B. Bradford
1916 F. A. Leavitt
1924 George G. Young
1925 George C. Young, Livermore
1927 Chester H. Sturtevant,
     East Livermore
1929 Chester H. Sturtevant,
     East Livermore
1931 Chester H. Sturtevant,
     Livermore Falls
1933 Francis S. Dow, Livermore
1935 J. Guy Coolidge, Livermore
1937 J. Guy Coolidge, Livermore
1939 George R. Grua
     Livermore Falls
1941 George R. Grua,
     Livermore Falls
1943 George R. Grua,
     Livermore Falls
1945 Lewis C. Berry, Livermore
1947 Harry C. Moulton,
     Livermore Falls
1949 Robert H. Boothby, Livermore
1951 Robert H. Boothby, Livermore
1953 Willard E. Riley
1955 William L. Kinch,
     Livermore Falls
1957 William L. Kinch,
     Livermore Falls
1959 William L. Kinch,
     Livermore Falls
1961 Leslie E. Boothby, Livermore
1963 Leslie E. Boothby, Livermore
1965 Forest S. Gilbert, Turner
1967 Edmund C. Darey,
     Livermore Falls
1969 Forest S. Gilbert, Turner

POPULATION

1795 - 400
1800 - 863
1810 - 1560
1820 - 2174
1830 - 2445
1840 - 2745

	Livermore	East Livermore	Total
1850	1764	892	2656
1860	1597	1029	2626
1870	1467	1004	2471
1880	1262	1080	2342
1890	1151	1506	2657
1900	1125	2129	3254
1910	1100	2651	3751
1920	1064	2636	3700
1930	1113	3148	4261
1940	1302	3190	4492
1950	1313	3359	4672
1960	1363	3343	4706

Appendix Two

Original Text of the Thomas Fish Journal, April 26, 1773 - June 26, 1773 and His Return to Port Royal, August, 1773

"Journal from Oxford to Androscoggen River April 26, 1773.
Left Oxford Dinner at - - - Loged at Framinham.
27 to Boston Spoak for a passage a Board of Capt. John Martins Sloop, Name the Salley, Belonging to Falmouth.
28 Got our Stores aboard waiting for a fare wind.
29 waiting for a fare wind.
30 Sailed 7 0 the clock in the morning came of against Dear Ireland head wind.
May 1 Day 1773 Saild half after 8 and at Sun Set of against Epswech bay Ninty six Saile of Vessels all In Sight at once pleasant weather fare wind but Small.
2 Sunday In at Falmouth at one of the clock afternoon three 0 clock come To an ancer at Town.
May 3rd Day 1773 got our stoares out of the Vessell and Stoard them In Mr Shattucks Store Left Famouth 2 0 the clock On the afternoon Traveld Eleven miles and cared our packs very heavey Loged at Mr Joseph Latens North Casco.
4th Traveld 4 miles 1/2 throw the woods before Breakfast killed one pigeon and Eat for Breakfast at Knight at Mr. Stinchfield of New Glouster Very hot weather met Mr. Livermores Team a going after thee Rest of the stoars Left Behind.
5th Set out for our township Mr. James Stinchfield our pilot D. Mixer Thos. Fish Willm Foster Ebiz Gleas (on?) Lieut. Livermore behind to bring up our Stores traviled to Little Amascoggen 9 mile from New Gloucester waided the River Willm Foster fell in to the River all over with 3 axes and a grait coat on his Shoulders Killed 4 pigeons one "patrage campt by great Wilson pond 30 miles to Little amascoggin (from Falmouth?) Meashuard by the chain 9 miles to wilson pond, In

wading I wet my watch in the works and Did Not stop and take water out.

6th Day began to clear our Road Set the woods af fire and burnt our gun stick Lay very coald for our Blankets is behind with our Stores.

7th Day Lieut Livermore and his hands come to us at Ten of the cloack with stores and had bad luck In crossing Little amascoggen River and fell In with one hors and our Stores (were) Very much wet and Left us at 2 of the Cloack and Returned after more Stores Claard the Road to a large Brook Very Bad passing till thare is a bridg built - the 1st Day of may Lieut Livermore Left Falmouth with his Team and hands.

8 Still at work on our Road Kild 2 patriges cetch Fish - Encampt by a pleasant pond our pilot Returned to us at Sun Set, marked the Road out.

9 Sunday morning our pilot Left us he was in our Employ 3 Days besides Sunday to goe home in - Delivrd Mr. James Stinchfield my Deed to Keep or Leave at the Registers office in Falmouth if he has opertunyty To Get Recorded Deed of my Land In port Royal Township - this Knight very sharp Litning and Thunder vary hard Til about 12 0 the clock.

10 Clearing our Road very much Tormented with the flys hot Day thunder and Litning veary hard and Sharp til midnite much Rain Lay uncomfortable this Knight Clead the Road within 1 mile of 20 mile River bad Logs by the mile to gather to cut out of the Road we have Not Eat but 2 meals of Solt provision Since we have been In the woods Fish and patridges plenty Saw where the thunder Struck a tree not far from our camp Last Knight.

11 Clearing Road - this Knight Phipses Cannaday Committees campt with us, bound up to theire Township to Loting out.

12 Lieut Livermoor and his hands carne to us about Ten 0 the clock forenoon. this knight Rany. 　　　　　　　　 .

13 Day Lieut Livermoor crost the Twenty mile River with 4 oxen 1 hors - this Day caryd our Baggage over Dito \River and Encampt near the River. crost with the Road at three 0 the clock. Rany Knight.

14 Rany morning Rany all Day Encampt on the East side of 20

324

mile River Fish plenty Trouts vary Large and plenty Lay hear
with our Blangkets Strecht all Day.

«15 Lieut Livermoor and I Sett out in order to view the Land
for the Rod In To our Township about 15 miles the way we
went and it Raind Some when we Set out and was as rainy a
Day as a most Ever I New and Lieut Livermoor went to goe
Round a Swamp to se if the Land would not beter acomadate
for the Road and got Lost from (us) and I flr'd three guns and
continu,d hollering for 2 hours and half by Times before he
-came to me and then we Sett out towerds and arived at our
ground camp at Dusk - but Like to have Layd in the wood all
Knight without fire but to our grait Jouy Mr How of pond
Town was thare a Sleep in myoId Saw bunk I had thare the
Last year and had a good fire and I puld of my Shirt and Rung
it as Dryas I could and warmed it and put on again and I Did
the same by my Blanket and Lay Down in my wet cloaths and
Rested as comfortable as I could - we wet our plan and it came
into 9 peces which cost us some Trouble having no other with
us.

16 Sunday Returned to our people to 20 mile River - by the
misforting we had a Satturday we was oblige to Return for want
of provistion and I Snapt my gun at a Large buck moose well
Loaded with a ball but the powder being wet a saterday and
Damp to my grait Sorow Did not goe off and Returd to our
peopell and all was well with them and found them Eating Som
hot patrige Broath whitch Did not com a mis to us also for we
had not Eat any hot victtuls Since we left them.

17 munday went with Lieut Livermoore to help him Drive his
cattle Into Town and got along vary well Except his hors fell
Down and cut his Knee and Lamed himself - got within about
one mile of camp at Dusk and haveing a grait mind to git in to
our camp (we) on yoak our oxen and I set my compas and it
being so Dark that I could not Se the Needle but Tuck East to
be West and Sheard of about one mile and Struck the grait
meadow and was oblige tp Lyon an Island in the meadow and
after Long Trail we got fire but had Noe ax with us Nor
provition - Sum Rany but we Campt Down as well as we cold
and Starved it our haveing eat Noe hot visttuls Since morning

In more recent years, this first home of Livermore Falls High School was enlarged and served as the town's Primary School only, until construction of a new Grammar School on Park Street.

Livermore Falls High School, 1900

This new building was the pride of the Town in 1900. It later became the Grammar School; and now, since construction of a new Grammar School on Park Street, it is occupied by the Primary School.

but wished for Day Light before it com - arived at our grand camp Eight 0 clock morning.

18 Tusday a Loocking over the Town to find whare will best acomo-"date for the Road - patridges or pigons almost Every Day the Dog came a croast a pocapine and filled his nose with Quills.

19 Wensday Returned to Silvester to our people and arived thare about 5 0 the dock and Jest before I got thare the Dog Stole Sum Chease and converted it to his own use and as he broak the Law he Recd his punishment Jest as I arived and in about one hour after he Tread a vary Large poco pine and I Shot it and Skind it and he Stoed the whole Body (in) to him that he need not Steal no moreprovition.

20 Thusday about the oald Task claring Road past a large Brook - about 12 0 the clock begane to Raine Set in araining and Beat us of from our worck before Knight Vary Rany and uncomfortable weather for our Busness 14 & 15th Days all our hands Lay by by Reason of Rain besides several other times part of a Day, this Day we had patrige for Diner and after we had Dind I tuck the gun and went about 100 Rods from the camp and Kild 2 more for the Next Day - our famyly is small Nobody Hear but Foster and Gleason and I - father Mixer and Lieut Livermore and his hands Left us the 17th Day to goe to our New Oxford Ryal to plant corn and prottous (potatoes) - this Time a Drawing a plan of our Town by the oald peacess that was wet and made out So as that it will answer our Town at this time.

21 Set out to goe for Stores to Little andrascoggen River to Mr Lanes arrived thare Jest before Knight and put up our Stores for marching the Next moning.

22 Day Satturday Set our heavy Load upon our Back But we had one cag we cald the Bull which helpt us cary the Rest at Every Spring we Bluded the Bull we come Twelve mile and Night com on.

23 Sunday arived at our camp this morning and found all things well.

24 Day monday moved forard on our Road about 1 file and haf about 2 0 the clock thare come up a Thunder Shoure and Raine

and Thunder Vary hard Sharp Litning, Rand till Knight.

25 Tusday pleasant and cold and the Hyes Did not bite so bad as useyal.

26 Wensday or Election and Vary Rany and noe Bread nor meal Some croas and crocked Went Into our Town. Rany all the way and "arived at the Grand Camp about Two 0 cloack - Lieut Livermore had Jest Killed a fat calf and the Sight of the calf with other good Neaccecarys made us (in) as good condition as Ever - hear we found Phipses cannaday men come to Se us also. To spend a few Soshable hours with us and Thay told us that they Kild a fat calf the Day before to Keep Election with, but thare cow Run away into the wood wild and thay had not milked hir since thay Kild the calf, but not Somuch to be wondered at for she was of the Natives of the Land thare So we had sam further Discorse about *Ryes* they asked me if I had Sean any and I tould them I had Sean a few but thay would believe me had not my check and face and hands ben almost Raw whitch proved that I Spoack the Truth. I Should not ben cald one of Varassatay by them So after a little past time In Eating Some fresh Veal and Drinking Some W. Enda Toddy we parted with our Neabours we went to grinding our axes for the Next Days Servis.

27 thusday the hands at work on the Road Next to the River for we cold not git any meal to cary out with us but expect Sam Tomorow from pond Town by Mr How and I went up to the meating house Lot and Layd out the Road and marked Down to the Entervale.

28 the auld Task and thar come a Scout of Gnats Down upon us this Day the first we have Sean and we expect thousands Directly, the Black *Ryes* Seam to abate, but the muscatoes are Vary Numer's among us and a grait many of them will weigh half a pound - not apeace tho' - the wind Vary high today So that we amagin (Imagine) Mr How could not eros ammascogen pond that our meal is not come.

29 Satturday at worck at the Road till 12 of the clock. Left Foster to fetch out Some meal and Gleason and I went out to our camp In Silvester for we was afraid the wild Beasts would Distrouy our Stores and cloaths if we Left the thare any Longer and we markd the Road 5 hundred Road aero ast 5 Lots and

Chester Moore beside his delivery wagon, about 1900

F. A. Millett, blacksmith

got to our camp Jest as the Sun Sot one mile and a half from our Town Line into Silvester and found all things well but Noe neal nor bread.

30 Sunday this morning made a Breakefast of Chocolate and Buter and Chease but noe Bread, Diner Noe Bread but about 2 a the cloack we heard a cracking in the Brush and I tuck the gun into my hand thinking it to be a moose but as sane it came in Sight Who Should it "be but our Nabour Foster with half a bushel of meal to his Back whitch Rejoyst us much as the Sight of a moose it Semes he thoat marcy was before Sacrifise tho it was Sunday he new we had Noe bread and Soe come out to us.

31 Monday unfortanate to and Remarkable - Foster cut his Knee or Jest above his Knee throuw 3 thicknesses of garter, Trowsers 1 thickness, Stocken 2 thicknesses. Not vary bad it was cut half after Nine and ten minets after Eleven he came vary Near being Kild and (was) Remarkably preserved. I was afelling a tree about 20 Inches throu varay Tall and when I found thee tree was agoing I give the word - Take care, and foster was about 4 Road frame me upon a Log about 3 feet from the ground and Stood and Looked of the tree as it was a falling and the tree fell on the Log he was on and gave it a cant and Turnd him Rite under the Tree he fell Right under a Log he was on and buckled him up Into a heep and the tree Settled on him and Struck the Breath out of his Body and Stounded him and the axe floe out of his hand about eight feet from him and he was In that posistion that he could not help himself and Gleason Lifted the Log about one Inch and I Turnd his head it being buckled under his Body So that as he come (to) he could Jest help him Self so as to get out - hurt his Shoulder Some and Beat his Leg Black and Blue and give his whole Body a univers (al) Shock.

June 1 Day Tusday Rany this morning till after Nine - went to worck and about three a cloack Beat of by Rane and a good Deal of thunder but bot Near - com home to our camp and Sett the girles to washing and Keep them washing till thare finger was Sore and the Bouys tended the Kittels with water the first time of washing Since we Left home, our Linnings and woolens Look vary White but our muslings and cambricks we that Not best to wash to Day becaze the weather looks Dowtfull for Driing and we are going to move to morrow and we that it would make them yalow So that thay would not be fit to be Sean in the meating hous.

2 Wensday Cloudy Loose Weather this morning Lowary all Day but we worcked all Day on the Road and fitting muscatoes till Dush - about Ten 0 the cloack a Bare came within few Road of our camp - all a sleep "in my hand and the Dog [umpt Into the Bruech (brush) about three Road and come back frited allmost to Death and yeald with his Brussels Stuck up and he Laramed (alarmed) all our camp and I Let him out and he folloed him of a spell and com back againe glad he was alive and we had Noe Little Laff of our Surprize and the fear the dog Sustaned for a fue minits - we cleard the Road into our Township this Day.

3 Day Thusday Rany amost al Day but we moved about 2 mile and)f mile into our Town.

4 Friday old worck Broak 1 Ax to Day.

5 Day Satturday I went into Town to Grind Fosters Ax broack yesterday and the flyes bit me the worst I have ben bit Since I have ben in the woods - a woolf com and hould Round our camp and made much Rout amongus.

6 Day Sunday.

7 Day monday about 10 of the clock Phipses Cannaday men come to us and thay Kooked thare Dinner at oure house and was bound home all harty and after we had Drunk a Little Brandy Toddy and Eat Diner to gather we parted. This after None I moved all our housing Stuff with our provision with a little help 2 mile.

8 Day Tusday this after Noon the Dog Kiled a pocopine and filled his mouth full of quiles and caused a good Deal of Truble to get them out of his mouth we tied his legs and gagged him and worcked about an houre upon him and he was vary glad after it was over.

9 Day Wensday this Day cloudy afternoon Rany Knight and the wind Blue So that we was afraid to go to Sleep but Keept awake all Night amost for feare of being Kild by the Trees.

10 Day Thusday Traviled in to Lieut Livermoores for we was

Celebration in 1890's on Union Street

afraid to Stay in the woods any Longer the Trees fell so cleared of about Noon and we Returnd again to camp.

11 Friday at work at the Road went in to our camp at Knight (Expected) whare Mr. How had marked our Road from Winthrop.

12 Day Satturday Rany in the forenoon afternoon at worck at the Road.

13 Day Sunday Set out to Wintrup 10 0 the cloak Struck our Town "Line In the Loar of Tyall somwar near whare it crosses a bever Dam and folod it about Two mile and Steard of ESE and struck a pond and thoat it was great andresscoggen pond and steard of ESE and Struck Dead River about half after one and Still Steard our corse and Struck Wintrup North oart of the Town one mr Earses (Sears?) Improvement - Vary Rany and Struck this improvement about foure 0 the clock hindred by the Raine so that we Did not git to mr Hows till Knight.

14 Day monday set out at one of the clock to mark oure Road to poart Royal and at Knight campt by grait anderascoggin pond as we was En camping we heard Something growling Like a bare and we went of from our camp and we found 2 cubs up on a Tree and I shot one of them and mr how Shoat the other and we had Som for brakefast and had a vary good brakefast. Road finished to Day.

15 Day Tusday Set out this morning and Struck the River by fishes Iseland about Eleven 0 the clock - 1 (o'clock) our hands Washing up for hom.

16 Day wensday after Lieut Livermoores cattle that was runaway Steard of about 12 0 the cloack Struck thare Tracks and follow of after them till Sun Set but could Not over take them our hands cutting a Road to the falls and campt with our Blanket or Victuals Next Day I got in Next Day.

17 Thusday at Eleven 0 the clock 24 hours without any victules Except one pan cake this afternoon packed up our things for marching home about the Sun Set foure miles on our Jorney Som Raine and thunder.

18 Fryday got into Mr Laines about the middle of the afternoon and Refreshed our Selves and Rested our Selves at Little andrew Soggen River.

19 Saturday crost the River and got to Mr. Stinchfield about

Eleven 0 the Clock and Refreshed ourselves and Sot of for falmouth Traveled to Mr. Wins lows in North casko and Loged thare. 20 Sunday at falmouth afternoon went church Quartered at Mr Shattucks.

21 Day Monday and Looking out for a passage found 2 Vesels Liakely "to Saile in 2 or three Days but it happend that a Vesel from Canybeck fell in with the Land in the fogg and put In to falmouth to fill water and we axadantally Se the Capt and agreed with him for a pasage and put our Stores a bord in about 15 minits and Sailed down the harbour but for want of wind we was oblige to come to an anker againe we Sailed at Sunsett and come to about Nine 0 the clock.

22 Day Tusday Lay wind bound and went a shoare againe about five 0 the clock the wind com Rould to the Norord and we com to Saile and went out of the harbour fare wind but Small.

23 wensday Still on our pas age Small wind but pleasant the Sun about an houre high thare com up a Small Squall Som thunder and Raine plasant Knight.

24 thusday this morning Round cape pan Beating all Day Small Brease part of the Time Lashed to a vesell Becalmed about Teno the clock got within the Light and Run up to Gorges Island and it Died away calm and we Run on the Island but the Tide being flowing we got of Sone without any Damage - and com too above Long Island for want of winde about Day Light and Lay till the Next Tide.

25 Fryday about 2 0 the clock com to toing in Leue (lieu) of coming to Saile for we had Noe wind and at fore 0 the clock we Landed our Bagage and Foster and I Set out for home and went to Lieut Livermoore of waltham about 10 0 the clock **In** the Evening.

26 Satturday vary hot - and Traviled home - Vary hard Days work for me."

[Major Fish returned to Port Royal in August, 1773, as shown by the following notes copies from his Journal.]

"August 23 Day to winthoop to attend Town meeting to Se if they would Layout road to meat ours 29 Sunday 30th at Town

Celebration in 1890's: Depot Street.

meeting 31 monday hom againe.

Sept. 3 Day 1773 To vew the Road Mr How mard to Se if I could not Sheer the Swamppy land But foud Noe way Nor found Noe way to erose fishes Brook with a bridge.

4 Day to the Southard of the marks but found Noe way for the Road to goe Near the marks.

6 Day up fishes Brook and found it could be pasd by a Bridge about 1 "mileli from the River Struck of for Bever Brook and found whare it could be forded about 2 miles from the River.

7 Day marked from fishes Brook to Bever Dito and vewd to Se if the Road could come from fishes Brook to the River and found vary good Land for a Road.

8 Day went to Beaver Brook and marked ESE and Struck our Town Line about 3 miles from grate Andarsscoggen Pond and went to 30 mile River to Se if the Road could not goe further to the E and North to Bring it Strait with my marks but found a vary Swamp.

9 Day Tuck a beach hill Near our Town Line and found it went up with a modret assent and Down with a modoret Desent and markd North about 2 miles to Beaver Brook and Struck my marks about half a mile to the west of our Town Line.

October 5, 1773 to wintrup to Let out and See a Bout a Bridge.

6 Up to Mr Craigg Let out the Bridge to Mr Craigg Struck of west and by Southard and Struck Brags Lot.

7 Day home and vewed the Road with Mr How.

"A Memarandom From Oxford to Po art Royal (1774)

April 18 Day Sett out for Boston Dind at Grafton at Knight at waltham at Deacon Livermores.

19th to Boston to Look for a passage Lodged at the Sign of the Lamb - Vary hard Thunder and Lightning.

20th found a pasage a Bord of Capt John Campbell Sloop her Name the Polly Traveled up to waltham to Deacon Livermores and thared Lodged.

21 Thusday to Boston a bying Stores Lodged at the sign of the Lamb.

22d Bying Stores and waiting for a pasage.

23 Satturday got oure Stores aboard and a q. after 8 Eight in the

Evining come to Sail.

24 Sunday maid wood Island and at Six 0 clock in the Evening Stode in for Seguin at 12 0 the clock com to an anker in the mouth Kanebeck River at Knight.

25th Nine 0 the clock in the morning come to Saile the wind a head beat up the River about five mile the tide faileing us we come too.

26 Beat up the River to Long Reach Left the Sloop and went up the River with Mr Suel in his Boat Arived at Mr Agraves at ten 0 the clock at Knight at Pownalborough much vary Soar hands a Roing.

27 Road up the River against a very Swift freshet to Deacon Clarks Travelled to winthrup to hyer a Teame to fetch up our Stores hyerd Mr Brag.

28 Back to Kenebeck River and up to Winthup again Lodged at Mr Whiteonge (Whitings?).

29 to Mr Hous Set out to goe to Mr Fullers Towards our town mised the Right Road and went out of our way about one mile and then struck through the woods about 4 miles in order to Strike a bridge cald craiggs Bridge and Struck within Ten Rods of said bridge kiled one patterage on our march Encampt by fullers meadow Vary Rany Day Rany Knight Mr Willington Taken not well.

Satturday went to Shoe Mr Ballard own town Line we left Mr John Badcok with Mr. Willington Vary Rany Returned to our camp found Mr Willington Violently Seized with a pain in his head and much Distresd at him Stummuch got him into Mr 'Braggs.

May ye 1st Sunday Rany went to Mr hows to Lodg. While I am now writting I heard credibly that 4 men was Drawnded at Versalboraugh Lieut Warring from pepperell Deacon Browns Son of Concord the others unnone to me.

2nd Day went to Mr Hopkins after my Instrements Left behind in our chist Bought a vary (large?) pack, come to Mr Chandlers found Mr Willington moved from Mr Braggs to Mr Chandlers vary sick and Staid with him this Knight,

3 Day measured the Road from Mr Chandlers and mard every mile on the Tree that is came out against on the Tres tht South

Side of the Road found the Road to be 18 mile and 1/2 wanting 13 Rod found our people campt whare 30 mile River Empties into grait Ammascoggen pond.

4 Day Set out with part of our stores and crosed Ammascoggen Pond went Down Dead River to greait Ammascoggen River Land our Stores and fired 2 guns for a token that we had arived and with much Joy thay Recved the token and maid the best of thare way to us for they haud Not Eat any victules cooked with water.

5 Day Set out to Run a line to the west part of our town.

6 Day Surveying and Saw Some Ice in a back cove of our River Laid on the Bank by the freshet out of the Sun.

7 Day went up the River and found all things well at my chest and Deacon Livermore well at his camp."

Some of the town's few owners of automobiles gather in 1910
to display and compare their vehicles.

The sign on the pole to the right of the Express wagon reads; "Automobiles not to exceed 10 miles per hour."

Appendix Three
Excerpts from the History of
THE FIRST BAPTIST CHURCH
Livermore Falls

On an October day in 1811, twenty-eight men and women were gathered in a small schoolhouse on Moose Hill, in the town of Livermore, County of Oxford, District of Maine, Commonwealth of Massachusetts.

The crisp fall air forewarned of more formidable cold to come, and all who gathered there shared a common concern. They talked of the physical hardship involved in traveling the many miles to their churches. Church attendance, for those God-fearing people, only a few generations removed from their Puritan ancestors, was a much-treasured privilege and an unquestioned obligation: the Church was the very center of their lives.

Most of the twenty-eight were members of either the First Baptist Church of Livermore (now North Livermore) or the Fayette Baptist Church. With dread, they contemplated another winter of traveling the round trip distance of six to sixteen miles required in attending these churches ... struggling on foot, or by horse, through drifted roads that were often little more than ill-defined paths. Sixteen miles under these conditions could well entail a full day of exhausting travel; and, 'Worse, it could even mean the occasional inability to worship in their respective churches.

All present readily agreed that it was necessary for them to request dismissal from their churches, in order to form a new church, "owing to the distance they lived from meeting."

After having successfully obtained their dismissals, the newly formed council met, on the 20th of November,

1811, at the house of Theodore Marston: formalities were completed, and the moderator gave the hand of fellowship, instituting an organization known 150 years ago as the "Third Baptist Church of Livermore", which later became "The First Baptist Church of East Livermore", and still later, "The First Baptist Church of Livermore Falls". One of the twenty-eight, Elder Thomas Wyman, was fortunately a competent minister, and was asked to take the pastoral charge of the Church, to which he consented.

Meetings were held in the schoolhouse near Wyman's Ferry (now known as Shuy) and at the Moose Hill schoolhouse, on alternate Sundays. In September of 1812, the Church was admitted to the Bowdoinham Association.

In December, 1812, the pastor's salary was given attention; a committee was appointed to determine what sum the Church ought to give Elder Wyman-- and then to determine how to proportion it equitably among the brethren. It appears that Elder Wyman's salary was set at $100 a year, and for this the committee assessed the brethren proportionately according to the value of their property, as shown by the Town Assessor's books. If any member wished to pay his assessments in grain, the price was fixed: wheat $1.17, rye 83 cents and corn 75 cents per bushel. There were frequent neglects and refusals to pay these assessments, resulting sometimes in exclusions.

The records of the Church in its early years are quite full of accusations and disciplinary action. But, this is not at all surprising when we consider some of the rules enforced at that time. For example, it was required that every member who shall be absent from any meeting shall, at the next church meeting, give a reason for such absence; a confession before the whole congregation was required from every member who wished the forgiveness of the Church for a sin; it was required that any member who should do anything to publicly reflect ill on the cause of God, should make confession of his fault in public meeting; evidence of family prayers was required under penalty of exclusion; and, as stated before, every member was required to pay an assessment for expenses of the Church, as levied on him by a committee.

One member, accused a second time of stealing, confessed privately to one offense of the kind, but then refused to confess publicly; accordingly, he was promptly excluded. In conference, one brother confessed to a quarrel, but was unwilling to confess before the congregation; after repeated demands, he was excluded. Another brother was accused of neglecting family prayers; he was excluded after having been denied the time to consider a change of course.

This item appears in 1814: "voted to give Brother Bassett a license to use his gift in Public." The records fail to state just what his gift was; but, from Brother Cushman Bassett's subsequent career, we know that his license was to preach. He was the first of five men who have gone from this Church into the ministry.

For six years, 1811-1817, Elder Thomas Wyman served as pastor and, notwithstanding all the discipline and exclusion, a gain of 78 members is shown. However, Elder Wyman "joined himself to the Masonic Fraternity of this Town", which aroused dissatisfaction among the members and resulted in a church meeting to discuss the matter. A few days later, Elder Wyman requested to be dismissed from his office as pastor, and the Church, with no hesitation, was quick to oblige.

Brother John Smith was one of the strong supporters of the Church in its early struggles. He was baptized in 1822 and continued in membership for 58 years. At prayer meetings, the pastor was always certain of Brother Smith's presence and equally sure of his prayer and testimony. Much of the time he served as Church Clerk. His son, Caleb Smith, although not a member, was always interested and helpful in the affairs of the Church.

In 1824 the Church discussed the building of a Meeting House. All seemed to think it best to build, but could not agree on where to locate it. Later, another discussion was held with same result. The first allusion to any agreement as to site occurs a few months later when a certain brother asked for dismission, "on account of the distance he lives from the meeting house which is building." His request was not granted, "Because he says the brethren have taken his privilege from him for that they do not build the Meeting House in an equitable place." After much controversy, as was customary in matters of dispute in those days, a council from other churches was called for advice on the whole question. Four churches - Fayette, Jay, and the two Livermore churches - sent messengers and elders. This council held that the Meeting House was located in the most equitable situation (this was at Shuy) and recommended that Brother Bumpus first retract whatever he may have said and then the Church grant his dismission. This advice was followed.

Others, however, feeling disgruntled at the location of the Meeting House (apparently believing it should have been built at or near Moose Hill), began to attend a meeting "set up in opposition", and this led to the exclusion of Deacon Farrington and others. The council was again called, and again voted that the situation chosen was the most equitable one; but some refused to be pacified by this decision and continued to go to the opposition meetings in the Moose Hill schoolhouse. Then exclusion went on in due process for some time, and in 1828 the Free Will Baptist

Church, with eight members, was organized at Moose Hill, and their church was erected in 1829. As the years went by, and transportation to and from church became less grounds for rational argument, feelings between the churches mended. Today, there is complete cooperation between the two: the same pastor

Moose Hill Free Will Baptist Church, erected in 1829

serves both churches, and considers both to be in his parish; members of both churches attend joint social meetings and participate in the same Bible study groups; joint services are regularly held at the Moose Hill Church on Easter morning; -- all of these things would have been unthought of in 1828.

The agitation over church members associating themselves with the Masonic fraternity still continued. It was voted that joining the Masonic Society should be made a matter for discipline; and, in 1832, another member was excluded for this reason. The ensuing disturbance resulted in another call for the council, which disapproved the action of the Church and declared that the matter might be safely left to a man's conscience.

Apparently the Church of that period dealt as summarily with its pastors as with erring brethren. Elder Robert Low was pastor 1825-1832, and the following record of his dismissal was made at a meeting in January, 1832.

Again, in 1839, we find a council of five ministers called "to advise what should be done with all the unburied difficulties of the past." They must have been men of sound judgment, for their advice was to restore an excluded member and to forgive and forget everything else; this advice seems to have been generally followed thereafter, as this is the last instance of councils being called to settle disputes.

In 1840, the Church received into its membership Brother Thomas Record and his wife by letter from Jay. This accession meant much to the welfare of the Church. His parishmen brought most of their problems before him; his counsel was always sought and his advice valued, for he was a peace loving man.

In 1844, the pastor's salary was increased to $150, and the Church's name was changed to the "Baptist Church of East Livermore.

With the development of industrial life in the community and the utilization of power at the falls, the center of village settlement moved northward to about its present location. Consequently, in 1854, it was decided to move the Church edifice from the location at Shuy to the site which the present building occupies. The contract for removal and rebuilding was given to Samuel Lyford. His contract states that "the said Lyford agrees to underpin and finish the outside of the house in the modern style for such a house ... and the inside after the plan of the Baptist Meeting House at Livermore Corner." He further agreed to paint it outside and inside, put blinds on the windows and build a chimney, all for the sum of $635.

This undertaking was made possible by the substantial and generous financial assistance of Brother John Smith, whom we have previously mentioned.

Brother Thomas Record's three sons ...Gustavus, Alvin and Isaiah Record ... and his daughter Mrs. Sarah J. Wing were added to the Church in 1856 and 1858. All four were among those who held the interests of the Church to be pre-eminent to their own, and they freely gave of their time, strength and means. The daughter, Mrs. Sarah Wing, was a most faithful and devoted member for 44 years. Rev. Isaiah Record was educated for the ministry, and was another of the five who have gone out from this Church to preach the Word elsewhere. Gustavus Record was Church Treasurer, served on various committees, and figured prominently in the history of the Church during the entire period of this membership. But, of these four valued members of the Church, the most prominent and most helpful was Brother Alvin Record.

At the time of Mr. Alvin Record's conversion, the family was living at Moose Hill. The members of the Moose Hill Church were holding revival services that were concluded with a baptism, the circumstances of which are mentioned to this day. The pond was covered with ice thick enough to support the congregation: one man stood with a rake to draw away the anchor ice as it formed after the opening had been cut. Mr. Record was one of the twenty baptized at that time. Subsequently, he united with the Church at East Bridgewater, Massachusetts, and on his return to

FAYETTE BAPTIST CHURCH

On November 20, 1811, twenty-two members of this church were dismissed to form the Third Baptist Church of Livermore.

THIRD BAPTIST CHURCH OF LIVERMORE

This building, erected at Shuy in 1824, was moved to the Church Street location in 1854. In 1870, it was torn down to make way for the present edifice.

NORTH LIVERMORE BAPTIST CHURCH

On November 9, 1811, ten members of this church were dismissed to form the Third Baptist Church of Livermore.

Livermore Falls, was received into this Church by letter from the Bridgewater Church in 1856.

Although he consistently declined to accept office or honors in the Church, he nevertheless played a most prominent and active part in all its affairs, assuming, in measure, the position his father had held as councilor and guide. A man of strong character and influence, his memory will always be inseparable from The Baptist Church of Livermore Falls. The memorial window, second from the rear, is dedicated to him and his wife, Agrandece Record.

Elder Amos B. Pendleton, serving at this period, is particularly mentioned in the previous record as an ideal pastor, sympathetic and generous to a fault. He had two terms of service amounting to nearly ten years, 1844 -1846 and 1855 -1863.

The old frame building was outgrown as time went on, and in 1870, it was torn down to give place to the brick structure now standing.

It is related that when the time came for the work of demolition and the men were gathered, each seemed reluctant to be the first to attack the old house. It savored of sacrilege to tear down and destroy the edifice so long dedicated to divine worship, so they hesitated until Rev. G. M. Robinson, with zeal and energy, advanced and struck the first blow.

The work of construction was carried on under a parish organization as before. Alvin Record, R. C. Boothby, J. A. Rowell, Caleb Smith, Rev. G. M. Robinson, and C. Wadsworth were prominent in this work; owing to their efforts, as well as to the generosity of those who gave their money to the project, the Church was dedicated free from debt, at a cost of about $8, 000, in 1874. Mr. Samuel Eustis, then of Illinois, gave $2200; Hon, Abner Coburn of Skowhegan gave $250; the furnace, registers, etc., amounting to about $215, were the gift of Mr. B. F. Sturtevant of Jamaica Plain, Massachusetts. The whole amount received from out of town was $2778; the remaining amount was paid by the Church and people of this vicinity.

While the Church was being built, meetings were held in the vestry and there was no settled pastor. During this time, the services were conducted by an 80-year-old retired pastor, Rev. Charles Miller. The records reveal that he was greatly loved by all. Although not a regular pastor, the history would be incomplete without mention of this grand old man.

The dedication took place in March, 1874, and was a festival of rejoicing. Services were held through afternoon and evening. Rev. J. F. Eveleth had come as pastor of the Church; Rev. H. E. Robbins, D. D., of Colby University was guest speaker in the afternoon; Rev. Isaiah Record, then of Turner, preached in the evening.

In 1879 occurred the first ordination ceremony in our history ... that of Rev. E. F. Merriam, D. D., who served here one year, at the end of which time he entered upon the work of the American Baptist Missionary Union.

The vestry seemed to be inadequate to the needs of the Church, and, in May of 1885, it was voted to build an addition. The building committee chosen numbered eight: J. A. Rowell, Alvin Record, Gustavus Record, J. G. Ham, R. C. Boothby, E. S. Goding and Deacons Parker and Wing. Evidently no time was lost or wasted by this committee. Ground was broken in June and the building completed the last of September. Meanwhile, funds were being raised successfully; then furnishings were obtained. In December the present vestry was ready for occupancy. The cost was something over $1700.

It seemed a sad coincidence that the day the new vestry was first used, should also mark the date of the funeral of Brother Gustavus Record, who had done so much toward its erection.

The building of the vestry seemed to inspire rather than exhaust the efforts of the people, for in 1887 the subject of a new parsonage was discussed. At that time a small cottage, standing on the site now occupied by the Bank Building was the Baptist Parsonage. This had been largely the gift of Brother John Smith; he gave one-half the cost and the Church the other half. Brother David Anderson, in whose memory a memorial window is inscribed, bequeathed to the Church, in 1885, the lot and buildings adjoining the Church property. The buildings, excepting the stable, were moved off, and the present parsonage built in their place.

Rev. E. S. Small who had been with the Church as pastor for ten years resigned in 1890, concluding the longest pastorate in the Church history, to that date. He had tried to resign three years earlier, but the Church refused to accept his resignation and prevailed upon him to continue; ill health finally forced his retirement. Those who remember him speak highly of his work in and for the Church, and the records confirm them. During his pastorate, as we have mentioned, the vestry was built, extensive repairs were made to the Church, the Baptistry was added, the parsonage was built, and ninety new names were added to the Church Roll.

Following comparatively short pastorates of W. O. Ayer, A. T. Whittemore, F. H. Davis and H. R. Mitchell, Rev. Horace W. Tilden, D. D. was pastor for four years (1899-1903). Among the ablest preachers in the state, he

The Parsonage and the Men Who Built It
This picture was taken at the time of completion, in 1888.

This picture of the Church grounds shows the Parish house, as it appeared after its construction in 1915. It served as Sunday School and recreational building until 1919, when it was moved to Pleasant Street. where it now serves as the Nazarene Church.

endeared himself to the people of the Church and the congregation; the influence of his strong personality was not merely confined to his own Church or town. The course in Bible study, under his guidance and instruct-tion, was a rare and valuable opportunity to those who were privileged to attend it, and his name still lives on in the memorial window placed by the class he taught. He was a Civil War veteran ... a patriot as well as a preacher. His resignation was tendered in May, 1903, and after several unsuccessful efforts on the part of the people to have it withdrawn, was sorrowfully accepted in July.

During the pastorate of H. M. Ives (1904-1907), there was a substantial increase in membership, due partly to efforts of the evangelists, Hatch and Taylor, who conducted union services for a time in the community, Fifty members were baptized in 1905.

The Church was fortunate to secure, in 1908, the services of Rev. W. S. Holland, a young rnan of great ability both as a speaker and a leader, whose able contribution to the life of this Church many of us still remember.

In November, 1911, the Church, in a series of services attended each time by congregations that filled the house, celebrated its 100th Anniversary. At these services, the stained glass memorial windows of the Church were displayed for the first time, Four former pastors, Revs. Merriam, Small, Ayer and Mitchell, were present and took part in the exercises; and letters were read from two other ex-pastors, Bartlett and Tilden.

Rev. W. S. Holland, after four years of service, tendered his resignation in December, 1912. At that time, a large number of people, deeply influenced by him through those years and wishing to take the step before he should leave, presented themselves for Church membership: and in the first three weeks of December he baptized forty-five. These, with nine others accepted by letter from other churches, made a total of fifty-four new members ... the largest addition to membership in a single year since the earliest days of the Church.

Following the short pastorate of Rev. F. B. Haggard, Rev. Henry S. McCready came to us as pastor in June, 1914. Those who were privileged to be youngsters at that period have many happy memories of his work with the boys ...the camping trips to Wayne 'Pond, basketball games and oyster stew suppers. Deeply interested in young people and the Sunday School, he felt keenly the lack of adequate Sunday School classrooms and of any recreation hall. Accordingly, the Church decided, in February, 1915, to build a Parish house at the rear of the lot between the Church and Parsonage. A committee consisting of H. C. Whittemore, C. H. Sturtevant, J. A. Record, F. A. Leavitt and C. H. Gorden was appointed to raise the funds and plan the building, and within the year the Parish house was completed, at a cost of $3700. For over four years the building was in quite constant use ... for basketball games and social affairs on week days, and Sunday School classrooms on Sundays. But, while the building was useful and enjoyable (particularly to the younger generation of that period), it presented serious problems, partly of expense, chiefly of administration; and, in 1919, the Church decided to sell the building. It was moved to the corner of Pleasant and Wheeler Streets, where it is now the home of the Nazarene Church.

A new flag, gift of Mrs. Charlotte Sturtevant, appeared in our auditorium in 1917, having a border of red about a field of white on which were displayed sixteen blue stars, each representing a young man of the Church family serving in Army or Navy. Many more were added to the number, in the last of 1917 and 1918, probably more than doubling it; but we have no complete record of the total. Harold C. Abbott was pastor during these war years of 1917-1918, followed by Rev. F. P. Freeman for the period 1919-1924. Both men proved able and efficient leaders, well liked by the entire Church constituency. Each added to the Church Roll a substantial number of new members as tangible evidence of their influence and inspiration.

Permission was given, in 1924, to the families of Deacon and Mrs. Joseph G. Ham, Dr. and Mrs. Henry Reynolds and Mr. and Mrs. Winfield Treat, to place upon the wall of the Church auditorium memorial panels which are the work of Mr. Harry Cochran. Mr. Cochran, an internationally known artist, musician and architect, was born in Augusta, Maine, in 1860. His murals adorn over 150 Maine churches, as well as many Masonic halls and churches throughout the country. Art critics predict that, in years to come, his work will inevitably gain even greater recognition. Cumston Hall, in nearby Monmouth, is an example of the architectural abilities of this man who challenged the old adage, "Jack of all trades, master of none."

In 1946, the year of Mr. Cochran's death, the children of Chester and Charlotte Sturtevant had the artist paint a fourth mural (and, incidentally, his final one) as a memorial to their parents. We are fortunate to have four such fine examples of the work of this Maine artist.

Under the energetic guidance of C. Harry Atkinson, who accepted the call to this Church in December, 1924, it was again decided to take steps to remedy the lack of Church School facilities; this time by building an addition to the Church structure itself. A committee consisting of C. H. Sturtevant, C. M. Bailey, J. C. Ham and C. N. Mixer was appointed in 1926 to have charge of the matter. On February 22,

1927, the Church School addition, completed and furnished at a cost of over $15,000, was dedicated; Rev. Carl Herrick was the principal speaker of the evening. This addition, containing ten large well-lighted classrooms, gives us one of the best equipped Church Schools in the state. Mr. Atkinson also instituted the Daily Vacation School, open to all children in the Community, which was operated for several years with great success. It was the largest school of its kind in the state, with an enrollment of 276.

Rev. F. S. Kinley, coming in 1929, not only was destined to face with us the trying depression years, but also the equally difficult years of World War II. We could never have asked for a better man to lead us through those years of crises. That his service with us was successful and inspiring, it is unnecessary to state, for his work, which still continues in his retirement, is well known to all of us. We only trust that he realizes the deeply appreciative regard in which the Church holds both his work and himself.

Rev. Bernard Alderman assumed the pastorate in 1954. The energetic and untiring leadership of this young pastor in church and community affairs has quickly won for him the admiration of the entire town.

On May 29th, 1958, an interesting special meeting of the Church was called. The purpose of this meeting was to consider whether the Church should join the Judson Baptist Association of Maine ... an association formed to protest the authority of the state Ordination Committee to refuse a candidate for ordination because of his beliefs, when such beliefs were consistent with those of his church. In decisive support of the autonomy of our church, it was voted: "We affirm our belief in the historic Baptist principle of individual freedom of conscience in matters of religious faith (on the basis of our understanding of the Scripture)." It was also voted that we join like-minded churches in the Judson Baptist Association.

On November 15th, 1959, an Ordaining Council met at our church. The Council consisted of twenty-six delegates (including six pastors) from eleven churches. After Rev. Alderman presented his paper, he very ably answered the many questions of participating pastors and delegates. The records report that, "The questions were answered with a humbleness, honesty and dignity as befits a child of God." The council recommended that our church proceed as soon as possible with ordination plans.

On January 18th, 1960, at a colorful evening service attended by over 300 persons, Rev. Alderman became the second pastor to be ordained in this church.

Thus, the Church has evolved from a group of twenty-eight men and women, convening in a public schoolhouse, to a roster of two hundred and ninety-seven members, possessing a beautiful church with all the necessary additional facilities, including a parsonage. It has progressed from a budget of slightly over a hundred dollars (collected partly in produce) to a budget of over twelve thousand dollars. But, the history of a church should not be expressed in dollars and cents, or in cubic capacity. Its temporal prosperity is only incidental, and conveys little idea of its real worth.

Who can measure the influence of one hundred and fifty years of sermons? How can the work of one faithful pastor or Sunday School teacher be adequately estimated? What can be said of the many who, influenced by the teachings from this Church, have gone on to other parts of the country, carrying that influence with them? And, what of the lives uplifted and the characters formed through a century and a half of time? Obviously, these are impossible questions to answer adequately. However, many will agree that, despite frequent discouragements, there has been registered a certain and indisputable progress. Although this progress has not been as fast as many must have desired, it has nevertheless, been in the right direction. It is undeniably true that the Church today has gained greater breadth of view, larger tolerance of others' opinions, and more charity for others' weaknesses, than existed one hundred and fifty years ago. We have before us far greater opportunities than did those twenty-eight men and women so long ago; but we also face correspondingly greater dangers.

In the hope that the relating of these past achievements will not appear empty boasts, but rather reminders of the responsibility that is ours, in meeting these increased dangers, we pass this brief record on to the next generation.

Pastors
First Baptist Church
Livermore Falls, Maine

Rev. Thomas Wyman	1811-1817
Rev. Elias Nelson	1818-1820
Rev. Joseph Adams.	1820-1822
Rev. John Haynes	1822-1823
Rev. Joseph Adams	1823-1824
Rev. Robert Low	1825-1832
Rev. Nathan Mahew	1833-1835
Rev. William Wyman	1836
Rev. O. B. Walker	1839-1842
Rev. D. Hutchinson	1842-1844
Rev. Amos B. Pendleton	1844-1846
Rev. William Wyman	1846-1850
Rev. Rufus Chas e	1850-1853
Rev. A. B. Pendleton	1855-1863
Rev. A. Bryant	1863-1866
Rev. Asa Perkins	1867-1868
Rev. E. M. Bartlett	1869-1871
Rev. J. F. Eveleth	1873-1878
Rev. E. F. Merriam	1879-1880
Rev. E. S. Small	1880-1890
Rev. W. O. Ayer, D. D.	1890-1893
Rev. E. T. Whittemore	1893
Rev. F. H. Davis	1894-1896
Rev. H. R. Mitchell	1897-1898
Rev. H. W. Tilden, D. D.	1899-1903
Rev. H. M. Ives	1904-1907
Rev. W. S. Holland	1908-1912
Rev. F. B. Haggard	1913-1914
Rev. H. S. McCready	1914-1916
Rev. H. C. Abbott	1917-1918
Rev. F. P. Freeman	1919-1924
Rev. C. H. Atkinson	1924-1928
Rev. F. S. Kinley	1928-1954
Rev. Bernard Alderman	1954-

Appendix Four

Historical Sketch of

EATON MEMORIAL

METHODIST EPISCOPAL CHURCH

of Livermore Falls

The United States had its beginning when the Constitution was adopted by the several states. But in writing a history of our country, we would have to go back of the adoption of the constitution and relate other events of historical importance. So it is with our church, it had its beginning when the first Methodist class was organized at Stone's Corner; yet previous events bear a relation.

Jesse Lee, the apostle of Methodism in New England, was the first Methodist minister to preach the gospel in this vicinity. In 1793 he organized the first circuit in Maine, known as the Readfield circuit. And it was from this circuit that our predecessors on these lands received their first Methodist gospel. It was at the house of Otis Robinson, at Gibbs' Mills, that the first Methodist sermon was preached, February 12, 1794. This sermon was preached by Jesse Lee, and he took for his text Romans eighth, thirteenth, "For if ye live after the flesh, ye shall die." Later in the same year Philip Wager, the first pastor stationed in Maine, preached at the home of Deacon Livermore—one of the two first settlers in town. Deacon Elijah Livermore, his wife, and one daughter, became members of the Methodist class which was formed about this time. In 1807 the Livermore Circuit was formed separate from the Readfield Circuit, and thenceforth until the Fayette Circuit was formed, our forefathers received what preaching they got from representatives of the Methodist church from the Livermore Circuit preachers. Jacob Haskell, father to Orrin Haskell, one of the officials of our early church at Livermore Falls, was one of the first members of this Livermore church. In 1815 we have record of the first quarterly meeting appointed at Livermore Falls. It was held in the barn of Mr. Whittemore about a half of a mile north of the village. Oliver Beale was presiding elder at this time and Samuel Hillman preacher of the Livermore Circuit. But before this time our church had really had its own organization.

Knowing what a large part evangelical religion played in the colonization of America, and having seen how early Methodism reached this section of the state, it is not surprising to find our organization closely following the blazed path of the pioneer. In 1797 Moses Stone of Watertown, Massachusetts, erected one of the first buildings in the town of Jay on the east side of the road just above what is now Stone's Corner. Later he erected the first framed building in town, and in 1802 his eldest son, Moses, known as "Major Stone," came to settle on his father's land. It was only two years later, 1804, that the first Methodist Class was formed at Stone's Corner by Rev. Joseph Baker, then pastor of the Readfield church, the first Methodist Episcopal church erected in Maine, being dedicated by Jesse Lee June 21, 1795. The first class leader was Scarborough Parker, another pioneer settler. It is interesting to note that two of the trustees of the present church are grandsons of this first class leader—Henry D. Parker and Jonathan Pike—and other church workers are his descendents. Scarborough Parker served as class leader until his death in 1814, when Moses Stone was appointed to fill the office left vacant. We

1 Methodism in Maine by Allen and Pilsbury

have no records to show the size of the class when it was first started in 1804, but the names of eight persons composing the class have come down to us. They were: Scarborough Parker, Hannah Parker, Moses Stone, Elizabeth Stone, Sally Dascomb, Sarah Richardson, Mrs. Eunice Whittemore and Mrs. Abigail Weston. (2) "Major" Stone began preaching soon after he became class leader, and the flock which gathered at these services made up for what they lacked in number by their strong hallelujah spirit. Moses Stone was ordained deacon by Bishop Roberts at Bath, July 2, 1822. These local preachers played a very important part in these early days. And their field of service was by no means confined to their own community.

Twenty years after the Livermore Circuit was set off from the Readfield Circuit, 1827, the Fay-

A favorite sport of auto owners in 1910
was attempting to make Church Street hill in as high a gear
as possible; going downhill was much easier.

ette Circuit was created an independent Circuit. This Circuit included North Fayette, East Livermore, Stone's Corner, and later Livermore Falls was added to the Circuit. The first pastor to come to Stone's Corner under this system was Philip Ayer. The Circuit preacher came to Stone's Corner once in four weeks, as did also James Smith, a local preacher from Fayette. Moses Stone filled the pulpit the other two Sundays until later when a prayer meeting was held at the time of the Sunday service once in four weeks (3). Elder Morrill of East Livermore, also a local preacher, conducted the services part of the time. Moses Stone always had charge of the prayer meetings except when the Circuit preacher was present.

During these early years and for many years following, it was the custom to hold what were known as "quarterly meetings," alternately at the different places on the Circuit. And the people from the whole Circuit would gather in the one place, often staying over night for the next day's meeting with some of the "brethren." The meetings began on Saturday and the people from North Fayette and East Livermore would gather at Stone's Corner—or vice versa—for what might be called religious banquet, where the words of the minister, local preacher, class leader and Presiding Elder were grasped by the hungry people, and the good old fashioned Methodist songs served for refreshments. However, tradition has it that Major Stone's orchard added its fruit between services. Saturday afternoon there was preaching by the Presiding Elder, which was followed by the business meeting of the quarterly conference. Sunday morning at about nine o'clock the "Love Feast" was held. Then the Presiding Elder preached in the forenoon, and generally the Circuit preacher in the afternoon, followed by the Communion service (3).

The home served as the first meeting house during the early history of the church, this in turn was followed by the school house. At what date the Methodists at Stone's Corner began to hold meetings in the school house is uncertain, but in an old letter dated November 27, 1836, the school house is mentioned as the meeting

3 Letter of Moses Stone

place for the Sunday services, apparently as an old story. It was not long after this that the people must have begun to talk of a meeting house of their own. On April 1, 1842, the trustees of the church met to decide upon the nature of the new meeting house and to let it out to contractors. The contract was let out to Jonathan Pike and Jacob True, who were to receive seven hundred dollars for the completed work—one-half to be paid in February following, the other in February, 1844. The contract called for a meeting house similar to the North Fayette

Church except for the following alterations:

"1st. To finish the singing gallery square with three seats.

2nd. To have no walk from entry to entry.

3rd. To have the windows without pointed arches on the outside.

4th. The pews to have doors with brass buttons.

5th. The cornice to be plain, the pulpit to be made of the most approved model."

(4)

The church was built in what is now the southeast part of the Stone's Corner Cemetery at about the place where the Grose monument now stands. The land for the church was given to the society by Moses Stone, Aaron Stone who lived on his father's farm signing the deed. The meeting house was accepted by a vote of the trustees December 20, 1842 (4). The board of trustees of the church at this time were: Moses Stone, Jr., Henry Parker, Isaiah Rich, William Grose, Aaron Stone, Otis Cole, David Bartlett, Jonathan Pike, and Jacob True. Henry Parker was secretary and David Bartlett treasurer (5). The pews were sold at auction, the names of the pew holders at the time of the first sale were: Grose and True Pike, Cyrus Parker, Henry Park-

er, Joel Parker, Francis and William Bryant, Reuben Basford, Elbridge Dascomb, Allen Cabb, David Bartlett, Aaron Stone, Jacob True, Jonathan Pike, Chase and Paine, William Sylvester, Isaih Rich, J. Crose, John Crose, Otis and Amos Cole, E. Basford, M. Basford, N. Pierce, Warren and Mitchel, Reuben Grose, Moses Stone, Moses Stone, Jr., William Grose, and W. Pike. The price received for these pews ranged from fourteen dollars up to thirty-three, about twenty-five dollars being the average received. Each purchaser received a deed of his pew, made out and signed by David Bartlett, acting for the trustees as a whole (4).

The new church was dedicated on Wednesday, December 28, 1842, C. W. Morse preaching the sermon. The sermon was followed by a quarterly meeting of several days length. Thomas Smith was pastor at this time and was spoken of as a strong preacher (7). He was, however, somewhat inclined to the Millerite doctrine, and in the spring of forty-four had completely jumped overboard (6). This added to the hardships of the then struggling members, who had erected a church in a sparsely settled community. Five and a half pews remained unsold (4), and six pews came back on the hands of the trustees. (6) These six pews were paid for by the trustees themselves. But a community of such pioneer stock does not know failure. And in spite of the struggle of church building, dissension during the Millerite tidal wave of forty-three, and other hardships of the church, it grew throughout the Circuit, until under "Ben" Foster the Fayette Circuit in 1845 numbered three hundred and thirty-two, a membership exceeded by only three charges in the state—Durham, Bangor and Portland.

6 A letter by Rev. Moses Stone of March 25, 1844
7 A letter by Rev. Moses Stone of December, 1842

In 1841 Cornelius Stone, son of Moses Stone and a graduate of Bowdoin College in the class of 1840, entered the Maine Conference. He was the first preacher to go out from the church, but has since been followed by two others. He continued to preach the gospel until, in 1856, his health gave out and he retired from the active ministry.

At what time the Sunday School began its career we do not know, but it was at least at an early date in the history of Methodist Sabbath Schools. The Sunday School was held at noon except in the winter when none was held because the children had to come so far. The first superintendent of whom we know was Moses Stone, Jr., later Franklin Strout served as superintendent.

Even after the church was built the class meetings and the Sunday evening prayer meetings were held in the school house. At what date Moses Stone gave up the leadership of the class is not definitely known, but in 1836 David Bartlett, was class leader having a class of fifty-three members (8). Joel Parker served as leader a few years later, and he was followed by Orrin Haskell. During all these years Moses Stone, who lived very near the school house, was always there to take the class in case the leader did not arrive, as a result the class was held with great regularity up to the time of his death, February 17, 1860. After the church was moved to its

8 Class Records

present foundation, the class still continued to be held at the Corner under Levi Daggett as leader, later under J. F. Strout. Other classes were held in different localities during the later history of the Stone's Corner Church. Cyrus and Henry Parker were leaders in the Stubb's Mills neighborhood. A class was also started at Livermore Falls under William Snow as leader (1).

The old Methodist hymns were a source of joy to these staunch christians, and many of them are remembered by the songs they used to sing. Captain Rich was one of this type whose name suggests that old song, "We'll stem the storm, it won't be long. We'll anchor bye and bye." We do not know the names of those composing the choir at any one time, but of those who sang in the choir at some time we offer the following: Cyrus Parker (leader), Nelson Pike, Jonathan Pike, Hannah J. Sylvester, Helen J. Sylvester, Smith Thompson and Frank Strout. These were accompanied by Otis Cole on the bass viol, Aaron Stone on some other instrument, and later Fred Cole on the violin.

In 1863 a second person brought up in the Stone's Corner Church entered the Conference and began to preach the gospel. This time it was a grandson of Major Stone, Cyrus Stone, D. D. Previous to his entering the ministry Cyrus Stone had served as tutor in ancient languages at Bowdoin College, his Alma Mater. He was a scholar, and, at the time of his death in 1889, was considered one of the ablest preachers in the Methodist Church in Maine.

But the church was not long to remain at Stone's Corner because of the greater centralizing of the population at Livermore Falls, only two miles south of the Corner. The movement had been on foot in many places in the state toward gathering in the country charges into villages where more regular preaching services could be conducted by the pastor. On May 15, 1866, the members of the Methodist class at Livermore Falls, which had been in existence for some time, met and organized themselves into a church. The stewards elected for the year were: Orrin Haskell, Moses Stone, Jonathan Pike, Cyrus Parker, Charles Richardson, D. B. Doyen and L. H. Daggett (9). In this list the Stone's Corner church had several of its old officials. The list of trustees at this time is not available, but with the exception of E. H. Brown—who had not moved to Livermore Falls at that time—the trustees were probably the same as they were in 1869: Orrin Haskell, J. W. Eaton, Cyrus Parker, Jonathan Pike, E. H. Brown, Jacob Haskell, Thomas Eustis, Moses Stone and Stephen J. Burgess (10). Under this regime James Armstrong was the first pastor. His charge was not limited to Livermore Falls, but included North Fayette and East Livermore. But he probably preached at Livermore Falls each Sabbath. The Quarterly Conferences were held as follows: First—North Fayette, Second—Livermore Falls, Third — East Livermore, Fourth — Livermore Falls (9).

The meetings were held in Lothrop Hall—the class meetings had previously been held in the school house and occasionally preaching service. But these Methodists were not long to remain

9 Steward Records
10 Old Deed of Church Property

contented with a hall for a house of worship and this same year 1866 saw material activities toward building a church. Orrin Haskell, John Eaton, Samuel Baldwin, Charles Richardson and several of the strong supporters of the Old Stone's Corner Church were those through whose active exertion and liberality the building of the church was made possible (1). During this first year of the church at Livermore Falls the members were very busy with the building of the church. John Eaton was a member of the building committee and rendered very valuable assistance in the work. The lumber was for a large part given by the members of the church from the old Stone's

Corner Church among whom were Captain Isaih Rich and Moses Stone. The underpinning for the church was hauled from the John Eaton farm on the other side of the river, where A. D. Brown lived for so many years. There was a great deal of work given which kept the building expenses from mounting up too high. The timber was hewed at a hewing bee held on a then vacant lot a short distance north of the church property. After the lumber had been collected and the timbers hewed, the building began on land—the present site of the church—deeded to the trustees by Charles Richardson. The work progressed under a Mr. Sanicher as the one in charge. During the erection of the steeple, which was built and then hoisted up, the town's people were startled by what some might have though an earthquake. The steeple, having been insufficiently fastened, came down through, causing slight damages but fortunately injuring no one. At last the church was completed and ready for occupancy. It was dedicated in the winter of 1867, the pastor Rev. James Armstrong preaching the sermon. He chose for his text, "And he smote the rocks and the water gushed forth." To what extent Elder Armstrong assisted in building the church is not definitely known, but, at least, he must have been a man of some mechanical ability, for he built the pulpit which was used for some years and which was later used in the vestry of the old church.

During these early years after the building of the church the Class Meetings still continued to play a very important part, especially since the several neighborhoods could each be accommodated by their own class. Charles Richardson was the first class leader at the Falls after the new church was built. The meetings were held at his house, the house next to the parsonage today, each Friday evening. Soon after the church was built Charles Richardson passed to his reward and James Baldwin became class leader. After a few years of service the leadership of the class passed on to Merritt Baldwin who served as leader only a brief period. He was followed, in April 1873, by Augustus Brown, who remained leader of the class for a few months over forty years—until his death on the fields of Gettysburg, June 29, 1913. During all these years Augustus Brown was at the class meeting each week through bad going and good with most faithful regularity—though he lived a mile and a half from town on a road very hard to travel in the dark. Since the death of this faithful leader, the church has been without a class leader, a fact to be regretted. Other classes were held at Stone's Corner, Jay Bridge and Jay Intervale. Orrin Haskell was the first leader at the Corner, he was soon followed by Levi Daggett, and J. F. Strout followed him. The class at Jay Bridge died young, mainly probably because of the lack of a good leader—the

records show, "no leader." Henry Gray was leader of the class at the Intervale for a good many years. J. L. Morse was appointed class leader in May 1869, but of what class the records do not show.

From the time the church was built the Sunday School began to play an important part in church life. S. J. Burgess was the first superintendent of whom we know. He served in this office until 1883, in which year he was followed by Charles Loring. A Sunday school was started at Jay Bridge having Marshall Gray as superintendent. It had about thirty scholars. In 1886 F. P. Stone took the leadership of the Sunday school, J. L. Morse having the Jay school. The next year E. C. Dow became superintendent, Osmond Gray having the Jay school The next year R. L. Richardson took Gray's place. In 1895 H. D. Parker was chosen superintendent. He was followed in 1897 by Dr. C. W. Brown. In the summer of 1897 a Sunday School was organized at Jay Intervale with Everett Paine as superintendent. In March 1900 a kindergarten class was started in the Sunday School by Miss Sarah Story with Louise Brown as assistant. In 1902 the Sunday School had increased to an average attendance of one hundred and twenty-one. Dr. Brown served as superintendent until he moved away, when he was succeeded, in 1904, by Frank Brown, who has filled the office up to the present time (9).

During the years following the building of the church the organization was not idle in making improvements on the church property. May 25, 1877 Moses Stone was appointed an agent to see if the pew owners of the Stone's Corner Church would relinquish their rights in the property for use in the Livermore Falls Church. A short time later the pews were installed in the vestry of the church. In 1881 the society built a cottage on the East Livermore Camp Ground at a cost of one hundred and fifty dollars. On March 19, 1888, the trustees appointed a committee to solicit funds for building a parsonage consisting of D. C. Searles, E. C. Dow and C. R. Loring. April 6, 1888 the building committee was chosen, consisting of C. R. Loring, E. C. Dow, J. Pike, D. C. Searles and A. D. Brown. It was later decided to build a stable in addition to the parsonage. In 1893 a horse shed was erected in the rear of the church (4). During the first year of Rev. George Palmer's pastorate the church was remodeled inside. The walls and ceiling were frescoed, opera chairs took the place of the old pews and new carpets, altar-rail, pulpit, draperies and chandeliers were put in. The church was re-opened March 6, 1898, the pastor preaching the sermon (9).

The choir since the church came to this place has for the most part been of very good size. The early choir consisted of the following: William Doyen (leader), D. B. Doyen, A. D. Brown,

Mary Brown, Emma Brown, George Eustis, John Eustis, Mrs. S. J. Burgess, Sarah Knight, Rhoda Sears, and Hattie Doyen (accompanist). Later Vesta Burgess served as organist for many years. The present leader of the choir, Dr. George H. Rand has served as such some thirteen or fourteen years.

The church has not been lacking in organizations such as are commonly found, although, perhaps, in some casese somewhat late. In October of 1902 a Ladies Aid Society was organized, which has continued until the present day, rendering valuable assistance to the church. On November 7, 1887, an Oxford League was organized by Rev. C. E. Bisbee. Under the pastorate of A. E. Parlin the Oxford League was converted into an Epworth League, March 21, 1890. In 1889 the King's Daughters were organized and this was converted into a Junior League July 15, 1895. Other organizations such as Women's Foreign Missionary Society, Women's Home Missionary Society and Organized Classes are found in the church. Under Rev. George Howard the men's class was organized into the Brotherhood of St. Paul which in turn was converted into the Methodist Brotherhood under the pastorate of Rev. J. A. Betcher.

On February 12, 1881, E. C. Strout was licensed as a local preacher by the quarterly conference. Later Mr. Strout entered the Conference and became an able preacher of the gospel. He was the last of the three preachers who have gone out from the church, and it was with deepest regret that the church received the news of his death a few months ago.

During the pastorate of Rev. S. E. Leech occurred the death of Rev. William Foster for so many years connected with the church. He had four times preached in charges where he was brought into contact with people of the Livermore Falls Church. In 1845, the year he was received in full by the Conference, he was pastor in Livermore Circuit. In 1858 and '59 he was preacher on the Fayette Circuit (preaching at Stone's Corner), in 1873-'75 he was pastor in our own church, and in 1884-'86 again pastor in the Fayette Church. Soon after this he retired from active service and came to Livermore Falls to live Here he was a great aid to the pastor and remained remarkably active until the last. He preached from the pulpit on his ninetieth birthday.

Soon after the twentieth century set in it began to become evident that the church would soon be too small and something woud have to be done. At times when Rev. J. R. Clifford was pastor seats had had to be brought in to accommodate the crowd Sunday morning, and after the evangelists, Hatch and Taylor, had been in the town during the pastorate of Rev. S. E. Leech, it became a certainty that the church was insufficient.

The officials who had served the church during the years intervening between the building of the first church, 1866, and the building of the second, 1906, include the following: Trustees: Orrin Haskell, J. W. Eaton, Cyrus Parker, Jonathan Pike, E. H. Brown, Jacob Haskell, Thomas Eustis, Moses Stone, Stephen J. Burgess, Nelson Pike, David Elliot, George Tarr, J. L. Morse, A. D. Brown, J. F. Strout, Jonathan Pike, Jr., H. L. Ellis, A. R. Nelson, C. K. Haskell, H. D. Parker, B. F. Barker, G. W. Stone, C. R. Loring, James A. Moore, D. C. Searles, E. C. Dow, D. W. Bailey, J. F. Jefferds, R. C. Stone and A. L. Holley. Stewards: Orrin Haskell, Moses Stone, Jonathan Pike, Cyrus Parker, Charles Richardson, D. B. Doyen, L. H. Daggett, J. F. Haskell, Nelson Pike, J. M. Baldwin, E. H. Brown, J. W. Eaton, A. D. Brown, J. L. Morse, D. M. Elliot, J. F. Strout, B. F. Parker, James Ridley, John Mayo, A. R. Nelson, Mrs. A. J. Morse, Mrs. L. Ellis, S. J. Burgess, E. C. Basford, E. C. Dow, Osman Gray, F. P. Stone, Joseph Rich, George Tarr, H. D. Parker, Marshall Gray, B. F. Parker, C. K. Haskell, George Stone, Jonathan Pike, N. B. Pottle, A. L. Holley, Wallace Dow, L. Lothrop, Horace Dow, Roscoe Richardson, O. L. Hardy, J. A. Moore, Willis Pike, C. W. Brown, C. H. Pike, Willis Hardy, Frank Dudley, T. R. Williams, L. M. Lothrop, Winslow Fuller, Fred Shipley, Dr. H. L. Holt, Dr. G. H. Rand, S. A. Nelke and William Bunten. Doubtless this is not an entirely full list as certain of the records cannot be found.

In April 1905 Rev. George Howard became pastor of the church and as matters materialized the building of the new church fell upon him— in so far as the pastor's share was concerned. During the summer Mrs. O. P. Thompson of Hollistown, Massachusetts, a native of the town of Jay, signified to the pastor her desire to present to the Methodist Episcopal Church of Livermore Falls, a pipe organ suited to the capacities of its auditorium and adapted to meet the need of its worshipping congregation (11).

The official board met at the call of the pastor, August 23, 1905, to take action regarding the gift of the organ and to consider the matters of repairs or possibly the erection of a new house of worship. The pipe organ was accepted with much gratitude expressed to the donor. It was voted to build a new church to cost not less than eight thousand dollars and that work should not begin until three-fourths of that amount had been raised. On April 3, 1906, the following building committee was appointed by the official board: E. C. Dow (chairman), J. A. Moore, D. C. Searles, Dr. G. H. Rand and H. D. Parker. Subsequently at a meeting held July 31, 1906, J. F. Jefferds and A. L. Holly were added to this committee.

May 24, 1906, work began preparatory to

364

moving off the old church to a lot purchased on Reynolds Avenue—the old church now serves as the Grand Army of the Republic Hall. The first bricks laid on the concrete foundation of the new church were laid July 18, Tracy and Parcher being the master masons in charge of the work.

"Without being unjustly invidious, and in full recognition of the merit of all, it seems only fair to say that the one man, who from the start, saw the major possibilities of the moment, and except for whose indefatigable effort and masterful management the church could never have been built, was Everett Dow" (12).

"Another man indispensable to the enterprise was J. A. Moore, who surprised all his friends by becoming the architect and superintendent of construction, exhibiting a knowledge and skill rarely equalled by those who have spent a life time in such work. The new church on the hill will ever remain a worthy monument to the genius of James A. Moore." (12)

The church edifice is a large and imposing structure, one of the most magnificent and serviceable of any in the State of Maine. The building is ninety-eight feet by sixty-six feet over all and the Gothic style of architecture predominates. Memorial windows were placed to honor the memory of Mrs. Elizabeth Grose, John Richardson, Henry and Harriet Norton Parker, John W. and Harriet N. Eaton and Family, Robert and Mary A. Moore, Elias H. and Hannah D.

12 Words of Rev. George Howard

Brown, Rev. W. H. Foster, Henry and Nancy Parker, Francis L. and Melinda K. Dow; also Sunday School Class No. 12 (Blanche Andrews-Brown, teacher).

The dedicatory exercises began Friday evening, May 24, 1907, with an organ recital by Mr. Fred Bearce of Boston, assisted by Miss Jennie Chenry of Livermore, Contra'to, and Miss Alice Chapman, of Boston, reader. Saturday afternoon, the 25th, the first sermon delivered in the new church was preached by Rev. George B. Hannaford of Rumford—"the Bishop of Oxford County." Sunday congregations were large and able sermons were preached during the day by presiding elder, G. D. Holmes and Rev. W. F. Berry, D. D. Among others who spoke during the dedication were Rev. George A. Martin and Rev. John R. Palmer. Tuesday May 28 was the day set apart for the dedicatory services proper and Bishop Goodsell was the man who formally dedicated the church to God and to His service. The Bishop preached an able sermon on "Sacrifice," after which some thirty-six hundred dollars was secured in cash and pledges to further liquidate the indebtedness.

The next year, to the deep regret of all Rev. George Howard was appointed to another charge. He had served the church well throughout his three years of pastorate—during a time when the greatest undertaking in the history of the church

was accomplished. Mr. Howard proved himself a man of the highest administrative ability and an indefatigable worker. He was unquestionably the man of the hour and the man for the hour. His early death was a source of great sorrow to his former parishoners.

The officials, members and friends of the church had responded liberally towards freeing the church from debt, yet when the dedication of the church, which represented a cost of twenty-five thousand dollars, was over there still remained a debt of several thousand dollars. During the first few years after the church was built the church was striving to diminish the debt, the most of the members had given about all they felt that they could afford, at the time of the dedication, and money came in slowly.

On January 5, 1911, while Rev. J. A. Betcher was pastor, another dedication took place—the naming of the church. At this time Rev. George Howard delivered the address in which the church was named, "Eaton Memorial Methodist Episcopal Church," in honor of Mrs. Harriet Eaton, who had contributed most toward the building of the church. On this occasion Bishop J. W. Hamilton was present and before the large crowd, which had gathered, left the church, the debt of sixty-four hundred dollars had been lowered to about two thousand dollars—in pledges materializing within three years. Since this time new pledges received have just about made up for former pledges unpaid, so that at the beginning of the conference year, April 1915, a debt of two thousand dollars was on the church.

Since the church was built the different organizations in the church have not been idle in raising money towards the debt. The money paid in by the different organizations up to the present time is as follows: Ladies Aid Society $1957.66, Epworth League $1,358.24, Brotherhood of St. Paul (re-organized into Methodist Brotherhood) $199.00, O. S. S. Society (Blanche Andrews-Brown S. S. Class) $100.60, Helping Hand Society of Jay Intervale $80.00, Fred O. Shipley S. S. Class $71.00, S. S. Birthday money $87.59, Brotherhood of David $5.00 and nearly every other class in the Sunday School added their contributions. Mrs. G. C. Howard's S. S. Class furnished the Ladies Parlor. Through the activities of the Ladies Aid and Epworth League the interest money on the debt and four hundred dollars of the principal have been raised during the present year.

The church has found that it has many friends and not least among these is the one whose name the church now bears. Mrs. Harriet Eaton is now the oldest living member of the church, having past her ninety-fifth birthday on the fourteenth of last January. She and her husband, John Eaton, aided in building the first church in

1866, and she has furnished financial aid towards the present edifice numbered in thousands. Until recent years she has been a faithful attendant at church, and only in the last year or two have we failed to find her at church, when the weather permitted. Other people have shown their genuine friendship and interest in the church, and rendered themselves indebted to the gratitude of the church by the gift of Memorial Funds. At present the church has three Memorial Funds which constitute a valuable aid in the financial struggle of the church. These funds are: The Richardson Memorial Fund, The Haskell Memorial Fund and The Stone Memorial Fund.

A watchword which anticipates an ever present need is that favorite old slogan of the Rev. George C. Howard: "A long pull, a strong pull and a pull all together."

"1st Methodist Church building; dedicated in 1867; moved to Reynolds Ave. in 1906, to serve as Grand Army of the Republic Hall (now the American Legion Hall)."

"2nd Methodist Church building, dedicated May 24, 1907."

Appendix Five

Catalogue of Scholars

In Livermore, made by Benjamin Foster. Mr. Foster was a popular and successful teacher of schools in Livermore from 1806 to 1810 or 1811. For which of these years the subjoined list was made does not appear.

Allen Eben.
Abbot Hull.
Abbot Bill.
Abbot Elizabeth.
Abbot Bethiah.
Abbot Anna.
Abbot Polly.
Basford Reuben.
Basford Nabby.
Basford Anna.
Boardman Sally.
Boardman George.
Boardman Holmes.
Bond Hannah.
Bigelow Polly.
Bigelow Eliza.
Bigelow Caroline.
Barton Asa.
Barton Catherine.
Barton Sally.
Barton Eunice.
Barton Aaron.
Benjamin William.
Benjamin Nathaniel.
Benjamin Betsy.
Benjamin Patty.
Benjamin Polly.
Benjamin David.
Benjamin Charles.
Benjamin Elisha.
Benjamin Ruth.
Basford Ebenezer.
Basford Joanna.
Basford Mercy.

Blanchard James.
Beals Jennet.
Beals Olive.
Britton William.
Bartlett Cyrus.
Bartlett Nathan.
Billings Abijah.
Billings Munro.
Commins Sally.
Commins Lucy.
Commins Asenath.
Cooper Sally.
Cooper Sukey.
Cooper Polly.
Chase Betsy.
Chase Nabby.
Chase Charles T.
Chase Lydia.
Chase Olive.
Cochran William.
Cochran Nancy.
Cochran Stephen.
Carver Eleazer.
Child Lewis W.
Child Joseph.
Child True.
Child Elisha.
Clark William.
Clark Samuel.
Clark Mary.
Chase Munro.
Chase Sarson.
Chase Jane.
Chase Mary.

Child Manson.
Child Bloe.
Clark Lydia.
Dolbier Polly.
Dennett Moses.
Dennett Nabby.
Delano John.
Delano Jabez.
Delano Samuel.
Edes Phebe.
Edes Eliza.
Edes Maria.
Edes Nabby.
French Betsy.
French Sally.
Fuller Philenia.
Fuller Hannah.
Fuller Anna.
Fuller Betsy.
Fuller Jesse Lee.
Fuller Orin.
Fuller Samuel.
Foster Asenath.
Fuller Nabby.
French Rebecca.
Fuller Rebecca.
Fuller Sally.
Fuller Ruth.
Gibbs Patty.
Goding Rhoda.
Goding Hannah.
Goding Zebulon.
Griffin Obed.
Griffin Hezekiah.
Griffin Sally.
Griffin Betsy.
Hathaway William.
Hubbard Nathaniel.
Haskell Hezekiah.
Haskell Polly.
Holman Dolly.
Holman Samuel.
Holman Daniel.
Hathaway Luther.
Hathaway Patience.
Hathaway Eben.
Hersey Mary.

Hersey Samuel.
Hersey Eliza.
Hersey Isaac.
Hersey William.
Hurd Polly.
Hurd Betsy.
Hurd John.
Hurd Hannah.
Hains Francis.
Hains Jerusha.
Hains Peter.
Hains Hannah.
Hains Henry.
Hains Henry.
Hains Rossetta.
Holmes Clark.
Hamlin Anna.
Hamlin Greene.
Jackson Nancy.
Judkins Fanny.
Judkins Asa.
Judkins Anna.
Judkins Hannah.
Judkins Patty.
Kenny Maria.
Kimball Jane.
Kenny Rachel.
Kenny Elisha.
Livermore Granville.
Livermore Hannah.
Livermore Eliza.
Livermore Elijah.
Learned Samuel.
Learned Charles.
Learned Maria.
Lovel Luther.
Leavitt Myloza.
Leavitt Sukey.
Learned Edward.
Leadbetter Luther.
Leadbetter Thomas.
Leadbetter Charles.
Leadbetter Huldah.
Mayhew Eliza.
Mayhew Phebe.
More Sally.
Merrill Eunice.

Merrill Joseph.
Merrill Silas.
Merrill Richard.
Monroe Sally.
Monroe Luda.
Monroe Hannah.
Monroe Nathan.
Monroe Isaac.
Merrill Salome.
Mills Sally.
Mills Persis.
Mills Appy.
Mills Julia.
Mills Lewis.
Morrison Cybil.
Norton Sukey.
Norton Jones.
Norton Jethro.
Norton Mary.
Norton Nabby.
Norton Ira.
Norton Patty.
Norton Moses.
Norton James.
Norton Tristram.
Philbrick Hannah.
Philbrick Jane.
Philbrick Eliza.
Philbrick Betsy.
Philbrick Charlotte.
Philbrick Harriet.
Philbrick Eunice.
Philbrick Anna.
Philbrick Thomas.
Philbrick Stephen.
Philbrick Maria.
Pratt Sally.
Pitts Polly.
Pitts Anna.
Pierpont Robert.
Pierpont George.
Pierpont Elijah.
Pratt Lucy.
Parker Benjamin.
Parker Jesse.
Parker Lucy.
Parker Rupanna.

Parker Nancy.
Parker Clarissa.
Packard Alanson.
Packard Sylvanus.
Parker Simon.
Packard Jerusha.
Paul Phebe.
Paul Ellis.
Paul Olive.
Rowell Betsy.
Rowell Bulia.
Rowell Abijah.
Reed Lucinda.
Reed Phillips.
Rose Zebedee.
Rose Church.
Randall Samuel.
Randall Mary.
Randall Joshua.
Randall Asa.
Stevens Clarissa.
Stevens Hannah.
Stevens Nabby.
Stevens Wealthy.
Stevens Markwell.
Stafford Moses.
Stone Sally.
Stone William.
Stacy Dolly.
Stacy William.
Stacy Hiram.
Stacy Sukey.
Strictland John.
Strictland Isaac.
Strictland Hastings.
Strickland Polly.
Sawtelle Lavinia.
Sawtelle Elmira.
Sawtelle Nathan.
Sawtelle Joanna.
Sawtelle Harriet.
Sawin Patty.
Sawin Samuel.
Sawin Rebecca.
Sawin Daniel.
Sawin John.
Sawin Abijah.

Sawin Polly.
Thompson Roxanna.
Turner Nabby.
Turner Persis.
Turner Arethusa.
Winter Olive.
Wyman Sally.
Wyman Eliza.
Wyman Witham.
Wyman Sukey.
Wyman Thomas.
Wing Mary.
Wing Susanna.
Wing Daniel.
Wing William.
Wing Emory.
Wing Samuel.
Wyer Diana.
Wyer William.
Wyer Sally.

Wyer George.
Woodbury Polly.
Woodbury Asa.
Waters Eliza.
Warren Aurelia.
Wing Hannah.
Washburn Cynthia.
Washburn Olive.
Washburn Abner W.
Wyman Peter.
Whitman Freelove.
Whitman Snow.
York Gideon.
York Shadrach.
York Rachel.
Young Jacob.
Young Moses.
Young Aaron.
Young William.

LIVERMORE SCHOOL, 1810, EAST SIDE.

Abbot Hall.
Abbot Bill.
Abbot Elizabeth.
Abbot Bethiah.
Abbot Anna.
Abbot Polly.
Abbot Rachel.
Bomp Zephaniah.
Benjamin Nathaniel.
Benjamin Patty.
Benjamin David.
Benjamin Polly.
Benjamin Charles.
Benjamin Elisha.
Benjamin Ruth.
Black William.
Basford Ebenezer.
Basford Johanna.
Basford Mercy.
Basford Elvira.
Barton Asa.
Barton Katherine.
Barton Sally.

Barton Eunice.
Barton Aaron.
Barton Lavinia.
Chandler Belinda.
Chandler Polly.
Chandler Dudley.
Clark Oliver.
Dutton Thomas.
Eastman Caleb.
Fuller Philena.
Fuller Hannah.
Fuller Anna.
Fuller Betsy.
Fuller Jesse Lee.
Fuller Selah.
Fuller Orin.
Fuller Samuel.
Fuller John.
Foster Asenath.
Fellows Benjamin.
Fellows Stephen.
Hobbs Jonathan.
Hains Francis.

The Umbagog Mill was dismantled in 1910; one machine and many of its brick were used in the Otis Mill.

Hains Jerusha.
Hains Hannah.
Hains Peter.
Hains Henry.
Hains Arabella.
Hains Harvey.
Hains Rosella.
Judkins Lavinia.
Judkins Asa.
Judkins Hannah.
Judkins Polly.
Judkins Anna.
Judkins Lucy.
Leadbetter Thomas.
Leadbetter Charles.
Leadbetter Huldah.
Leadbetter Benjamin.
Morrill Elijah.

Morrison Cybil.
Morrison Ruth.
Pillsbury Eben.
Randall Samuel.
Randall Joshua.
Randall Asa.
Swift Sally.
Whitaker Stuart.
Washburn Cynthia.
Washburn A. Waterman.
Wyman Daniel.
York Rachel.
York Gideon.
York Shadrach.
Young Aaron.
Young William.
Young Joshua.

The spelling of the names, though not in all cases according to the usage of the parties themselves, stands as written by Mr. Foster.

#9 machine at Otis Mill in 1909; Raoul Duguay, A. LeRiche and R. Simard.

By the favor of Z. K. Harmon, Esq., of Portland, the following lists of officers and soldiers of the militia from Livermore, who went to the defence of that town in the war of 1812, are given.

In the war of 1812–14, when the State militia were called out for defence of the sea-coast towns, two companies were called out from this town and marched to Portland for the defence of that place. These companies were commanded by Capts. Elias Morse and William Morison and were attached to Lieut. Col. Samuel Holland's regiment. A copy of Col. Holland's staff roll is given below; those marked with a * were from Livermore:

Samuel Holland, *Lieut. Col.*	*John Briggs, *Paymaster.*
Moses Stone, *Major.*	Cornelius Holland, *Surgeon.*
*Joshua Soule,† *Chaplain.*	Ebenezer Ellis, *Sergeant Major.*
*James Chase, *Adjutant.*	Daniel Austin, *Quartermaster Sergt.*
*Henry Wood, *Quartermaster.*	John Hearsey, *Drum Major.*

When the militia had been in the service at Portland about two weeks, not much prospect for a fight appearing, the three Oxford County regiments were consolidated into one, which regiment was commanded by Col. William Ryerson and continued in service from Sept. 25, to Nov. 5, 1814. The following are the Livermore men who served under Col. Holland 14th to 24th Sept., and also under Col. Ryerson 25th Sept., to 5th Nov., 1814.

CAPTAIN MORSE'S COMPANY.

Elias Morse, *Captain.*	*Privates.*
Henry Aldrich, *Ensign.*	Samuel Ames.
Nathaniel Soper, *Sergeant.*	Lucius Andrews.
Thomas Haskell, "	Lescom Andrews.
Daniel Child, "	John Bigelow.
—— Hardwick, "	Samuel Beals.
John Fisher, *Corporal.*	Luther Beals.
John Hayes, "	Samuel Boothby.
John Griffith, "	Thomas Bryant.
Bradish Turner, "	Simeon Brown.
Nezer Bailey, *Musician.*	George Chandler.
Seth Ballou, "	Joshua Campbell.

---

†Afterwards Bishop Soule.

From Washburn's "Notes of Livermore," published 1874 by Bailey and Noyes.

Caproni's fruit and confectionary store, 1910: many of the hardest decisions of the day were made here — whether to spend the hard-earned
nickel for "Cherry Phosphate," ice cream, or a nose-tingling soda.

In the early 1900s, "Livermore Falls always had a good baseball team —
and spent more money (on the sport) in about ten weeks than was paid
the three ministers of the Baptist, Universalist and Methodist Churches
for a full year."

Didymus Edgecomb.
Warren Dailey.
Daniel Edgecomb.
Joseph Foss.
Elijah Fisher.
Grinfill Fisher.
Seth Foster.
Samuel Fuller.
Daniel Graffam.
Eli Hathaway.
Josiah Hobbs.
Joseph Jackson.
Stephen Jones.
Oris Morse.

Luther Lovewell.
David Morse, Jr.
Jonathan Merrill.
Simeon Putnam.
Paul Robinson.
David Rich.
John Strickland.
Daniel Safford.
John Safford.
Gad Soper.
Alexander Soper.
William Saunders.
Abijah Sawin, Jr.
James Starbird.

The following were Livermore soldiers who served after the draft from Sept. 25, to Nov. 5, 1814.

Elias Morse, *Captain.*
Henry Aldrich, *Ensign.*
John Griffith, *Corporal.*

Privates.

Lucius Andrews.
Luther Beals.
Simeon Brown.
Elijah Fisher.
Daniel Edgecomb.

Daniel Graffam.
Eli Hathaway.
Joseph Jackson.
Luther Lovewell.
David Morse, Jr.
David Rich.
James Starbird.
Alexander Soper.

CAPTAIN MORISON'S COMPANY.

William Morison, *Captain.*
Thomas Davis, *Lieutenant.*
Billy Benjamin, *Ensign.*
Alden Wellington, *Sergeant.*
Martin Farrington,   "
Obed Wing,   "
Timothy Eastman,   "
Francis F. Haynes, *Musician.*
Daniel Dolley,   " '
John Clark,   *Corporal.*
Samuel Randall,   "
Nehemiah Knowles, "
Jacob Lovejoy,   "

Privates.

Datus T. Allen.
Ebenezer Burgess.
Charles Benjamin.
David Bartlett.
Samuel Burgess.
Amos Carver.
Samuel Dunn.
Stephen Dutton.
Benjamin Farrington.
Abraham Fuller.
Stephen Freeman.
John Hodgdon.

Samuel C. Hodgdon.
Abraham Hodgdon.
Paul Hammond.
Amos Hobbs.
Thomas Leadbetter.
Oliver S. Lyford.
Samuel Lyford.
Joseph Lyford.
Jonathan Libby.
Joseph Morrill.
Elijah Morrill.
Jeremiah Knox.
Simeon Norris.
William Norris.

Samuel Norris.
Moses Page.
Edmund Phillips.
Nace Smith.
William Smith.
William Stinchfield.
Ebenezer Tanner.
John Wyman.
Elijah Wellington.
Adam Wilbur.
Lewis White.
Geo. Walker.
Moses Young.
Moses Young, Jr.

The following were Livermore soldiers who served after the draft from Sept. 25, to Nov. 5, 1814.

William Morison, *Captain.*
Thomas Davis, *Lieutenant.*
Alden Wellington, *Sergeant.*
John Clark,　　*Corporal.*
Jacob Lovejoy,　　"
Francis F. Haynes, *Musician.*

Privates.

Datus T. Allen.
David Bartlett.
Ebenezer Burgess.

Amos Carver.
Didymus C. Edgecomb.
Abraham Fuller.
Abraham Hodgdon.
Thomas Leadbetter.
Samuel Lyford.
Joseph Morrill.
Elijah Morrill.
Edmund Phillips.
Elijah Wellington.
Moses Young, Jr.

There were a large number of Livermore men who enlisted into the United States army for one year and during the war, and served in the 34th and 45th Regiments of Infantry, whose names cannot now be obtained to insert in this work.

THE END

Index: A History of Livermore
(excludes listings found in the appendix)

379

395

www.ingramcontent.com/pod-product-compliance
Lightning Source LLC
Chambersburg PA
CBHW030759150426
42813CB00068B/3257/J

* 9 7 8 1 4 2 6 9 3 5 6 8 8 *